EVOLUTION OF INFORMATION TECHNOLOGY IN EDUCATIONAL MANAGEMENT

IFIP – The International Federation for Information Processing

IFIP was founded in 1960 under the auspices of UNESCO, following the First World Computer Congress held in Paris the previous year. An umbrella organization for societies working in information processing, IFIP's aim is two-fold: to support information processing within its member countries and to encourage technology transfer to developing nations. As its mission statement clearly states,

> IFIP's mission is to be the leading, truly international, apolitical organization which encourages and assists in the development, exploitation and application of information technology for the benefit of all people.

IFIP is a non-profitmaking organization, run almost solely by 2500 volunteers. It operates through a number of technical committees, which organize events and publications. IFIP's events range from an international congress to local seminars, but the most important are:

• The IFIP World Computer Congress, held every second year;
• Open conferences;
• Working conferences.

The flagship event is the IFIP World Computer Congress, at which both invited and contributed papers are presented. Contributed papers are rigorously refereed and the rejection rate is high.

As with the Congress, participation in the open conferences is open to all and papers may be invited or submitted. Again, submitted papers are stringently refereed.

The working conferences are structured differently. They are usually run by a working group and attendance is small and by invitation only. Their purpose is to create an atmosphere conducive to innovation and development. Refereeing is less rigorous and papers are subjected to extensive group discussion.

Publications arising from IFIP events vary. The papers presented at the IFIP World Computer Congress and at open conferences are published as conference proceedings, while the results of the working conferences are often published as collections of selected and edited papers.

Any national society whose primary activity is in information may apply to become a full member of IFIP, although full membership is restricted to one society per country. Full members are entitled to vote at the annual General Assembly, National societies preferring a less committed involvement may apply for associate or corresponding membership. Associate members enjoy the same benefits as full members, but without voting rights. Corresponding members are not represented in IFIP bodies. Affiliated membership is open to non-national societies, and individual and honorary membership schemes are also offered.

EVOLUTION OF INFORMATION TECHNOLOGY IN EDUCATIONAL MANAGEMENT

Edited by

Arthur Tatnall
Victoria University
Australia

Adrie Visscher
University of Twente
The Netherlands

Andrew Finegan
University of Adelaide
Australia

Christopher O'Mahony
Uppingham School
United Kingdom

 Springer

Evolution of Information Technology in Educational Management

Edited by Arthur Tatnall, Adrie Visscher, Andrew Finegan, and

Christopher O'Mahony

p. cm. (IFIP International Federation for Information Processing, a Springer Series in Computer Science)

ISSN: 1571-5736/1861-2288 (Internet)
ISBN: 978-1-4419-4716-1
eISBN: 978-0-387-93847-9

Printed on acid-free paper

9 8 7 6 5 4 3 2 1

springer.com

Table of Contents

Preface

Evolution of Information Technology in Educational Management

As the editors of this volume we are very happy to publish a selection of the papers that were presented at the eighth Conference of Working Group 3.7 of the International Federation for Information Processing which was held in July 2008.

The focus of Working Group 3.7 is on ITEM: Information Technology in Educational Management (for more information, please visit our website http://item.wceruw.org/), and the theme of its 2008 conference was on the *Evolution of Information Technology in Educational Management*. Our Working Group started its activities (officially we were not an IFIP Working Group at that time) in 1994 in Israel, so it made sense to look at how ITEM has evolved over the years and to reflect on what its future may be.

The conference took place in Darwin (northern Australia) which even during the Australian winter is a very pleasant location for having a conference. The town of Darwin was given its name by the Captain of the Beagle (the ship on which Darwin travelled when he made the investigations on which he based his Theory of Evolution) who came to the area and named the town after the giant of science he admired.

The conference had the same structure as the previous conferences of our Working Group: the presentation and discussion of research findings in combination with discussion groups in which a specific topic was discussed in greater depth several times during the conference. The results of both activities are included in this conference book.

Contributions to the conference varied considerably, for example from forms of data visualisation in ITEM systems to integrated school performance feedback systems, systems for university administration, information systems for pupil transfer, human-computer interaction in ITEM, strategic planning for ITEM, and the use of web portals in university administration.

The discussion group reports included in this volume focus on three topics: the evolution of ITEM, University ITEM systems, and the future of school performance feedback systems.

Contributions to the conference came from all over the world: Spain, Australia, England, Finland, China, Germany, Uganda, Japan, Slovakia, Switzerland and The Netherlands. All papers in this book have been peer reviewed. Papers were selected from those presented at the conference and the authors were given an opportunity to improve them, based on conference feedback, before publication.

Last but not least, the reader is invited to one of our future conferences. The next one will be held in Botswana in 2010. For more information, please have a look at our website (http://item.wceruw.org/).

Arthur Tatnall (Victoria University, Australia)
Adrie Visscher (University of Twente, The Netherlands)
Andrew Finegan (University of Adelaide)
Christopher O'Mahony (Uppingham School, UK)

Bringing Order into Chaos

Building an Integrated School Management Information System – A Case Study from Germany

Angelina Lange and Andreas Breiter
Institute for Information Management, University of Bremen, Germany

Abstract: How can a public educational organization deal with new information requirements from outside the organization when there are problems with the internal data flows? The German school system is currently changing towards data-driven decision-making for school improvement and accountability. Data becomes an important asset and building large-scale information systems becomes a necessity. In other countries and especially in corporate organizations data warehouses have already been implemented to support analytical data processing for high-level decision-making. These existing approaches will be used to transfer some findings to the German education system. Based on the methodology of information needs analysis, we will introduce a case study from the German State of Bremen. Its department of education is under way of building an integrated school management information system. With the help of qualitative interviews and ethnographic methods, we elicited the requirements and suggested a step-by-step participatory design approach to combine information demand and supply.

Keywords: Integrated school management information system, case study, information needs analysis, interoperability, data warehousing, organizational problems

1. BACKGROUND

Throughout the last decade, the German school system has moved towards stronger accountability. In order to reach the goal of higher student outcomes, quantitative and qualitative measures of quality have been introduced. While other countries, especially the U.S. and the U.K., have a long tradition in using data, this is a fairly new field in Germany. Currently, the major trend moves towards State-wide standardized student achievement tests, often copied from large-scale assessments such as PISA, TIMSS or PIRLS. As the German school system is decentralized on the federal level to the 16 Laender (States) and centralized within the States, we can find 16 different set-ups of strategies and objectives for data use. As Visscher (2002) pointed out, there is a general distinction regarding the use of data: for

Please use the following format when citing this chapter:

Lange, A. and Breiter, A., 2009, in IFIP International Federation for Information Processing, Volume 292; *Evolution of Information Technology in Educational Management*; Eds. Tatnall, A., Visscher, A., Finegan, A., O'Mahony, C., (Boston: Springer), pp. 1–14.

accountability or for school improvement. The current approaches in Germany have the claim for school improvement but are often used exclusively for accountability.

Both cases, the school system in general and building-level management in schools, have to deal with large amounts of data. This data can only be collected, processed and visualized with the help of information systems. Hence, most school districts and State Departments of Education are working on database systems to support the "thirst for data" by politicians, the general public as well as school administrators and education research. The existing information systems are isolated "island solutions", which have been developed internally to serve a single purpose in a specific situation. They are mostly incompatible, and this leads to heavy manual work with severe problems in data quality.

In this paper, we will introduce a case study from the small German State of Bremen (160 schools, 80,000 students), which is currently in the process of designing an integrated school management information system that should serve as the major data pool for all relevant decisions. As other countries and corporate organizations are far more advanced, we will take a look at some of the developments. Already in the beginning of the process, it became obvious that the major obstacles are not technical but organizational. Hence, the starting point was an in-depth information needs analysis with all stakeholders, which was compared to the data supply from the existing information systems. This gap analysis led to a specification of the data model and the definition of data exchange processes between different data owners and database systems. We will introduce the basic results of the information needs analysis and describe our step-by-step-solution.

2.   INTEGRATION OF INFORMATION SYSTEMS

Based on Visscher's (2001, p. 4) original definition on school information systems, we have developed an extended version:

"Within an integrated school management information systems (ISMIS) the data from different school information systems and different scopes of the school management and administration are joined and prepared for the different stakeholders. The basis constitutes the administrative school information systems which include both the master data of schools, students, teachers and other aspects..." (Breiter et al. 2006, p. 5).

Even if there are still information systems for different purposes needed, e.g. management of assessment data and making them available for different stakeholders, an integrated school management information system seems to be needed (cf. figure 1). It allows the combination of information as it is more and more claimed by public, policy and media in the discussion of school quality.

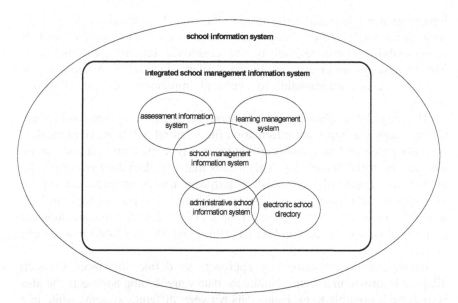

Figure 1: Typology of School Information Systems (Breiter et al. 2006, p. 6, fig.1)

Compared to other countries the history of school information systems in Germany is rather new. There is a body of empirical research on the use of school information systems in other countries, like the case study in New Zealand (Nolan, Brown, & Graves, 2001), Visscher's and Bloemen's (1999) examination of data-systems in Dutch schools, an examination of experiences with a widely used school information system in the UK (Wild, Smith, & Walker, 2001) and in Hong Kong (Fung & Ledesma, 2001). Selwood (2008) has thoroughly analyzed the development of school information systems in the UK. He pointed out that they evolved from small-scale, self-tailored individual school-based systems to large-scale, commercial products, which resemble enterprise resource systems (ERP) in corporate organizations.

Since the 1980s, the integration of heterogeneous information systems became an important topic for many corporate organizations (e.g. Inmon 1996). Enterprise application integration (EAI) is translating data and functions from the format of one application into the format of another. It is a continual conversation between mutually incompatible systems. This is exactly the problem that many school districts are facing. Basically, there are three technical solutions for this problem:

(a) Building a completely new, all-in-one information system;
(b) Developing an intermediate system layer in which all data from the source systems is mirrored and later processed (data warehouse);
(c) Defining interfaces between all the different existing information systems to allow data exchange (interoperability framework).

The idea of the "perfect" information system, which includes all data, functionalities and organizational needs, is old. For some Ministries of

Education it might make sense to start the use of information systems for some tasks totally new. Today there is more sensibility for the need of interoperability. But there is always the question of importing the "old" data into the new system or even let this be available in parallel. Additionally, it is expensive and interminable to plan and implement such an all-in-one system.

The idea of a data warehouse is to leave the operative systems as they are and just copy the important information for a central database. Here the data is consolidated and merged according to data type, general unit and others. The data is stored historically. This means that new data does not overwrite the old one. Especially for statistical purposes this is an important aspect. This idea of data management has already been an important topic in U.S. school districts, e.g. Spielvogel and Pasnik (1999) describe the development of a school data warehouse in Florida, Thorn and Mayer (2006) in a tri-state project.

Interoperability describes an approach to define interfaces between different information systems. Unlike the data warehousing approach, the idea is to make it possible to exchange data between different systems while in a data warehouse there is no connection between the systems. The European Interoperability Framework for e-government distinguishes between three different dimensions of interoperability (European Commission 2004): The basis is the technical interoperability, which defines the physical linkage. In the dimension of semantic interoperability, metadata is added, so a meaning for a specific context is created. On the third organizational dimension, coordination and reorganization of processes are addressed. This spans from the identification of all stakeholders, which are involved and the definition of roles and responsibilities to questions of legal compliance such as privacy and security. In a white paper with the title "Standards for Business", the European Standardization Institute (ETSI) introduces the layer of syntactic interoperability between the technical and the semantic one (Van der Veer & Wiles 2006).

In other countries, there are projects to define the interoperability of school information systems. The School Interoperability Framework (SIF) in the U.S. and the sister project in the UK are both trying to set standards for data interchange between school information systems (http://uk.sifinfo.org). Due to the federal structure of the German education system, there is no comparable approach in sight. Some of the standards can be transferred while others need to be redefined. Up to now, there has been no real need to build integrated school information systems, as only few stakeholders were interested. This has dramatically changed due to the bad performance of German students in international assessment studies.

3. CASE STUDY: BREMEN STATE DEPARTMENT OF EDUCATION

As there are no central responsibilities on education by the federal government in Germany, each of the 16 States is developing its own system. Some are more advanced than others. All systems are domain specific applications mostly addressing the administration of student and teacher records. They represent good solutions for the problems of communicating with schools about their personal resources and the students as well as creating statistics for different internal or external needs. The problem is that these systems are not integrated with other systems.

3.1 Methodology

In our methodology, we follow the information needs analysis as suggested by Winter & Strauch (2003, 2004). This approach deals with the special issues of building a data warehouse. The way of building a data warehouse instead of building an all-in-one system was preferred because of financial considerations and the lack of software companies which can provide an integrated system. In Germany there is still no framework or definition of exchange formats in place so the third variant of interoperability with standardized data exchange was not really available for this case.

In the initialization (cf. box 1 in fig.2, next page), we identify key stakeholders as well as targeted decision-making processes. The second step is the analysis of the state-of-the-art (cf. box 2 in fig.2). Based on the know-ledge about the organization and the state-of-the-art the next step is the information needs analysis (cf. box 3 in fig.2). Finally on the basis of the requirements a data model is created (cf. box 4 in fig.2). The information needs analysis and the data modelling are recursive and hence allow the adjustment of the system on changing general conditions.

3.2 Context and Current Situation

The Department for Education in Bremen has taken up the challenge to introduce an integrated school management information system (ISMIS). It is confronted with new internal and external requirements. Bremen has to deal with new data from the standardized tests to meet education policy goals. By moving towards school autonomy in recent years, the controlling mechanisms require data collection. Bremen has introduced a guideline for school quality to help schools in self-evaluation as well as with external inspectors. For the current legislative period the State of Bremen will publish its first "report on education". It should inform the parliament and the public about the performance and the challenges of the educational system and the individual school.

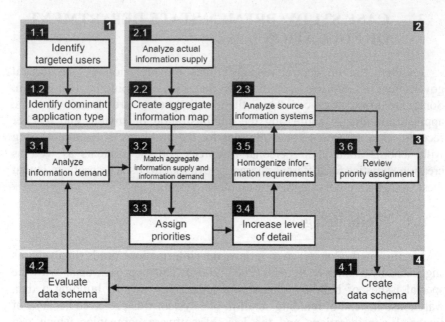

Figure 2: Activity Model for information needs analysis (Winter & Strauch 2004, p. 1365)

External requirements are defined e.g. by national statistics, which are currently in a change process. The KMK[1] has decided a new method to track every individual from kindergarten to adult education with the help of a unique student-ID. This development is highly disputed by privacy protection institutions and it would require a complete change of the information systems in each State (KMK 2006). A second external requirement is derived from the Bremen Freedom of Information Act, which regulates the rights of the citizens to access any (non-confidential) government information (see Kubicek 2006). School and student achievement data seems to be highly attractive.

3.3   Initialization

In our case study we are dealing with different stakeholders inside the school system especially inside the ministry of education. Beneath the needs of the highest level – the Minister for Education – there are different departments with special views on the subject. The following list gives an idea about the variety of information needs:

---

[1]   The KMK is a working committee of the ministers for education and research of the 16 States. Its goal is to coordinate educational policies in Germany.

- Statistics
- Human resources
- Facility management
- Transportation
- Curriculum
- Teacher training
- School improvement
- Inspections
- School supervisors for the different school types
- General education policies
- Professional development
- Quality management

With the help of an international workshop on school information systems (Breiter et al. 2008), the key stakeholders developed an initial idea about the relevant concepts and approaches from other countries.

3.4   State-of-the-art

By creating an inventory of documents and reports in use, we can achieve a first match between subjective information demands and information supply. This leads to an aggregated "information map", which is a model of the relevant information subjects on an aggregated level. This will serve as the basis for the analysis of all relevant data sources. This is a necessary condition to ensure a sufficient level of data quality. It is necessary to review the respective legal and regulatory framework and the "data culture" in the specific context (e.g. no public school ranking in Germany).

The as-is analysis of the existing database systems has uncovered a heterogeneous ICT infrastructure. The existing information systems were created from the different departments to solve current problems without taking into account requirements from other departments. The existence of several systems with intersecting content led to redundant data and communication problems between departments. Besides the central administrative system for students records, there are domain specific applications e.g. for finance, facility management or teacher records. This led to large problems with data quality. In the different systems for school management, the same teacher is connected with three different index keys, which makes data integration impossible. Apart from three major commercial information systems, there are a lot of individual workarounds in place. Even in the same department every employee has his/her own self-made "databases" for special purposes. A direct count came up with more than 1,000 different databases for 300 employees. This produces redundant and outdated data. Hence to be sure, data is collected again directly from schools, leading to confusion and additional workload. Additionally, there are old databases which are "retired with their administrator". It is often unclear if the information is available at all. As most information is individualized, work is done multiple times and redundant data is created.

Our research also shows that there is no real trust in the data which is in place. Most of the employees already had bad experiences working with wrong or outdated data. For this it is very important to only let data into the central system which is of high data quality. If there are bad experiences in the first time of using a new system or access to the data the trust and hope invested will be gone.

3.5 Information needs analysis

On the basis of individual and group interviews as well as participant observation during decision-making meetings, a basic understanding of the processes has been developed. We addressed this issue by splitting up the discussion into different levels. The general questions were discussed in groups with only one or two members (mostly the leaders) for every department. To get everybody with the process and to take into account their needs we additionally had individual interviews and group discussions within the departments. Information needs analysis addresses this challenge by trying to stimulate a negotiation process between different stakeholders (data managers, technology providers, decision-makers etc.). It tries to link those who are involved in producing information with the target audiences (users) who need – or are perceived to need – information to improve the quality of their decisions.

During the interviews and the group meetings, we found a large degree of misunderstanding about the use of data. The requirements of the two internal departments (Education & General Services) are diverse and partly contradictory. One department's focus is on individual schools in their everyday work, the other one on aggregated data. So it was not only important to break down the ideas to the everyday work of the involved employees and avoiding technical terms but also introduce possibilities for the different departments to discuss with each other. By using concrete examples for the general concepts and visualizing every step of the process we reached a basis for finding a common understanding.

Another issue is that not everybody should be able to see, edit or even delete all data. There is some kind of fear to lose power if the data is no more secured by the person himself/herself but everybody can get it from the central system. It also might be that there is the idea to be controlled if everybody can see the results of the work. So a well defined identity management with specific roles and rights to see the data and to update it is not only important for security issues but also for organizational ones.

3.6 Future system

This step is about matching information supply and demand. It will end in a set of homogenized information requirements, defining information gaps. By identifying typical questions, which stakeholders have in mind when using imaginatively a "black box", we tried to get a first impression of information demands. As we know from prior research (Gorry & Scott Morton 1989), decision-makers have difficulties in defining their needs. They tend to overestimate their needs or are not able to specify concrete data. We observed that not missing data was the primary problem for decision makers as nearly all information is available somewhere in the organization. Instead, it is important to identify the 'right questions'. After defining the goal it is necessary to assign priorities to the information requirements based on development costs, implementation time, data security and privacy, information granularity, refresh frequency and many more.

With the results of the first three phases (phase 4, data modeling is still ongoing) in mind, we defined a step-by-step-approach (see figure 3). The different requirements were assigned with priorities of creating a system which reduces the workload, increases data quality and reduces redundant data.

The core idea is to make data available which was so far individualized or only available to one department. Data which is relevant to others will be copied into a central database. First this database will be a central entrance to information, which will serve for building internal registers or information system for the public. Second the database will be extended with the functions for reporting.

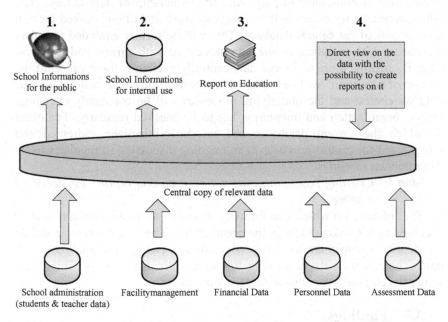

Figure 3: Architectural model of the integrated management information system

Step 1: *Automated processing of the public information system*

The most pressing requirement was to provide basic data about individual schools to the public. As the quality of this data is crucial for any other information system, we put a lot of effort into the data flows and the ownership. We defined "godparenthoods" for specific data items. Individuals have the responsibility to update the information if it changes. They are reminded of this task by regular e-mails. The data is copied out of the source systems on a regular basis. Schools have the possibility to check and expand the information.

Step 2: *Expanding public information about schools for internal uses*

After creating a central storage for finding information about schools, this was expanded for internal use. As the employees in the departments for school supervision and inspections need more confidential details about the school additional data is copied regularly to the central database. In this step, there is also data introduced which is not directly connected to a specific school.

Step 3: *Reorganizing responsibilities for data and implementing regular copies of the data into the data warehouse*

This step is an ongoing task for the whole project. We address the core information of every department and, hence, the core power element. Analyzing the inter- and intra-departmental information flows is affecting the power balance within the organization what Crozier & Friedberg (1977) called "micro-politics". Although human interaction is highly cooperative, competition is constantly in play. And the ownership of data is key. Data which is needed for others in their everyday work and often is asked for will also be part of the central database. This will be further extended to a data warehouse with analytical online data processing with current and historical data. By making more and more data centrally available, the creation of the "report of education" will be easier – at the same time - with better data. The data warehouse and the underlying processes will be constantly changing. Hence, organization and integration has to be checked regularly. The order in which the current databases and responsibilities are addressed and reorganized for central provision is an ongoing discussion in regularly inter-departmental meetings.

Step 4: *Creating possibilities for data search and reports for decision-making*

The information which was formerly available to individuals can now be accessed by all stakeholders in the organization. There is the need to define an identity management to clarify who can see, change and analyze which data. There will be the possibility to create individual reports. This is the future development for high-level decision makers.

3.7 Findings

As already introduced by Davis in 1982 there is a difference between the general information requirements of an organization and the specific information needs for a specific task. Addressing the issue of an integrated school information system we are facing the problem that these issues merge. This is already known from enterprises who try to build an ERP system. Information and knowledge became assets and therefore the management of these issues is a strategic and tactical task (Mentzas et al. 2003).There is a need for an overall information strategy. In our case we try to introduce two approaches of addressing this problem:

First we argue that information management is a task for the management. The implementation of a Chief Information Officer (CIO) might be a good idea. There is a need for a role which has an overview of all activities concerned with information management in the organization and has the freedom and power to make general decisions. As Rau (2004) puts it, the CIO is responsible for three areas and has to find a balance between them:

(a) costumer requirements/interaction with the users
(b) every-day-work (efficient and effective)
(c) strategic decision on information systems as selecting new technologies etc.

Philip (2007, p.253f.) describes the tasks as: "play the role of technology scout within the organization" and be the "technology interpreter" – fluent in two languages: the business language and the language of technology.

Second we give the advice to have an Information Audit in place. The strategic Information Audit tries to map and to analyze the relationship of information resources and organizational goals. Core of this is the identification of the organizations missions and goals as well as the role information and information systems play. These overall goals are broken down to specific and attainable short-term targets. Also the critical success factors (CSF) for the achievement of the objectives are addresses. The next step is to define activities which should ensure the meeting of the CSFs. At least the information resources, which are required for this are identified (Buchanan 1998). The like will be done for core processes, resources and content (Buchanan 2007). In table 1 you can see the general matrix which will be filled with the detailed results of the Information Audit.

Table 1: Information Audit Scope Matrix (Buchanan 2007, p.171, fig.8)

	Management	Technology	Systems	Content
Strategic				
Process				
Resource				

4.   CONCLUSIONS

Due to massive external pressure, the German education system is currently changing with high speed. The ultimate goal is to increase school quality. One major challenge is to collect the relevant data and to use it for system-level and building-level decision-making. Most States are building up large-scale databases in order to support this process. As we have pointed out, interoperability is in the first place an organizational rather than a technical challenge. Our case illustrated the problems of finding the same language to deal with the new situation and historically grown infrastructure. Information needs analysis is a highly interactive process which is necessary to define a priori the technical system requirements. In parallel, this leads to a common understanding of what should be done with data.

From our empirical findings, it became obvious, that education departments will need an overall information structure and to fill the position of a Chief Information Officer (CIO) at the top-level management. The more data becomes available, the more external pressure will force the education system to publish data and the more efficient and effective information management is necessary. Even with our approach of introducing a central database for reorganizing the information flow and building up a data warehouse there is the risk of information overload. Building an effective and efficient identity management will be a key future endeavour. Other countries are some steps ahead and Germany's school system should take the opportunity to learn.

5.   REFERENCES

Breiter, A., Lange, A., & Stauke, E. (2006). Introduction and Analytical Framework. In A. Breiter, E. Stauke, N. Büsching & A. Lange (Eds.), *Educational Management Information Systems - Case Studies from 8 Countries* (pp. 5-16). Aachen: Shaker.

Breiter, A. et al. (2008). *School information systems and data based decision making.* Berlin et al.: Peter Lang.

Buchanan, S. & F. Gibb (1998). "The information audit: An integrated strategic approach." *International Journal of Information Management* 18(1): 29-47.

Buchanan, S., & Gibb, F. (2007). The information audit: Role and scope. *International Journal of Information Management, 27*(3), 159-172.

Crozier, M., & Friedberg, E. (1977). *Actors and systems: the politics of collective action.* Chicago: University of Chicago Press.

Davis, G. B. (1982). "Strategies for information requirements determination." *IBM Systems Journal* 21(1): 4-30.

European Commission (2004). *European Interoperability Framework for Pan-european eGovernment Services.* Luxembourg: European Communities.

Van der Veer, H. & A. Wiles (2006). "Achieving Technical Interoperability - the ETSI Approach" *ETSI White Paper* No. 3, October 2006, European Telecommunications Standards Institute.

Fung, A. C. W. & Ledesma, J. (2001). SAMS in Hong Kong Schools: A Centrally Developed SIS for Primary and Secondary Schools. In A. J.

Visscher, P. Wild & A. C. W. Fung (Eds.), *Information Technology in Educational Management. Synthesis of Experience, Research and Future Perspectives on Computer-Assisted School Information Systems* (pp. 39-53). Heidelberg: Springer.

Gorry, G. A., & Scott Morton, M. S. (1989). A Framework for Management Information Systems. *Sloan Management Review.*

Inmon, W. H. (1996). *Building the Data Warehouse.* New York, NY: John Wiley & Sons.

KMK (2006). *Zur langfristigen Sicherstellung der Datenbasis für die Bildungsberichterstattung.* Frankfurt a.M.: Konsortium Bildungsberichterstattung.

Kubicek, H. (2006). Informationsfreiheitsgesetze vor einem weiteren Paradigmenwechsel. In D. Klumpp, H.

Kubicek, H. & R. Cimander (2007). Three dimensions of organizational interoperability. *Online proceedings of the eGovInterop'07 Conference, Paris 2007.*

Mentzas, G., D. Apostolou, et al. (2003). Process and Product Approaches in Knowledge Management. *Knowledge Asset Management: Beyond the Process-centred Approaches.* London, Springer: 1-18.

Nolan, C. J. P., Brown, M. A. & Graves, B. (2001). MUSAC in New Zealand: From Grass Roots to System-Wide in a Decade. In A. J. Visscher, P. Wild & A. C. W. Fung (Eds.), *Information Technology in Educational Management. Synthesis of Experience, Research and Future Perspectives on Computer-Assisted School Information Systems* (pp. 55-75). Heidelberg: Springer.

Philip, G. (2007). "IS Strategic Planning for Operational Efficiency." *Information Systems Management* 24(3): 247-264.

Rau, K. G. (2004). "Effective Governance of IT: Design Objectives, Roles, and Relationships." *Information Systems Management* 21(4): 35-42.

Selwood, I. (2008). Managing with ICT in Education. In: Breiter, A., Lange, A., & Stauke, E. (Eds.) *School information systems and data based decision making* (pp. 71-80). Berlin et al.: Peter Lang.

Spielvogel, B., & Pasnik, S. (1999). From the School Room to the State House: *Data Warehouse Solutions for Informed Decision-Making in Education.* New York: EDC/Center for Children and Technology.

Thorn, C. A., & Meyer, R. H. (2006). *Longitudinal Data Systems to Support Data-Informed Decision Making: A Tri-State Partnership Between Michigan, Minnesota, and Wisconsin* Madison, WI: Wisconsin Center for Education Research, University of Wisconsin.

Visscher, A. J. (2001). Computer-Assisted School Information Systems: The Concepts, Intended Benefits, And Stages of Development. In A. J. Visscher, P. Wild & A. C. W. Fung (Eds.), *Information Technology in Educational Management: Synthesis of Experience, Research and Future Perspectives on Computer-Assisted School Information Systems* (pp. 3-18). Norwell, MA: Kluwer.

Visscher, A. J. (2002). A Framework for Studying School Performance Feedback Systems. In A. J. Visscher & R. Coe (Eds.), *School Improvement Through Performance Feedback* (pp. 41-72). Lisse: Swets & Zeitlinger.

Visscher, A. J. & Bloemen, P. P. M. (1999). Evaluation of the Use of Computer-Assisted Management Information Systems in Dutch Schools. *Journal of Research on Computing in Education, 32*(1), 172-188.

Wild, P., Smith, D. & Walker, J. (2001). Has a Decade of Computerization Made a Difference in School Management. In C. J. P. Nolan, A. C. W. Fung & M. A. Brown (Eds.), *Pathways to Institutional Improvement with Information Technology in Educational Management. IFIP TC3/WG3.7 Fourth Working Conference on Information Technology in Educational Management, Auckland, NZ* (pp. 99-120). Norwell, MA: Kluwer.

Winter, R., & B. Strauch (2003). A Method for Demand-driven Information Requirements Analysis in Data Warehousing Projects. *Journal of Data Warehousing, 8*(1), 38-47.

Winter, R. & B. Strauch (2004). Information requirements engineering for data warehouse systems. *Proceedings of the 2004 ACM symposium on Applied computing. Nicosia, Cyprus*, ACM: 1359-1365.s

ITEM Strategic Planning
Two Approaches

Christopher D. O'Mahony
Uppingham School, UK

Abstract: Best practice in IT for Educational Management (ITEM) promotes the value of robust strategic planning. In schools, however, the experience of the 1980s and early 1990s suggested that school senior management teams were inadequately trained and prepared for managing the development of an ITEM Strategic Plan and driving its implementation. From around 1995 to the present day, school management teams have been becoming more sophisticated in their approach to ITEM Strategic Planning. This paper considers the approaches of two schools to ITEM Strategic Planning – one in Australia and one in England – and compares the advantages and disadvantages of the two approaches. The paper discusses issues surrounding governance, collection of evidence, approaches to professional development and feedback mechanisms. Similarities and differences between the two approaches are highlighted, and recommendations made that are of relevance to schools that are seeking increased effectiveness in their ICT efforts.

Keywords: School information systems, Strategic Planning, Professional Development, Educational Management, information technology

1.   INTRODUCTION

It was Harry Mintzberg who once wrote that "strategic planning" as a process was inherently doomed, since it attempted to integrate two fundamentally different mindsets (Mintzberg 1994, 2005). From his point of view, "strategy" is about inspiration, intuition, vision, whereas "planning" is about perspiration, persistence, and sheer plod. The author would argue that, although this disconnect can explain why so much strategic planning fails, genuine organisational growth depends on effective synergy between these two mindsets. A similar dichotomy often exists between "leadership" and "management", and between "effectiveness" and "efficiency". Other authors argue that, by harnessing the dynamics of these apparent opposites, they in fact become complementary (Covey 1990, 1992, 2004; Bossidy & Charan 2002). That is, one depends on, relies on, works with the other to achieve true organisational improvement. Leaders need managers, and managers need leaders; efficiency depends on effectiveness, and vice versa; strategy

Please use the following format when citing this chapter:

O'Mahony, C.D., 2009, in IFIP International Federation for Information Processing, Volume 292; *Evolution of Information Technology in Educational Management*; Eds. Tatnall, A., Visscher, A., Finegan, A., O'Mahony, C., (Boston: Springer), pp. 15–22.

relies on planning, and planning starts with strategy. Leaders are into strategy, managers are into planning.

In schools, another dichotomy exists – between two quite different organisational cultures. Academic members of school staff tend to function in a professional, collegial mode, whereas non-academic support staff tend to function in a more bureaucratic, mechanistic mode. Schools, like universities and hospitals, demonstrate an organisational culture described as a "professional bureaucracy" (Mintzberg 1994, O'Mahony 2000). Given that most school senior management teams are academics, strategic planning skills often tend to be under-developed.

IT for Educational Management (ITEM) has had a very brief history of implementation in schools, dating from the mid-1980s. During the period from 1985 to 1995, ITEM strategic planning was generally unsophisticated. In educational ICT, change is the one constant. For the most part, educational institutions have been on the receiving end of ICT innovation, responding to change rather than driving change. As a result, the adoption of ICT innovations in schools more often follows ad-hoc diffusion models, rather than as an outcome of specific decision-making strategies. Thus, investments by schools in products/solutions such as school administration systems, email systems, local area networks, laptop programmes, intranets, VPNs, VLEs and the like, can be isolated decisions rather than forming elements of some wider strategy (Jones 2003).

From 1995 onwards, however, as ITEM has become more embedded into educational institutions, school efforts at robust ITEM strategic planning have been improving. This paper investigates the efforts of two schools at building comprehensive ITEM strategic plans, noting their similarities and differences, and discussing the positive and negative aspects of each.

The following sections consider the two case study schools in terms of:

- Base school profile comparisons
- Overall strategic directions
- Governance mechanisms
- Consultative processes
- Key components of the plans
- Professional Development themes

The paper concludes by exploring those dimensions that characterise a good ITEM strategic plan.

2.   SCHOOL PROFILES AND STRATEGIES

The Australian case study school is an independent day and boarding college for boys in Sydney, Australia, established in 1880. Although initially hesitant to embrace ICT innovations in the early 1990s, the school's management realized in 1994 that a number of factors were at work which required a whole-school strategy for ICT. The school tabled its first ICT Strategic Plan in late 1995, with a focus on core network connectivity, hardware supply, staff training and support services. From that time onward, the school has produced successive ITEM strategic plans on a triennial basis.

The UK case study school is an independent boarding school for boys and girls in the East Midlands area of England, established in 1584. The school's journey with ICT has been quite haphazard in approach, moving from a low base in the 1990s to a significant investment in networks and hardware in 2000. Despite this one-off capital injection, ongoing support for ICT in the school has been piecemeal, and the first formal ITEM strategic plan was only tabled in 2007. A useful comparison of the two case study schools is as follows:

Dimension	UK Case	Australian Case
Pupils	760	1550
Pupil gender	Boys and Girls	Boys
Academic Staff	110	190
Support Staff	370	60
Acres	120	110
Computers	1400	750
ICT suites	10	14
Servers	14	35
Printers	300	80
ICT Support Staff	8	10
Computers - to - ICT Support Staff	1-to-175	1-to-75
Internet connectivity	2mbps	10mbps
Annual fees income	GBP 18,000,000	GBP 14,000,000
Annual ICT expenditure	GBP 500,000	GBP 1,000,000
% ICT spend vs. income	2.8%	7.1%

Figure 1: Comparative profile of case study schools

Each of the case study schools has encapsulated its vision for ICT with a visual device that brings together the disparate elements of their respective ITEM strategic plans. These models assisted in providing visual links with each school's over-arching development plans, ethos and mission statements. These 'top level' models are shown in the following figures:

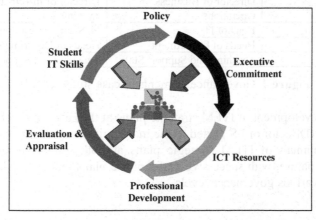

Figure 2: Australian strategic model

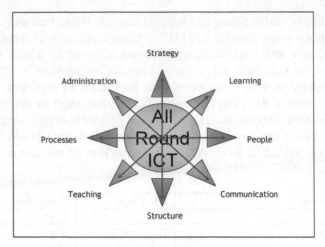

Figure 3: UK strategic model

3.   GOVERNANCE MECHANISMS

One of the critical success factors for an ITEM strategic plan is the degree of ownership or 'buy-in' from various stakeholder groups within a school. An ITEM strategic plan does not spring fully-formed from the mind of a single individual, but is the result of much consultation, both horizontally across many people at the same organisational level, and also vertically across many people at different authority levels in the school.

Governance mechanisms in place in the two case study schools showed many similarities, but also some key differences (see Figure 4 below):

Organisational Level	Australian case study school	UK case study school
1	College Council	Trustees
2	Headmaster	Headmaster
3	Finance Committee	SMT
4	IT Committee	Bursar
5	Director of Business Operations	Director of Information Systems
6	Head of IT	IT Steering Committee
7	Heads of Department	Heads of Department
8	Teaching and Support Staff	Teaching and Support staff

Figure 4: Governance elements in case study schools

In the development of ITEM strategic plans at the case study schools, the Head of IT (Director of I.S.) acted as the main point of contact in both cases. The development of ITEM strategic plans at both schools tended to be iterative in nature, with successive drafts of the plans requiring critique and sign-off at various governance levels.

An indicator of the evolving sophistication of ITEM strategic governance was the increasing degree of rigour and justification required in successive plans over the period 1997 to 2007. In 1997, the Australian ITEM strategic plan achieved sign-off at level 3, whereas in 2006 this sign-off was reserved for level 1. In 1997, the UK school did not have an ITEM strategic plan, but in 2007 sign-off was at level 2.

A further point of divergence is the organisational positioning of the IT Committee within this governance structure. In the Australian school, the IT Committee was a sub-committee of the Finance Committee, which in turn was a sub-committee of College Council. As a result, the IT Committee had a predominantly finance-loaded composition, tending to favour the 'bureaucratic' over the 'professional' culture. The Head of IT acted as secretary to this body. In the UK school, the IT Committee was a sub-committee of SMT, had a stronger composition of academic staff. In this case, the Director of I.S. chaired this body. Understandably, given these differences, accountability in the Australian case tended to be quantitative, whereas accountability in the UK case tended to be qualitative.

Each of the schools investigated engaged in wide consultation in the development of their ITEM strategies. As can be seen in the tables below, each sought to engage in dialogue with as many relevant parties as possible. Each school also went through multiple iterations of the draft strategic plan, before achieving final sign-off.

The components of each school's ITEM strategic plan were carefully compared. Many elements were seen to be common between the two plans – strategies for hardware acquisition, software acquisition, business continuity and disaster recovery, learning management systems, database strategies, professional development programmes, and the like. A detailed analysis of the two ITEM strategic plans suggested that ICT efforts at the two case study schools was at differing levels of sophistication. In this regard, 'stages of growth' models of ICT evolution would suggest that the Australian case study school was at a higher stage of growth than the UK counterpart (Nolan 1979, Galliers & Sutherland 1991, O'Mahony 2000). This is unsurprising, given that the Australian ITEM strategic plan was in its fourth triennial phase, whereas the UK school had only just completed its first plan.

4. PROFESSIONAL DEVELOPMENT COMPARISONS

Other papers presented at ITEM conferences by the author have highlighted the crucial nature of ICT professional development to achieve effectiveness in ITEM efforts (O'Mahony 2002, 2004, 2006). Other authors acknowledge that merely providing hardware and software resources in schools is not sufficient to generate effective use (Cuban 2000, Kennewell et al 2000, Mumtaz 2000, Lambert & Nolan 2003, Kennewell 2003.)

All schools acknowledge that, in addition to the provision of ICT hardware and software, it is crucially important to provide ICT training for staff. Broad-brush initiatives such as ECDL have always been a useful starting point, but it is increasingly recognized that staff ICT training must be customized, both for individual schools and for individual staff. A growing body of empirical evidence makes it clear that there are genuine and measurable improvements in ICT use through a robust ICT PD programme and strategy.

In both case study schools, staff were asked to complete ICT competence surveys, in an effort to discern professional development needs. Staff were asked to self-evaluate their current competence on a range of applications, and then asked to indicate their desired future competence on the same application set. By analyzing the difference between 'current' and 'desired', a set of PD priorities can be established. Key points in both schools were:

- Staff believed themselves generally competent with websearching, email and wordprocessing;
- Staff were seeking to improve their skills with Excel, Powerpoint, Intranet and digital whiteboards.

In both case study schools, staff were asked in the same survey to rank a set of 'ICT inhibitors' – elements that may be holding them back in their use of ICT. In rank order, these were as follows:

1. Time
2. Quantity of ICT Training
3. Quality of Staff ICT
4. Quantity of ICT Support
5. Quality of classroom ICT
6. Quantity of Staff ICT
7. Quality of ICT Training
8. Quality of ICT Support
9. Quantity of classroom ICT
10. Willingness

This result is consistent with similar research in other educational establishments (ACCAC 1999). "Time" and "Lack of Training" are seen as the two biggest areas preventing effective ICT use. Any ITEM Strategic Plan needs to genuinely address items ranked 1 to 5.

5.   CONCLUSIONS

There are many lessons learned by schools, and in particular by school management teams, through the development of ITEM strategic plans. Some of these lessons are summarized below:

- Good ITEM strategy must be informed by robust research and well-exercised methodology;
    - An ITEM strategic plan is much more likely to receive acceptance across a school community, and to achieve its

> objectives, if it is based on validated evidence and if it is developed using methods designed to articulate comprehensive goals and objectives;

- Good ITEM strategy must be continuously evaluated and reviewed;
  - An ITEM strategic plan needs to include relevant checks and balances. Regular review checkpoints needed to be included at all stages – development, implementation, and post-implementation. Strategies and programmes need to have specific and measurable (SMART) targets associated with them, enabling clear analysis of return-on-investment and other metrics.
- Good ITEM strategy leads to improved organisational agility and effectiveness;
  - By ensuring clear articulation with school-wide development plans, by ensuring 'ownership' of the strategy by all relevant stakeholders, by ensuring that the strategy is grounded in firm evidence, and with appropriate control mechanisms, it is highly likely that the plan will be a valuable tool in taking the school forward.

Characteristics of a good ITEM Strategic Plan, as seen in the two cases discussed in this paper, include:

- Articulation with school-wide development plan
- Clearly-articulated governance mechanisms
- Evidence of wide consultation
- Development of the Plan should be iterative
- Initiatives linked to programmes linked to strategies
- SMART targets
- Feedback mechanisms
- Built-in regular review process
- Well-communicated with all relevant stakeholders

A robust ITEM strategic plan demonstrates to school leaders and the wider school community that ICT efforts are genuine and sincere, and that the strategy is an expression of collective will. It is also a clear indicator that a school is willing and able to evolve its ITEM efforts to more complex levels, ultimately with visible benefits in teaching, learning and administration.

6. REFERENCES

ACCAC (1999), Whole school approaches to developing ICT capability. Cardiff: ACCAC.

Bossidy, L.A., and Charan, R. (2002), "Execution: the discipline of getting things done" New York: Crown Business.

Covey, S.R., (1990), 7 habits of highly effective people. New York: Free Press.

Covey, S.R., (1992), Principle centred leadership. New York: Simon & Schuster.

Covey, S.R., (2004), The 8th habit: from effectiveness to greatness. New York: Free Press.

Cuban, L. (2000), Oversold and Underused: Computers in the Classroom. Cambridge, MA: Harvard University Press.

Galliers, R.G. & Sutherland A.R., (1991), Information systems management and strategy formulation: the 'stages of growth' model revisited, Journal of Information Systems, 1, 1991.

Jones, A.J., (2003), "ICT and future teachers: are we preparing for e-learning?", Proceedings: IFIP Working Groups 3.1 and 3.3 Working Conference: ICT and the Teacher of the Future, Melbourne, 2003.

Kennewell, S., Parkinson, J., and Tanner, H., (2000), Developing the ICT-capable School. London: Routledge Falmer.

Kennewell, S., (2003), "Developing research models for ICT-based pedagogy", Proceedings: IFIP Working Groups 3.1 and 3.3 Working Conference: ICT and the Teacher of the Future, Melbourne, 2003.

Lambert, M.J., & Nolan, C.J.P., (2003). Managing learning environments in schools: developing ICT capable teachers. In Management of Education in The Information Age - The Role of ICT. Edited by Selwood I, Fung A, O'Mahony C. Kluwer for IFIP. London

Mintzberg, H., (1994), The rise and fall of strategic planning. London: Prentice Hall.

Mintzberg, H., Ahlstrand, B., Lampel, J., (2005), Strategy bites back. London: Prentice Hall.

Mumtaz, S (2000), "Factors affecting teachers use of information and communications technology: a review of the literature", Journal of Information Technology for Teacher Education, 9, 3, 2000.

Nolan, R.L., (1979), Managing the Crises in Data Processing, Harvard Business Review, 57, 2, March 1979, pp 115-126.

O'Mahony, C.D., (2000), The evolution and evaluation of information systems in NSW Secondary schools in the 1990s: the impact of values on information systems. PhD Thesis (unpublished): Sydney: Macquarie University.

O'Mahony, C.D. (2002), Managing ICT Access and Training for Educators: A Case Study, Proceedings: Information Technology for Educational Management (ITEM2002 conference), Helsinki.

O'Mahony, C.D. (2004), Reaping ITEM benefits: a link between staff ICT access, ability and use., Proceedings: Information Technology for Educational Management (ITEM2004 conference), Las Palmas.

O'Mahony, C.D. (2006), ICTPD 4 ME!, Proceedings: Information Technology for Educational Management (ITEM2006), Hamamatsu.

University Web Portals
Patterns and Policies

Audra Lukaitis and Bill Davey
School of Business Information Technology, RMIT University, Australia

Abstract: A two-year study of Web portal use in a large university has found a number of results that can help in management decision making about the use of university Web portals as a communication channel. The study involved the collection and analysis of Web usage statistics for a business information technology school in a large city university over a two-year period. Findings initially indicate that: it is likely that some students and prospective students prefer personal contact (or face to face communication) to information provided by the portal; students use the portal mostly during critical phases in the academic calendar; students use the portal "at the last minute" or "just in time"; students are only interested in information absolutely specific to their immediate needs; students are not interested in multimedia per se. These findings should help us in improving Web portal use as a communication channel. Preliminary findings can contribute to our understandings of student information seeking behaviour and choice in the use of administrative educational information systems and communication channels.

Keywords: Web portals, university administration, communications channels, management decision making

1.   INTRODUCTION

Information technologies continue to evolve and develop at ever-increasing rates. *"While radio took over 40 years to reach 30% of North America's population, television took 17 and the Internet only 5"*. (Forgas and Negre, 2004). Madell and Muncer (2005) in a study of Internet and mobile phone use by young people found that usage was "complementary", in that *"... young people use the Internet and mobile phone strategically to meet different communication needs"*. Smoreda & Thomas (2001) indicate that Internet users' social networks are more extensive and active than those of non-users, as there are more opportunities on the Internet for social connectivity through email, chat rooms, e-groups, instant messaging, and personal spaces.

Likewise, Jung, Kim et al. (2005) found that the most popular Internet usage among youth was related to email, chatting, games, mailing list,

Please use the following format when citing this chapter:

Lukaitis, A. and Davey, B., 2009, in IFIP International Federation for Information Processing, Volume 292; *Evolution of Information Technology in Educational Management*; Eds. Tatnall, A., Visscher, A., Finegan, A., O'Mahony, C., (Boston: Springer), pp. 23–30.

newsgroups, or surfing Web sites, maintaining a personal Web page, listening to or downloading music and reading online newspapers (Suryani, 2007).

If communication between students has become increasingly technology based, then the educational administrator and academic must become aware of how students seek out information and get their messages from a university, and hence develop systems that meet the communication expectations and information seeking behaviour and preferences of students.

Changes in Australian Government education policy, direction and funding mechanisms, and amalgamations of Australian universities and colleges of advanced education, mean that university student participation rates have been steadily rising; likewise, there has been growth in onshore and offshore international student enrolments. Consequently universities have become bigger, more complex organisations spanning geographical and cultural boundaries. Pressures to contain or reduce expenditure, pressures to do more with less, efforts to improve and deliver quality and efficiency in the context of multi-campuses, and student preferences in communicating with their university, underlie the importance of understanding how and why students use various academic information systems and communication channels.

2.   WHAT OTHERS HAVE FOUND

The literature of Web use by University students does not give a unanimous picture. Aiken, Martin et al. (2003) put this very strongly

"...much is still unknown about how college students use the Internet, Web, and campus information systems for academic work and leisure."

Similarly Uçak (2007) remarks that while there has been much research on the internet, few studies have looked at internet usage and university students.

In a recent study of Indonesian students studying in Victorian-based universities, when participants were asked about how often they visited certain Websites over a two-week period, approximately one third of respondents checked their own university Websites more than 40 times but more than half (55%) didn't look at other university websites at all. (Suryani, 2007) When the participants were asked about what was the most useful item to get information to support their study, 50% preferred the Internet, 25% opted for lecturers or tutors, while 21% sought information in books, and others consulted the advice of friends. (Suryani, 2007)

Results indicate that the majority of students now have access to a computer at home (91%) and most of these students have access to the Internet (86%) Sherry & Fielden (2005). Likewise, a study of Internet use habits of students in a department of information management in a Turkish university revealed that the majority of students used the Internet every day, and preferred electronic media to printed media, and sourced information mostly from the Internet and from their department's computers. (Uçak, 2007).

When looking for information on the Internet, the students consider most how easy it is to access. The students find the quality of easy access of information more important than its other features and they use search engines most in seeking information (Uçak, 2007).

Young people value the Internet's inbuilt immediacy – in accessing information, in communicating, etc. – as one of it most basic and positive elements. Thus, they choose the more immediate possibilities the Internet facilitates compared to those with slow reaction times and results which are not immediately generated (Forgas and Negre, 2004).

Interestingly, Spennenmann (2007) in a recent study of Internet usage by nine Australian universities (students, administrators and academics) found that the majority of users (81 per cent) used the service between the standard office hours of 8.00 and 5.00 with another slight peak after dinner (7.00 p.m.).

Huang, Chen & Chen (2004) in carrying out a study of communication channels used in a graduate program at an American university asked students how often they checked their E-mail accounts and the school Website. The researchers found that 96.25% of participants checked their E-mails at least once a day, where 83.75% visited the school Website at least once a week. The researchers also found that students appreciated the rich content of their school's Website and were aware of constant updates. The researchers highlight comments made by one student who said that as a prospective student, he got all his information about the program from the school's Website, but relied more on information distributed via E-mail once enrolled (E-list servers). Interestingly the study also found that 12.5% of participants preferred oral announcements, often preferring to clarify or confirm a message with the sender.

3. THE STUDY

In this study, we examined an aspect of Web usage behaviour of students over a two-year period, looking for trends in student access (or prospective students or visitors) in a school in a business faculty. We were seeking "general usage trends". The portal under investigation was open to public access; visitors are not controlled by authentification. As a result we have identified some policies that our University can use to ensure maximum impact from the Web site as a portal for communication with students. The impact of the study comes from a subsequent examination of how an educational manager might approach the same task in their institution. It seems that the patterns we have found are general; however, the method we have used to conduct the analysis could be useful in other places.

The school WEB portal studied consists of three main content areas, each with a known cycle of activities (e.g. timetable updates, annual brochure production etc.):

- **Current student and staff administration** (timetables, course and general program information, program brochures, information for prospective students, open day, orientation, elective course information, forms, important links to university services such as the library, faculties, schools, administrative services etc.). This works as both an intranet and Internet. (See Appendix A)
- **Prospective student marketing/general information** – prospective students, program promotion, key links to Faculty and University marketing endeavours (news stories etc.), special one off promotions (this area also crosses over with student and staff administration).
- **Research** – (major research projects etc.), research training scheme, publications. Also includes extensive staff profiles with publications, particularly for research staff, information for prospective Masters and PhD research students.

The university has an array of policies and procedures relating to the creation, implementation and upkeep of electronic content and distribution. All electronic communications relevant to the University's products or services must comply with the University's communication, advertising and marketing guidelines.

Compliance is ensured through training, style guides, policies and procedures, and linking communication between three major organizational levels: schools, faculties and the university. Compliance and communication is maintained by close relationships between the three organizational units via designated staff.

For example the University Web Style Guide clearly defines style requirements for publishing Web content at the university in order that:

- Design and presentation of content is of a high quality and aligned with the authorised corporate identity of the institution;
- Web publishers are able to appropriately reflect and promote the University;
- Persons creating Web pages understand their responsibilities in relation to the design and content of university Web pages;
- Content on University Web sites is consistently presented to improve the experience of site visitors;
- A high level of accessibility exists on University Web pages;
- The university meets its obligations under legislation affecting Web content and presentation (RMIT Style Guide 2008).

What can and cannot be done is clearly communicated to relevant staff; policy is assured at faculty and university levels.

4.   ANALYSIS

One of the researchers – in addition to academic duties – is the school Web site manager and for many years in the past was a program coordinator.

Currently the Web role includes overseeing the school's Web presence, with an emphasis on accuracy, integrity and timeliness of information.

Further, the role entails ensuring compliance with relevant RMIT multimedia and marketing policies and managing the delivery of two school Web usage reports per annum with reporting to relevant stakeholders. Therefore the researcher is involved in the gathering, analysis and reporting of school web usage statistics as well as the direction of the school's Web presence, ensuring adherence to university policies and guidelines.

In this study, we have analysed clicks on a specific breakdown of pages in the Web site of a single school. Although this is a parameter at some distance from the intentions and motivations of visitors, Hofacker and Murphy (2000) assure us that clicks are a reliable measure of Web site performance.

Website performance metrics are indicators of whether or not the Website is successful. Measuring was implemented by tracking different traffic parameters associated with the Website. The most common parameter relates to the frequency of use of the Website, that is, how many people are using the Website. This is a fairly simple and straightforward measure of the reach of the Website in terms of hit numbers. The reach of a Website is an important aspect of performance because it measures the extent to which the Website is known, and accessed by different people. Website reach can be measured by measuring the number of unique visitors to a Website and has been used in previous studies on Websites (Tarafdar and Zhang, 2008).

Gathering of usage statistics took place at the beginning of a new semester over a two-year period, commencing one week before semester start and four weeks after semester start for semesters one and two. With a history of program coordination and administration experience, the first three-weeks of a semester time frame were known to be high student communication traffic periods (face to face, phone, email, reception enquiries covering a gamut of predictable and unpredictable enquiries). The week before semester start was used as a point of comparison.

The researchers used descriptive statistics only and hence have restricted our findings to those conclusions supported by overwhelming patterns. For instance, over a four month period hits at the University front page varied through 1099305 to 1139740 to 1428275 to 1360401. There may be some significant difference between these figures, but no pattern is strong enough for us to draw a conclusion. Alternatively, the Information Systems School Website was hit 2008 times in December but 4085 times in February. These figures are so different that it seems irrelevant to perform significance tests. In the case of each analytical conclusion stated here, the descriptive statistics are conclusive in the same way.

The following patterns were at these extreme levels:

- Hits on elective subject pages were 20 times higher than hits on core subjects.
- Hits on information pages related to specific subjects were twice as high in the three weeks prior to close of enrolments than after those weeks (weekly totals).

- Hits on individual academic staff pages were ten times higher than any other general contact pages.
- Hits on individual academic staff pages were twice those of any specific degree program page or other information page.
- Over five degree programs (including postgraduate and undergraduate coursework programs) hits were proportional to enrolment in each program.
- Over the two years of the study there has been a smooth increase, as measured over the same month each year in total hits. There is no evidence that significant changes in the Web site have changed hits.

5. CONCLUSIONS

Our conclusion comes in two parts. First there is a recommendation to the managers at RMIT. Secondly we have lessons learnt from our analysis that can inform other managers when inspecting their own records. From the very different hit levels we discovered there are a number of conclusions that we might be able to act upon.

5.1 Some students prefer personal contact to information provided by the portal

We were interested in the high levels of hits on individual academic staff pages. Although members of our staff are interesting people it seemed strange that students looking to overcome their information needs would be spending time looking at people pages. An informal interview of reception staff and people in charge of subjects or programs was conducted. These people told us that they are continually asked for information that is readily available on the Web site. Those interviewed believed that students have a "need" to talk to a person about their programs, even when that talk just reiterates information available on the Web. This may be a phenomenon related to specific students who do not trust the Web site, and should be investigated further.

5.2 Students use the portal mostly during critical phases in the academic calendar and students use the portal "at the last minute"

A seasonal trend was obvious over the four semesters represented by the study period. We were suspicious of the months where higher activity occurred and compared weekly statistics to the academic calendar. The hits were consistently very high in the weeks of enrolment and the last week before changes to enrolment are closed. This indicates that at least some cohort of students does actively use the Web site for information around the critical times of the semester, particularly when seeking information about "elective" subjects.

5.3 Students are only interested in information absolutely specific to their immediate needs

The Web site is very broad in content. There are stories of successful graduates, interesting advances in applied research, social activities sponsored by the University and a plethora of educational opportunities not immediately part of a degree program. None of these ancillary pages had hits approaching 1% of the hits to pages from degree programs. The existence of a Web site may allow distribution of the many aspects of a University, but these pages are accessed at a level that may indicate access by only the authors of the pages.

5.4 Students are not interested in multimedia per se

Over the two years of the study a number of initiatives have been taken to improve the "quality" of the Web site. These initiatives have resulted in redesign of sections of the site. There was no evidence from hits to "improved" and unchanged pages that these changes have resulted in additional use by students. Given the amount of effort required to make these improvements it seems from our figures that research should be conducted into the payback from formatting changes to information pages.

These findings should help us in improving use of Web channels as a communication tool for students.

5.5 Getting knowledge from hits

Educational managers, like those in any other industry, must make balanced decisions. The concept of perfect data and infallible decision making is silly. At some point every manager must decide how much effort to put into data gathering before making a decision. Our system of examining hits and paths seems to err on the side of simplicity. To use simple descriptive statistics, as in this exercise, will not yield robust results. To use these as an indicator of both policy direction and subsequently policy refinement seems a sensible balance between effort and outcome. In our case changes in architecture of the site, including searching and tree construction have resulted in significant gains in use and quality of communication.

6.   REFERENCES

Aiken, M., J. Martin, et al. (2003). College Student Internet Use. *Campus-Wide Information System* 20: 182-185.

Forgas, R. C. and Negre, J. S. (2004). The use of new technologies amongst minors in the Balearic islands. *AARE Conference proceedings 2004. "Doing the public good"*. Melbourne, Australia, AARE.

Hofacker, C. F. and Murphy, J. (2000). Clickable World Wide Web banner ads and content sites. *Journal of Interactive Marketing* 14 (1): 49-59.

Huang, Shen-Cheng, Chen, Chao-Hsiu, Chen, Hsin-Liang (2004). A Case Study of Communication Channels in a Graduate Program. *Proceedings of the 67th ASIS&T Annual Meeting*, Vol. 41, 147-155.

Jung, J.-Y., Y.-C. Kim, et al. (2005). The influence of social environment on Internet connectedness of adolescents in Seoul, Singapore and Taipei. *New Media Society* 7 (1): 64-88.

Madell, D. and Muncer, S. (2005). Are Internet and mobile phone communication complementary activities amongst young people? A study from a 'rational actor' perspective. *Information, Communication and Society* 8 (1): 64-80.

Nielsen NetRatings, Average Web Usage Month of March, 2002 U.S., 2002a, http://pm.netratings.com/nnpm/owa/ NRpublicreports.usagemonthly

Nielsen NetRatings, February 2002 Global Internet Index Average Usage, February 2002b, http:// www.nielsen-netratings. com/hot_off_the_net_ i.jsp

RMIT University Web Style Guide 3.0 (Staff log-in required).

Sherry, C. A. and K. A. Fielden (2005). The millennials: Computer savvy (or not?). *HERDSA*.

Smoreda, Z. & Thomas, F. (2001). "Social networks and residential ICT adoption and use", Eurescom Summit 2001 (3G Technicoliges & Application), Heidelberg 12-15 Nov. 2001.

Spenneman, Dirk H. R.(2007). Learning and teaching 24/7: daily internet usage patterns at nine Australian universities. *Campus-Wide Information Systems* Vol. 24 No. 1, 27-44.

Suryani, A. (2007). Exploring new media usage among Indonesian students in Australian universities. *2007 ISANA International Conference "Student success in international education"*. Stamford Grand, Glenelg, Adelaide, Australia, ISANA.

Tarafdar, M. and J. Zhang (2008). Determinants of reach and loyalty - a study of Website performance and implications for Website design. *Journal of Computer Information Systems,* 16.

Uçak, N. Ö. (2007). Internet Use Habits of Students of the Department of Information Management, Hacettepe University, Ankara. *The Journal of Academic Librarianship* 33(6): 697-707.

ITEM out of WG 3.7
Is there any life out there?

Javier Osorio, Jacques Bulchand and Jorge Rodriguez
Las Palmas de Gran Canaria University, Spain

Abstract: At the IFIP WG 3.7's Working Conference two years ago, we presented a paper offering a classification of the Group's published works by research topics and methodologies. The scope was exclusively internal and some conclusions about the output and future challenges were suggested. We now focus our attention externally, exploring the overall activity in the field of information technology for educational management. On the one hand, we have concentrated on practical works, mainly represented by computer applications for commercial purposes and, on the other hand, we have analysed high level theoretical works. After our review process, we became aware of the preponderance of practical activity in the field, with little support from the theoretical perspective. However, we have found a similar orientation when comparing the research topics and methodologies applied by authors in research journals with those adopted by authors who have contributed to WG 3.7.

Keywords: Information technology for educational management, research activity, research methodologies, practical work, computer applications for educational management.

1. INTRODUCTION

We have been able to find numerous references to the application of information technology (IT) in the business area dating from the first appearance of computers (McKinsey & Company, 1968; Wagner, 1970; Gorry and Scott Morton, 1971; Lubas, 1976). In effect, the first advances in computing, which basically focused on providing tools to support arithmetical calculation, were quickly followed by the development of informatic applications for business management. The high performance achieved in data processing, especially in areas of an eminently quantitative nature, such as accounting and payroll management, justified the high investments that large corporations made in IT (Corr, 1977; Clancy, 1978). Later, and encouraged by the apparent success achieved in private business management, other sectors also opted to invest in IT. One of the sectors that

Please use the following format when citing this chapter:

Osorio, J., Bulchand, J. and Rodriguez, J., 2009, in IFIP International Federation for Information Processing, Volume 292; *Evolution of Information Technology in Educational Management*; Eds. Tatnall, A., Visscher, A., Finegan, A., O'Mahony, C., (Boston: Springer), pp. 31–42.

joined the informatic wave was that of education, whose management needs were similar to those of business management, especially in the case of large institutions such as universities, ministries and education departments. Thus, accounting and payroll management similarly benefited from the implementation of IT within education organisations.

The use of computers in the education area really took off in the 1980s with the appearance of personal computers and later, in the early 1990s, with the growing popularity of an already mature tool, the Internet (Linn, 1998; Miesing, 1998). Focusing now on applications in the educational field, we have witnessed various phases in which most software production shifted from applications for education management to applications to support teaching and learning (William, 2002). The available power of computers at the time initially favoured the development of basic administration applications and, as that power increased, so did the development of highly complex applications where alphanumeric, graphic, sound and visual information combined to permit the development of effective applications for teaching and learning (Spencer, 1991).

One problem that has arisen in the education area is the efficient use of IT resources to optimise education management. In that respect, the lack of theories and know-how regarding how to plan or integrate IT for education management led to the appearance of numerous problems. The growth in investments by education authorities, particularly in the most developed countries, justified the initiation of studies of the problem in order to find empirically validated solutions. Thus, the specialist journals and forums began to address the problem of IT in education management in a different way. The increasing number of seminal works on the topic appeared alongside the growing presence of computers in the field of education (Heinich, 1970; Fleming and Levie, 1978). It should be stressed that this process did not take place in isolation; it benefited from the advances and contributions of the information systems (IS) area, which, to a great extent, fuels the area of study that concerns us. In that context, 1995 saw the creation of a working group within the Technical Committee for Education of the IFIP[2], under the auspices of UNESCO, that focused exclusively on the area of information technology for educational management, from which its acronym (ITEM)[3] is taken. However, the existence of this workgroup by no means meant that its members monopolised this line of research; there are numerous contributions from different areas that have helped enrich this discipline.

This work aims to contextualise the work of that working group in relation to the activity undertaken in other areas, and especially in the research published in journals listed in the Science Citation Index (SCI) of the Institute for Scientific Information (ISI).

---

[2] IFIP: International Federation for Information Processing
[3] The working group in question is identified by the initials WG 3.7 of IFIP TC-3 (www.ifip.org)

2. CONTEXTUALISATION

To conduct the proposed study, we performed an operation to find and identify works in the field of ITEM. At the same time, we moved away from the purely academic and research environment to explore the commercial context in an attempt to somehow link the reality of the use of ITEM with that reflected in the relevant research. To that end, we used several sources. One source was an Internet search for commercial software used for educational management. Another was a similar search for research and diffusion groups in this field and the third was a search of the ISI data base for articles related to the topic. In order to establish criteria of comparison, our reference was the work by Osorio and Bulchand (2007), which focused on studying the activity of working group WG 3.7 during its first ten years.

In general, we based the search for information on the descriptors of the field of study that concerns us, namely "information technology for educational management". Since the relevant publications often use synonyms, such as "computer" instead of information technology and "school administration" to refer to educational management, we also used those words in the searches by means of Boolean combinations. First of all, we conducted a generic search using the Google Scholar search engine in order to know, in general terms, the extent of academic production in this topic. We repeated that search using generic Google and the same search parameters. The aim was to identify whether we could find indicators of the production of relevant content outside the purely academic field that was appreciably different from those found using Google Scholar. The next step was to explore the offer of applications and software for educational management that is available on Internet. Thus, we considered the possibility of estimating the fundamentally commercial production and finding a dichotomy between the academic and the commercial components. Finally, we accessed the ISI data base and searched for similar terms in journals of academic excellence. In this case, the search focused on journals in the specific field of "education" within the area of social sciences.

3. RESULTS

3.1 General and Academic

One of the problems associated with an Internet search for information is the difficulty of filtering the resulting information so that the results match the established criteria. In effect, the search for the words represented by the acronym ITEM resulted in millions of documents that contained some of the four words but relatively few that specifically included the whole term. The problem becomes more complicated because documents that are not directly related to the term appear first since they have higher hit rate on Internet. However, when the search was refined, most of the results corresponded to academic documents and books mostly written by authors from the university environment, with few documents written by authors from the business field.

When we confined our search to the academic field and used a search engine like Google Scholar, after refining several times[4], we found a total of 35 references that complied fully with the criteria of the area that concerned us. The predominance of books published by WG 3.7 stood out as a result of its biannual meetings. This led us to conclude that, in the academic sector, that group constitutes a referent with outstanding production. However, the above does not preclude the presence of numerous authors who have undertaken work in this field and whose collaboration with the works of WG 3.7 could be very enriching.

3.2 Software

The search for specialist commercial software for educational management in primary, secondary and university education centres constituted a conclusive factor that supported the basically applied and practical nature of the field of ITEM. The high number of informatic applications available commercially on Internet reflects the importance of this activity and goes some way to explain the scarcity of works from the high level academic sphere, as we shall see later. Using a single search engine and taking the English language as the reference, we identified 155 commercial software packages. That number can be considered quite high and reflects, on the one hand, the commercial interest in this field and, on the other, the absence of a clear top-selling application in the sector, at least in the Anglo-Saxon context.

The applications for educational administration or management that we found cover uses for timetable management and classroom allocation, marks management, tracking student evolution as well as for accounting and financial management in education centres, although that last category displayed the lowest presence in the overall results. We should point out that the results of this search basically showed commercial applications and that there are numerous tools developed in-house by many education centres that, although operational, are not reflected in the search results.

In short, there is a strong imbalance between the practical dimension of ITEM, with its strong contribution in terms of investment effort and man-hours, and the more theoretical dimension, focused on publications that determine the achievement of better results in the application of informatic tools in the field of educational management. That situation is not repeated in the area of the use of information technology in the business world, where a great number of informatic applications are available, some of which can be considered sales-leaders in the sector. There is also a broad base of

---

[4] By way of example, a search using the terms "computer* education* management" obtained 2,442 references although most of them could not be classified as belonging to our field of study.

publications and references to strategies and recommendations to promote best practices in their application in business management.

There is a strong link between the ITEM field and the more generic field of information systems and information technology (IS/IT). Some answers to the problem related to the introduction of IT in educational management may be sought in the latter field, since its larger base of knowledge offers solutions that, in the main, can adapt to the area that concerns us by maintaining nuances that are unique in the discipline of educational management.

3.3   Journals indexed in the ISI

With regard to the results of the ISI data base search, the most notable is the date of the first publication on the topic, which was in 1967. This demonstrates the early interest in the field, well before personal computers became known. Another notable characteristic of this group of publications is the low number of published articles that can be considered wholly related with our area of study compared with the numerous publications within the education area. However, even more noticeable is the high number of publications within that area but outside what could be called the "high academic level". This situation may be due to the fact that the field of study has an eminently practical nature with little margin for a particular theoretical body to be established. In addition to the above, this field has reached maturity and it hardly seems necessary to produce new theoretical constructs except in the case of new paradigms or theories appearing in the fields of management or information systems, on which, to a great extent, our field of study draws. Moreover, it should be said that the most dynamic agent of change in this discipline is information technology, which is in a state of constant evolution and whose advances have more impact from a practical than a scientific perspective. Another factor that might explain the scarcity of high level publications is the fact that the low impact of these publications for the scientific community generates little personal and professional motivation. One of the most representative indicators of that low impact is the small number of times that an article has been cited. This is demonstrated by the fact that, of the 48 articles that can be considered to belong to this discipline, 31 (64.6%) have never been cited in another publication indexed in the ISI, against the 17 that have been cited, the most cited having been cited 8 times.

In order to compare the topics that were considered in the research on the ISI data base and that can be considered characteristic of ITEM with those undertaken within WG 3.7, that group's articles were classified into the following areas: (a) Strategies to integrate IT into educational management; (b) Assimilation and integration of IT into educational management; (c) ITEM state of the art: The discipline's present situation and trends; (d) Assessment of IT support to educational management; (e) National, regional and local experience in the use of IT for educational management; (f) IT applications in educational management; and (g) Teacher and manager training in the use of IT for educational management. Table 1 displays the data in absolute and relative terms of both samples.

Table 1: Papers classified by research subject

Topic	ISI Web of Science 1968-2007) N. %	IFIP WG 3.7 (1995-2005) N. %
Strategies to integrate IT into educational management.	6 12.5 %	9 8.7 %
Assimilation and integration of IT into educational management.	9 18.8 %	27 26.2 %
ITEM state of the art: The discipline's present situation and trends.	9 18.8 %	3 2.9 %
Assessment of IT support to educational management.	6 12.5%	20 19.4 %
National, regional and local experience in the use of IT for educational management.	6 12.5 %	18 17.5 %
IT applications in educational management.	10 20.8 %	20 19.4 %
Teacher and manager training in the use of IT for educational management.	2 4.1 %	6 5.9 %
TOTAL	48 100 %	103 100%

The following conclusions can be drawn from Table 1: the figures regarding the relative participation of the papers classified in the various research subjects show values in similar ranges for several of the identified categories. In some categories, the two figures are very close, as in the case of IT applications in educational management, where the difference is only 1.4%. It is this category that appears most frequently in the publications in the SCI of the ISI, with the peculiarity that it was quite a common topic in the 1970s and early 1980s. Hardly any papers that can be included in this category have appeared more recently. The reason for that chronological distribution may be that, during the mentioned period, information technology applications in educational management constituted a novelty and, since it was an innovative field, emphasis focused on of the announcement of new tools.

However, the greatest difference between the two groups of publications can be found in the group ITEM state of the art: The discipline's present situation and trends, in which the high presence of articles from the ISI data base, in percentage terms, contrasts with the almost token presence of WG 3.7 publications. The reason for that significant difference may lie in the editorial philosophy of the many journals that usually favoured the publi-cation of articles of an integrative nature that addressed the developments and paradigms characteristic of a determined area of knowledge. This was because such articles were of great interest both to experienced and to new scholars in the discipline who wished to know the views of other, more erudite, academics on the general situation of the discipline. Moreover, novice readers were also able to extract from a single article a compendium of knowledge that they would otherwise have had to read different articles to obtain.

Furthermore, focusing on research methodologies and making use of their classification into the following types: (a) Theoretical – conceptual; (b) Theoretical – illustrative; (c) Empirical – case studies; and (d) Empirical – field studies, we compared them with the methodologies applied in WG 3.7 publications, as shown in Table 2, and reached the following conclusions. Firstly, there is a strong similarity between the percentages of theoretical and empirical articles in the two categories, the difference being only 2.8% in both cases. Secondly, although in the case of empirical research, the proportions in the two groups are very similar, there is the paradox that the tendency between the two groups is inverse. In other words, the proportion of articles based on case studies in one group is very similar to that of articles based on field studies in the other, and vice versa, with articles using field studies as the methodology predominant in the articles from the SCI of ISI. One possible explanation for the above may lie in the tendency of publications indexed in the SCI to publish articles based on this methodology because it was considered "more scientific" due to the more universal conclusions that are usually associated with it.

Table 2: Papers classified by research methodology

Research methodology	ISI Web of Science (1968-2007) N. %	IFIP WG 3.7 (1995-2005) N. %
Theoretical studies	**21** **43.8 %**	**48** **46.6 %**
Theoretical – conceptual	9 18.8 %	18 17.5 %
Theoretical – illustrative	12 25 %	30 29.1 %
Empirical studies	**27** **56.2 %**	**55** **53.4 %**
Empirical – case studies	8 16.6 %	37 35.9 %
Empirical – field studies	19 39.6 %	18 17.5 %
TOTAL	**48** **100 %**	**103** **100%**

4. CONCLUSIONS

ITEM is a field that is strongly influenced by innovations in IT, as demonstrated by the content of a great number of publications that can be classified as belonging to this category. This contingent character regarding technology has aroused greater interest in the area related to the marketing of informatic products than at a scientific-academic level, and as the scientific level of the publications increases, that interest appears to obey an inversely proportional relationship to that level.

The community researching this topic could find a meeting point in WG 3.7 and that group could be open to the inclusion of new members by means of direct contact with other academics who have published articles related to the discipline.

Finally, and given the importance of this field in practice, there should be a debate within ITEM about what topics should be the object of future research. The aim would be to link research to market interest, in other words, not to widen the present gap between the direction taken by theoretical research works and that followed by practical application in the educational management activity.

5.   APPENDIX

Table 3 shows the results of articles found in the ISI Web of Knowledge. The search was performed combining the terms (compute* OR tech* OR IT OR information technology OR IS OR IS/IT OR inf* syst*) AND (education* admin* OR education* management). From the list obtained, a tighter search was carried out by reading the abstracts to select only those papers which better fitted the scope of ITEM.

Table 3: Papers extracted the ISI Web of Knowledge to perform the analysis

Title	Author(s)	Source	Date
Cyber schooling framework: Improving mobility and situated learning	Chen NS, Kinshuk, Wang YH	International journal of engineering education	2007
Development of eMed: A comprehensive, modular curriculum-management system	Watson EGS, Moloney PJ, Toohey SM	Academic medicine	2007
Improving the utilisation of management information systems in secondary schools	Bosker RJ, Branderhorst EM, Visscher AJ	School effectiveness and school improvement	2007
Systems limitations hamper integration of accessible information technology in northwest USK-12 schools	Wisdom JP, White N, Goldsmith K, et al.	Educational technology & society	2007
Data for school improvement: Factors for designing effective information systems to support decision-making in schools	Breiter A, Light D	Educational technology & society	2006
Complexity of integrating computer technologies into education in Turkey	Akbaba-Altun S	Educational Technology & Society	2006
All aboard-destination unknown:	Goldberg AK,	Educational	2006

A sociological discussion of online learning	Riemer FJ	technology & society	
School technology leadership: An empirical investigation of prevalence and effect	Anderson RE, Dexter S	Educational administration quarterly	2005
Using information and communication technology in secondary schools in Nigeria: Problems and prospects	Aduwa-Ogiegbaen SE, Iyamu EOS	Educational technology & society	2005
An approach to assisting teachers in building physical and network hybrid community-based learning environments: the Taiwanese experience	Chang LJ, Chou CY, Chen ZH	International journal of educational development	2004
Education project management in the information age: the case of the Kimberley Thusanang Project	Harvey S	International journal of educational development	2004
Examining teachers' decisions to adopt new technology	Sugar W, Crawley F, Fine B	Educational technology & society	2004
Meta-knowledge - a success factor for computer-supported organizational learning in companies	Herrmann T, Kienle A, Reiband N	Educational technology & society	2003
Evaluation of the implementation, use and effects of a computerised management information system in English secondary schools	Visscher A, Wild P, Smith D, et al.	British journal of educational technology	2003
Teacher training on technology-enhanced instruction - A holistic approach	Tan SC, Hu C, Wong SK	Educational technology & society	2003
Public school administrators and technology policy making	Nance JP	Educational administration quarterly	2003
The professional development of principals: Innovations and opportunities	Peterson K	Educational administration quarterly	2002
Information technology in dental education	Yip HK, Barnes IE	British dental journal	1999
New technologies and the cultural ecology of primary schooling: Imagining teachers as Luddites in/deed	Bryson M, DE Castell S	Educational policy	1998
Computer-based simulations of the school principalship: Preparation for professional practice	Maynes B, McIntosh G, Mappin D	Educational administration quarterly	1996
MIS implementation in schools: A systems socio-technical framework	Telem M	Computers & education	1996
Selecting a commercial clinical information-system - an	Wont ET, Abendroth TW	Journal of the American medical	1994

academic medical-centers experience		informatics association	
Staff usage of information technology in a faculty of higher-education - a survey and case-study	Schwieso J	Educational & training technology international	1993
Distance learning partnership	Brownridge IC	Education	1993
Campus computing - a big approach by a small college	NEAL CV, KELSEY DH	Education	1993
Brain train - professional-education and training requirements in developing-countries	Keenan S	Education for information	1992
The role of the British-council	Bate G	Education for information	1992
EMS - case-study in methodology for designing knowledge-based systems and information-systems	Zhang Y, Hitchcock P	Information and software technology	1991
Effectiveness of computer-assisted special-education administration simulations	Schloss PJ, Cartwright GP, Smith MA	Journal of special education	1986
Voluntary technological growth - an administrative challenge	Rhodes LA	Educational leadership	1984
A national status-report on the use of electronic technology in special-education management	Burrello LC, Tracy Ml, Glassman EJ	Journal of special education	1983
Harnessing the computer in educational management	Clemson B	Journal of educational administration	1980
Information-systems and educational-administration - totally inseparable and generally archaic	Simmons JR	Educational technology	1979
Application of computer to an educational management problem - from naivety to frustration, to victory	Schmitt NJ	Educational technology	1976
Considerations in design of information-systems for educational management	Bruno JE	Management	1975
Educational management information systems for seventies	Hayman JL	Educational administration quarterly	1974
Systems technology and operant conditioning in organization and administration of university affiliated facility for mental retardation	Throne JM	Educational technology	1973
Training educational managers via educational technology	Banghart FW, Harris E, Mcgee J	Educational technology	1973
Technology-based educational	Hayman RW,	Educational	1972

system using computer management	Lord W	technology	
Use of computer in educational management	Shaw DC	Educational technology	1972
Information system design for educational management	Turksen IB, Holzman AG	Socio-economic planning sciences	1972
Trends in administrative technology	Engel RA	Education	1971
Computer-aided education management - integrated records and counseling system	Thrasher CL, Campbell JH, Bennett GE	Journal of educational data processing	1971
Instructional technology and administrative decisions	Eye GG, Garrison Mb, Kuhn JA	Educational technology	1969
Technology of computers and systems analysis - impact on school management	Mcloone EP	Educational technology	1969
Educational technology - economics, management and public policy	Randall R, Blaschke C	Educational technology	1968
Computer concepts and educational administration	Caffrey J Marker,RW, McGraw,PP and Stone,FD	Educational record	1967

6. REFERENCES

Clancy, D.K. (1978). "The management control problems of responsibility accounting". *Management Accounting*, March.

Corr, A.V. (1977). "Accounting information for managerial decision". *Financial Executive*. August.

Fleming, M.L. and Levie, W.H. (1978). *Instructional message design. Principles from the behavioural sciences*. Educational Technology Publications. Englewood Cliffs, NJ.

Gorry, A. and Scott Morton, M. (1971). "A framework for management information systems". Sloan Management Review. Vol. 13, No 1.

Heinich, R. (1970). *Technology and the management of instruction*. Association for Educational Communication and Technology. Washington, DC.

Linn, M.; Bell, P. and Hsi, S (1998). "Using the Internet to enhance student understanding of science: The knowledge integration environment". *Interactive Learning Environments*. Vol. 6, pp 4-38.

Lubas, D.P. (1976). "Developing a computerized general ledger system". *Management Accounting*. May, pp-53-65.

McKinsey & Company (1968). *Unlocking the computer profit potential*. McKinsey, Mass.

Miesing, P. (1998). B-Schools on the I-way. *Journal of Management Education.* Vol. 22, No. 3, pp 753-770.

Osorio, J. and Bulchand, J. (2007). "Ten years of ITEM research: Analysis of WG 3.7's Publisher work (1994-2004)", in Tatnall, A., Okamoto, T. and Visscher, A. (eds.) *Knowledge Management for Educational Innovation.* Springer. New York.

Spencer, K. (1991). "Modes, media and methods: the search for educational effectiveness". *British Journal of Educational Technology.* Vol. 30, No. 1, pp. 12-22.

Wagner, G.R. (1970). "Decision Support Systems: computerized mind support for executive problems" *Managerial Planning.* Sept-Oct.

William, W. (2002). "Current trends in educational technology research: the study of learning environments.

E-Contents for Technological Literacy in a Pre-College Program

Yukari Kato

Tokyo University of Agriculture and Technology, Japan

Abstract: This study provided attractive course materials for technological literacy education for a wider audience, including first-year students, high school students, and foreign students in pre-college courses. This prototype e-Learning system is designed to engage a wider range of engineering faculty students paired up with Japanese language teachers to develop an e-Learning system, creating four modules that include video lectures, auto glossary for technical terms, reading materials with narration, and two types of comprehension activities. Evaluation results indicate that a multimedia e-Learning environment is effective and has the potential to better prepare students for engineering education, especially for advanced learners of Japanese in pre-engineering courses.

Keywords: Web-Based Training, Japanese Language Education, Literacy Education, Wider Audience, First-Year Program

1. INTRODUCTION

With the advent of technology, multimedia e-Learning systems are becoming ubiquitous for language learning on university campuses. Using these systems, the language learning process may be made more flexible, rich and individualized. However, in order to be successful, systems must be adapted to and take into account both learners' mental processes and academic requirements in their specialized fields.

There are questions about whether language teachers who are working in isolation can design appropriate courses for a wide variety of learners and their various needs, interests, and academic disciplines. Fukao (1994), from the viewpoint of Japanese language teachers, discusses the difficulties of selecting adequate materials and designing language courses for inter-mediate to advanced students who must be able to read academic articles. The first issue is that language teachers do not have enough specific knowledge to be able to cover all specialized fields. The second issue is that

Please use the following format when citing this chapter:

Kato, Y., 2009, in IFIP International Federation for Information Processing, Volume 292; *Evolution of Information Technology in Educational Management*; Eds. Tatnall, A., Visscher, A., Finegan, A., O'Mahony, C., (Boston: Springer), pp. 43–56.

foreign students are apt to lose interest in reading materials that are not closely related to their specialized field. This may be due to a lack of interest and knowledge in "teaching advanced skills" in Japanese language education. In other words, Japanese language programs for engineers and scientists have been struggling to meet student demand for advanced language courses due to a lack of adequate resources in funding and personnel.

A possible solution for the above difficulties is to base Japanese language curricula on literacy education for a wider audience, including functions that support both language and specialized learning. In fact, Yamamoto (1995) indicated in her report on a Japanese summer course at Massachusetts Institute of Technology (MIT) that cooperation between Japanese language teachers and the science and engineering faculty enhanced students' understanding of Japanese academic articles. This kind of teaching strategy holds promise for the development of an adequate curriculum for advanced Japanese learners in specialized fields. In another example, in China, Japanese language teachers and academic faculty have cooperated to support Chinese students' acquisition of necessary college skills prior to their study at Japanese universities (Kaji 1983)(Tsujii 1983). In contrast, in Japan, only a few attempts have been made so far at forging cooperation between language educators and researchers in specialized fields (Konishi 1983).

1.1 Japanese Language Courses for a Wider Audience

The question is: what and how do we teach to a wider audience? The wider audience is not limited to non-engineering students (Rover 2006). It encompasses high school students, foreign students in pre-college courses, and teachers in K-12 schools, all of whom are more diverse in their background and interests. To answer the question, we might consider what is taught to first-year students in technical colleges and universities and to the next generation of pre-engineering students. Additionally, given the content, how do these audiences learn about engineering? Interestingly, there are relatively few textbooks or trade books published on this topic.

To solve these types of problems, the e-Learning project for the Advanced Japanese Language Course was developed at Tokyo University of Agriculture and Technology in Tokyo, Japan though collaborations among professors from the College of Engineering and Agriculture and Japanese language teachers. The materials from the e-Learning project have already been published as a trade book to introduce to the next generation the specialized research topics in technology. Through cooperation between language teachers and professionals, e-Learning content has been under development since 2006.

This project was also motivated in part by a desire to develop new technological literacy e-Learning content for a wider audience. Shin & Wastel (2001) argue that the design of CALL (Computer Assisted Language Learning) should be 1) underpinned by a solid educational model, and 2) informed by a rigorous engineering approach ensuring that the design addressees the educational requirements of its potential users. It is significant that user goals are mentioned less frequently in CALL literature than user characteristics, needs, profiles and so forth (Colpaert 2006).

Watts (1997) mentioned that the goals of language education might be seen in terms of improved language skills such as increased proficiency in speaking and writing or acquisition of particular knowledge sets, or in general areas such as gaining a better appreciation of another culture.

In order to accomplish these requirements, this project aimed to develop e-Learning content that integrates linguistic skill with an emphasis on reading comprehension skills (Kato et al. 2002) and focuses on technological literacy for a wider audience. This paper is organized as follows: Section 2 describes the e-Learning courseware designs, which were implemented by combining four different strategic learning modules on an LMS Server (moodle, http://moodle.elp.tuat.ac.jp/moodle/login/index.php). Section 3 outlines the survey used to investigate the evaluations of 22 first-year engineering students and 21 foreign students in a pre-engineering course. Section 4 examines the results of the survey and discusses the design for system development. Finally, the paper closes with conclusions and intentions for future work.

2. E-LEARNING CONTENT DEVELOPMENT

This e-Learning development aimed to integrate Japanese language education with an emphasis on technological literacy in engineering education. It has been implemented with cooperation between Japanese language teachers and professionals in science and engineering.

Course design was decided by taking the following factors into account:

1) *Flexible learning environment for learners' diversity.* Technology would provide learners with greater opportunities for exposure to scientific documents, lectures and task-based activities, with the possibility of many hours of independent work at their own pace.

2) *Sharing knowledge for technical literacy education.* Content was developed through cooperation between Japanese language teachers and professionals in specialized fields. Through this collaborative work, knowledge for designing technical literacy curricula was discussed and shared.

2.1 Hybrid Online Course for Technological Literacy

The complete e-Learning content for technological literacy is made up of six modules implemented in the moodle platform (http://moodle.elp.tuat. ac.jp/moodle/login/index.php): (a) technical text reading with narration, (b) auto glossary of technical terms, (c) video clips with transcription, (d) comprehension tasks for streaming lecture, (e) comprehension tasks for reading material, and (f) comprehension tasks for graphical information, as shown in Fig. 1.

Through Modules (a) and (b), as shown in Fig. 2 and Fig. 3, students learn and understand meanings and pronunciations of technical terms in documents. In particular, narration is helpful in understanding how to pronounce words that are not used frequently in daily life. Complex sentence structures and Kanji characters that comprise a large portion of technical writing may cause problems for language learners' comprehension process in lower order decoding. Confirming sounds and meanings in technical documents is valuable for teaching advanced Japanese language (Yamamoto 1995).

Module (a) technical reading with narration (Fig 2) and Module (b) auto glossary of technical terms (Fig. 3) were designed to promote better understanding of linguistic features in academic texts.

These modules mainly focused on identifying and recognizing word meanings and grammatical forms.

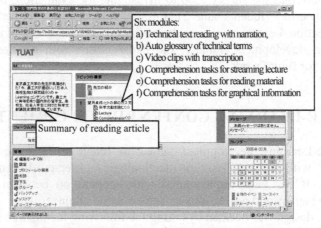

Figure 1: Top page of e-Learning system

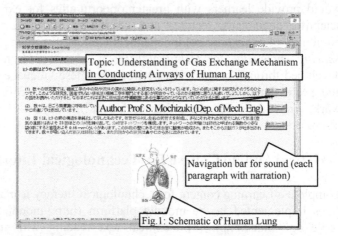

Figure 2: Technical reading with narration

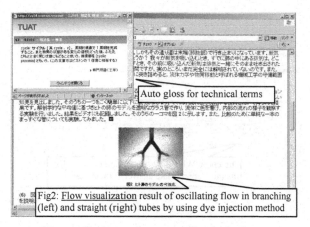

Figure 3: Auto glossary of technical terms

Module (c), as shown in Fig. 4, builds in video clips related to the main ideas of documents that were shown in Module (a). In order to promote listening comprehension in international students and beginners in the engineering department, video clips are linked to texts that describe the main ideas of lectures. The content of lectures is adjusted to the level of an introductory course for high school students and the first year students.

Module (d) includes lecture comprehension tasks that facilitate content understanding and language skills that lay the foundation of engineering education.

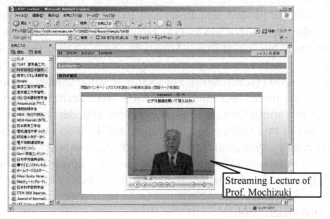

Figure 4: Video clips with transcription

Modules (e) and (f) were comprehension tasks for the reading material. Graphical information and video clips are embedded in textual documents as shown in Fig. 5. In our courseware, a total of six strategic modules, detailed above, were developed.

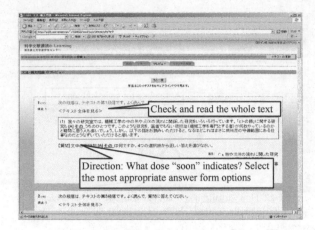

Figure 5: Comprehension tasks for the reading material

3. EVALUATION SURVEY FOR MULTIMEDIA COURSEWARE

This research aimed to consider specific practice guidelines that are research-based and implemented in educational settings (Foshay, Silber & Stelnicki 2003). An important criterion of success for e-Learning in language classrooms is whether it is acceptable to learners. However, few research studies have investigated learners' use of computerized reading modules (Ercetin 2003). Previous research suggested that foreign students show favourable attitudes toward new tasks and explanation with graphics in e-Learning reading content. Conversely, Japanese language teachers showed negative attitudes toward ordinary language tasks. During the post-survey debriefing, the teachers were particularly pleased with explicitness and validity of instruction (Kato 2005). For example, some teachers reported that multilingual dictionaries and multimedia tools were desirable when dealing with students of various language levels. In order to understand the strengths and limitations of this survey and to design and develop language-learning systems efficiently, systematic and consistent evaluation by both learners and teachers is necessary. Therefore, we developed a new e-Learning system (moodle: http://moodle.elp.tuat.ac.jp/moodle/login/index.php): that includes more multimedia resources and language tasks for a wider audience (Kato & Akiyama 2006)(Kato 2006).

We believe that the multimedia-based approach is effective and has the potential to better prepare students for academic life at colleges and universities.

3.1 Objectives

The purpose of the survey presented here was to elicit students' perceptions of how well the course was designed by language learning/teaching framework and their reactions to various methods used in multimedia e-Learning. The purpose of this survey was to systematically explore both advanced Japanese language learners' and native Japanese students' interaction with multimedia modules designed to promote understanding of academic writing and to support technological literacy in engineering. Additionally, by collecting data from non-engineering students, we were able to consider ways to teach technological literacy to a wider audience.

The survey investigated the following two questions:

(a) Are there any differences between engineering and non-engineering majors with regard to their preference for multimedia e-Learning?
(b) Are there any differences between foreign and native Japanese students in engineering with regard to their preference for multi-media e-Learning?

3.2 Procedure

3.2.1 Subjects

The research subjects were 43 native and foreign students studying in public universities in Japan; 34 students majoring in engineering, including 22 advanced learners of Japanese and 12 native Japanese students, and 9 non-engineering native Japanese students. Twenty-one students were native Japanese students, including 7 first-year engineering majors. All advanced learners of Japanese were from Kanji-using countries in Asia: China and South Korea. These students had already received 1-2 years of formal instruction and had passed the first (highest) or second level of the Japanese Proficiency Test.

3.2.2 Questionnaires and Data Collection Procedures

One of the most attractive features of e-Learning is that it is capable of allowing both the instructors and the learners to customize instruction and learning according to their needs (Itoh & Hannon 2002). Previous surveys (Nagata 1996)(Nagata 1998) and interviews (Kato 2005) point to the fact that today's students and teachers require a more interactive, media-rich learning environment. This student survey was used to capture students' reaction to various instructional methods used in an e-Learning system. The survey items targeted students' reaction to various modules implemented to teach understanding of academic writing and to support technological literacy in engineering. These survey items provide a link between students' perceptions of the implemented modules and our anticipated benefits of the multimedia-based methods.

3.2.3 Procedures of Data Collection

The same questionnaire was used for both foreign students and advanced learners of Japanese. Individual questions were designed to investigate users' subjective preference toward e-Learning systems (function, relevance, achievement, and motivation) in comparison to previous research (Kato 2005), (Obayashi at al. 2002) (Dansuwan et al. 2001)(Suzuki 2002).

Subjects individually used web-based courseware on the Learning Management System (LMS; http://moodle.elp.tuat.ac.jp/moodle/login/index. php). Each subject used four modules that include video lectures, auto glossary of technical terms, reading materials with narration, and two types of comprehension activities, as mentioned in Section 2.1.

After using the e-Learning courseware for one hour, students were asked to read the 29 questionnaire items and indicate their reaction by choosing a number from 1 (disagree) to 4 (strongly agree).

3.2.4 Factor Analysis

We conducted item analysis to investigate the discriminative power of 29 questions. Then, 29 items were submitted to factor analysis by using principal component analysis and varimax rotation was conducted. Five items that loaded at less than .54 were excluded: Items 3, 11, 12, 13 and 14. Five complex items for multiple-loaded factors were also deleted: Items 1, 10, 18, 24, 25.

Table 1 shows the 19 items loaded by each factor. The cumulative variance of the four factors was extracted 51.56%.

4.   RESULTS

The pattern matrix for loading greater than .54 as a criterion of factor salience appears in Table 1 (next page).
The first factor included nine items that loaded on 20.47 % of the variance.
We labelled this factor "Positive reaction to e-Learning content.

Representative items are Item 16: "The number of *auto glosses* is adequate," Item 29: "Studying e-Learning content is fun," and Item 28: "I would like to use other e-Learning content even if it is not in my field."

Factor 2 consisted of four items that loaded on 11.99 % of the variance. This factor was labelled "Effectiveness of Auto Glossary" and included Item 21: "I can answer *lecture listening comprehension tasks* by use of *auto glosses*" and Item 23: "I can answer *technical reading comprehension tasks* by use of *auto glosses.*" This factor seems to evaluate the function of auto glossary in Module (b) with regard to comprehension tasks (*lecture listening* and *technical reading comprehension tasks*).

Three items loading on the third factor accounted for 10.30 % of the variance. Examples include Item 8: "*Video clips* have high-quality sounds" and Item 4: "*Lecture listening comprehension tasks* are related to the topics of *video clips.*" This factor concerns "Positive Perception of Multimedia Effects," especially quality of sounds in video clips and narrations.

There were three items included in Factor 4, which was labelled "Positive Perception of Technical Reading with Narrations." One item, Item 22: *"Text comprehension tasks* are related to practice in the *technical reading with narration* module," showed users' perceived effectiveness for reading tasks in combination with narration.

Table 1: Items Arranged According to Factor

Items		Factor Loadings			
		Factor 1	Factor 2	Factor 3	Factor 4
Q16	The number of *auto glosses* is adequate	0.911	0.112	0.065	0.034
Q29	Studying e-Learning content is fun	0.863	-0.111	0.404	0.136
Q15	The content of *auto glosses* are easy to understand	0.821	0.408	-0.167	0.009
Q2	The content of text in *technical reading with narration* module are easy to understand	0.806	0.143	-0.214	-0.009
Q26	I would like to take courses at TUAT after I study e-Learning content	0.770	0.165	-0.156	0.256
Q28	I would like to use other e-Learning content even if it is not in my field.	0.747	0.031	0.378	-0.145
Q27	I would like to use more varied e-Learning content	0.746	-0.005	0.533	-0.168
Q9	*Video clip* modules are easy to access and watch	0.638	-0.283	-0.070	0.229
Q17	More *auto glosses* are desirable	0.577	-0.051	-0.674	-0.096
Q21	I can answer *lecture comprehension tasks* by use of *auto glosses*	0.051	0.935	-0.032	-0.171
Q19	More plain explanations and descriptions of *auto glosses* are desirable	-0.160	0.891	-0.001	-0.014
Q23	I can answer *technical reading comprehension tasks* by use of *auto glosses*	0.189	0.837	0.111	-0.038
Q7	*Auto glosses* are helpful to practice the *technical reading with narration* module	0.388	0.731	0.023	-0.048
Q8	*Video clips* have high-quality sounds	-0.052	0.071	0.785	-0.297
Q4	*Narrations with technical reading* have high-quality sounds	-0.051	0.148	0.671	0.157
Q20	*Lecture listening comprehension tasks* are related to the topics of *video clips*	0.111	-0.279	0.624	0.357
Q22	Practice in the *technical reading with narration* module is related to *text comprehension tasks*	0.254	-.221	-0.076	0.833
Q5	The sounds are helpful to study *technical reading with narration* module	-0.285	0.292	0.453	0.662
Q6	The sounds are helpful to continue studying *technical reading with narration* module	0.461	0.090	0.389	0.543
	Rotation Sums of Squared Loadings:	5.937	3.478	2.988	2.548
	Contribution rate (%)	20.47	11.99	10.30	8.79

4.1 Differences between Foreign and Native Japanese Students

To investigate the preferences of both foreign students and native Japanese students (including engineering and non- engineering majors) in using e-Learning courseware, we compared means and standard deviations on data for the four factors (Positive reaction to e-Learning content, Effectiveness of Auto Glossary, Positive Perception of Multimedia Effects, Positive Perception of Technical Reading with Narrations). Means and standard deviations for the four factors are shown in Table 2 and Fig. 6.

Concerning the first research question, "Are there any differences between engineering and non-engineering majors with regard to their preference for multimedia e-Learning?" we conducted a t-test on data for four factors.

Table 2: Average Scores and Standard Deviation of Native Japanese Students

	Numbers	Factor 1	Factor 2	Factor 3	Factor 4
Native Japanese (Engineering)	N=12	2.63 (0.64)	3.00 (0.92)	3.08 (0.71)	2.60 (0.73)
Native Japanese (Non-Engineering)	N=9	2.79 (0.56)	3.53 (0.46)	3.33 (0.62)	2.63 (0.58)
T		0.57	1.51	0.81	0.09

Table 3: Average Scores and Standard Deviation of Engineering Students

	Numbers	Factor 1	Factor 2	Factor 3	Factor 4
Native Japanese (Engineering)	N=12	2.63 (0.64)	3.00 (0.92)	3.08 (0.71)	2.60 (0.73)
Foreign Students (Engineering)	N=22	3.49 (0.53)	3.26 (0.72)	2.91 (0.95)	3.15 (0.66)
T		4.33**	0.89	0.53	1.87†

Factor 1: Positive Reaction to e-Learning Content, **Factor 2**: Effectiveness of Auto Glossary, **Factor 3**: Positive Perception of Multimedia Effects, **Factor 4**: Positive Perception of Reading with Narration.
** $p < 0.01$, †$p < 0.05$

Concerning the second research question, "Are there any differences between foreign and native Japanese students in engineering with regard to their preference for multimedia e-Learning?" we also conducted a t-test on data for four factors, as shown in Table 3 and Fig. 6.

There was no significant difference between foreign students and native Japanese students with regard to Factor 2 (Effectiveness of Auto Glossary) and Factor 3 (Positive Perception of Multimedia Effects).

On the other hand, in Factor 1, the mean for foreign students was significantly higher than that of native Japanese students majoring in engineering, which indicates that foreign students more positively evaluated "Content Effectiveness" of e-Learning courseware than native Japanese students (t (32)=4.33, p<0.01). Likewise, there was a slight difference between foreign students and native Japanese students for Factor 4, which indicates that foreign students prefer the function of "Reading with Narration" more than Japanese students do (t (32)=1.87, .0.05<p<0.10).

However, with regard to all four factors there was no significant difference between engineering and non-engineering students.

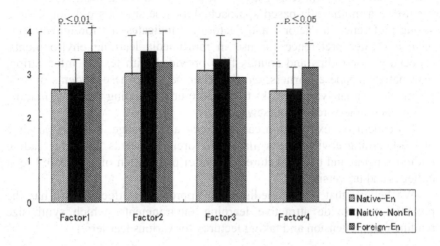

Figure 6: Comparison of Average Scores

5. DISCUSSION

Our proposed system has functions that lead students to learn both the traditional and original features typical to academic writing, and selects relevant tactics to activate students' comprehension of textual and graphical information.

Concerning the first research question, *"Are there any differences between engineering and non-engineering majors with regard to their preference for multimedia e-Learning?"* results indicate that there was no significant difference between engineering and non-engineering students with regard to all four factors.

This indicates that the two groups of Japanese students have very similar patterns for all four factors. Among four factors, the results of Fig.6 show that the average scores of Factor 2 and Factor 3 are higher than those of Factor 1 and Factor 4.

With regard to the second research question, *"Are there any differences between foreign and native Japanese students in engineering with regard to their preference for multimedia e-Learning?"* there was no difference between foreign and Japanese students with regard to Factor 2 (Effectiveness of Auto Glossary) and Factor 3 (Positive Perception of Multimedia Effects). This is due to the fact both Japanese and foreign students have very similar patterns for Factor 2 and Factor 3. In other words, both native and foreign students positively evaluate the items with regard to auto glossary (Factor 2) and multimedia effects (Factor 3) in courseware.

On the other hand, the mean for foreign students was higher than that of native Japanese students for both Factor 1 (Positive reaction to e-Learning content) and Factor 4 (Positive Perception of Reading with Narration). Though foreign student responses on the survey indicate a strong preference for use in a multimedia-based approach, Japanese students did not show a strong preference in Factor 1 and Factor 4. It indicates that foreign students have a greater preference for use in multimedia learning environments, especially video clips and sounds files provided with textual information, than native Japanese learners. On the other hand Japanese students did not positively evaluate various tasks to promote understanding technical reading and streaming lectures in courseware.

No conclusive explanation can be given at this stage, but it is possible that e-Learning environments may lead foreign students to study reading comprehension and taking lectures for better preparation of academic life at colleges and universities.

We believe that a multimedia-based approach is effective and has the potential to provide attractive learning environments, which synthesize reading comprehension and taking lectures for various learners.

6.   CONCLUSION

The results of the present study have relevance for instructional design for learners' diversity. The first implication derives from the fact that both native and foreign students positively evaluated the items with regard to auto glossary (Factor 2) and multimedia effects (Factor 3) in courseware. This suggests that auto glossary and streaming lectures are positively evaluated by both native and foreign students. Then, the contents' quality and difficulty should be carefully controlled with consideration for appropriate levels of both of users.

The second implication derives from the fact that the mean for foreign students was higher than that of native Japanese students for both Factor 1 (Positive reaction to e-Learning content) and Factor 4 (Positive Perception of Reading with Narration). Generally, foreign students evaluate e-Learning contents more positively than Japanese students. There was a gap between the two with regard to the function of Reading with Narration. Although this function was seen as effective for technical reading by foreign students, it was not by Japanese students.

The limitations of a single study that used only one content area, one text, and a limited number of participants cannot be ignored. Additional developmental research for e-Learning is required to more fully understand the strengths and limitations of this survey. We are developing a new reading e-Learning system (http://www.elp.tuat.ac.jp), which includes more language tasks and multimedia resources on various areas.

7. FUTURE WORK

We plan to incorporate both developmental and empirical approaches in our future studies. Since our system framework is, at present, still in its preliminary form, we are continuing to investigate how to implement the functions mentioned above. In order to prepare appropriate materials, we need to learn how multimedia effects are evaluated by the learner's language proficiency and background knowledge.

Another future research direction is to promote the cooperation between Japanese language teachers and professionals in specialized fields. Through this collaborative work, knowledge for designing technical literacy curricula will be discussed and shared for technological literacy education.

By use of Web-Based technologies, a faculty learning community is organized to share knowledge and improve teaching and learning. Web-Based Teaching/Learning Platform, such as Moodle and WebCT, provide busy teachers with an opportunity to work with other teachers and exchange their ideas on strategic teaching and learning. Web-Based Teaching/Learning Platform can be also used for instructional design databases in higher education.

8. REFERENCES

Colpaert, J. (2006): "Pedagogy-driven design for online language teaching and learning", CALICO Journal, 23, 177-497.

Dansuwan, S., et al. (2001): "Thai language learning system on the WWW using natural language processing and the evaluation", CALICO, 19, 67-88.

Ercetin, G. (2003): "Exploring ESL learner's use of hypermedia reading glosses", CALICO Journal, 20, 261-283.

Foshay, W. R., Silber, K.H. & Stelnicki. (2003): "Writing Training Materials that Work", San Francisco: Jossey-Bass/Pfeiffer.

Fukao, Y. (1994). "Teaching Japanese in reading comprehension class in technical literature", Journal of Japanese Language Teaching, Vol.82, 1-12.

Itoh, R. & Hannon, C. (2002): "The effects of online quizzes on learning Japanese", CALICO Journal, 19, 551-561.

Kaji, A. (1983). "Teaching Japanese to Students of Chemistry", Journal of Japanese Language Teaching, Vol. 51, 49-52.

Kato, Y. & Akiyama, M. (2006): "Development of E-learning contents for reading scientific and technical documents as subject matter of guidebook to research topic in TUAT for high school students", The Journal of Japanese Language Education Methods, 13(1), 38-39.

Kato, Y. (2005): "Differences of criterion for evaluating Japanese reading support system between Japanese language teacher and foreign students" Journal of Multimedia Aided Education Research, 2(1), 175-187.

Kato, Y. (2006): "Teacher's collaboration for development of e-Learning contents for reading technological texts", Proceedings of the22nd annual conference of JSET, 803-804.

Kato, Y. et al. (2002): "A relevant learning framework for nonnative speakers: a proposal for integrating textual and graphical information in Japanese academic reading", Information and Systems in Education, 1, 70-79.

Konishi, H (1983). "Problems in instruction of primary science subjects in the foreign students' course", Journal of Japanese Language Teaching, Vol. 51, 27-36.

Nagata, N. (1996): "Computer vs. workbook instruction in second language acquisition", CALICO Journal, 14, 53-75.

Nagata, N. (1998): "Input vs. output practice in educational software for second language acquisition", Language Learning & Technology (Online), 1, 23-40. Available: llt.msu.edu.

Obayashi, F. at al. (2002): "A study of learning support system for integrative study", Journal of Information Processing, 43(8), 2764-2773.

Rover, D.T. (2006): "The Academic Bookshelf: Teaching engineering to a wider audience", Journal of Engineering Education, 95, 347-349.

Shin J-e. & Wastel, D. G. (2001): "A user-centered methodological framework for the design of hypermedia-based CALL systems", CALICO Journal, 18, 517-538.

Suzuki, K. (2002). Instructional design manual, Kyoto: Kitaoji.

Tsujii, J. (1983). "Experiences of teaching information sciences for Chinese students", Journal of Japanese Language Teaching, Vol. 51, pp.49-52.

Watts, N. (1997): "A learner-based design model for interactive multimedia language learning packages", System, 25, 1-8.

Yamamoto, K. (1995). "The acquisition of advanced Japanese reading ability for material science students at the MIT summer course", Journal of Japanese Language Teaching, Vol. 86, 190-203.

Note: This work has been partly supported by E-Learning Projects at TUAT : http://www.elp.tuat.ac.jp

On the Utilization of a New Class of School Information Systems
School Performance Feedback Systems

Adrie J. Visscher
University of Twente, the Netherlands

Abstract: Given the internationally increasing trend to feed back information to schools and teachers on their performance to improve their quality, the characteristics of so-called school performance feedback systems (SPFS) will be analysed here along with the factors which have contributed to their international growth. A theoretical framework is presented which includes the factors assumed to influence the utilisation of SPFS-information. The findings of a longitudinal study into the use of a Dutch SPFS called ZEBO are summarized here, and finally, some reflections are presented on the complexity of SPFS use and on how SPFS utilization may be promoted further.

Keywords: School self-evaluation, school improvement, school performance feedback, evaluation utilization

1. INTRODUCTION

Internationally seen, there is an increasing trend to feed back information to schools and teachers on their performance. School improvement is often the main objective, however, accountability and the promotion of parental/student school choice also play a role.

The features of so-called 'school performance feedback systems' (SPFSs) will be analysed here just as the factors that have contributed to their international growth. Thereafter, the characteristics of the Dutch school performance feedback system ZEBO will be presented briefly, followed by the brief presentation of a theoretical framework including the factors assumed to influence the utilisation of SPFS-information and its effects. Based on this framework a longitudinal study into the use of the Dutch SPFS called ZEBO was carried out of which the research findings are summarized here. Finally, some reflections will be presented on why SPFS use is complicated and how the utilization of SPFSs can be promoted further.

Please use the following format when citing this chapter:

Visscher, A.J., 2009, in IFIP International Federation for Information Processing, Volume 292; *Evolution of Information Technology in Educational Management*; Eds. Tatnall, A., Visscher, A., Finegan, A., O'Mahony, C., (Boston: Springer), pp. 57–67.

2.   THE NATURE OF SCHOOL PERFORMANCE FEEDBACK SYSTEMS

School performance feedback systems are defined here as information systems providing schools with confidential information on their performance and functioning as a basis for school self-evaluation. Such systems have become widespread in education in many parts of the world. They share a goal of seeking to maintain and improve the quality of schools, and arise out of a belief in the power of feedback to learn, and to produce change, often accompanied by a sense of disillusionment at the lack of impact of other models of school improvement.

This definition excludes informal, self-generated feedback and separates SPFSs from systems for *public* school performance accountability and for the support of school choice, which have rather different aims and contents.

The content of the information on the school's *performance or functioning* must be taken broadly. 'School performance' here is likely to mean some kind of contextualised measure for fair comparison, adjusted to take account of factors beyond the control of the school ('value added'). 'Performance' may also include absolute performance measures and may equally relate to non-academic outcomes of schooling (e.g. behavioural and affective). Information on the *'functioning'* of schools relates to school process measures like the resources spent, the subject matter taught, the instructional methods used, and the nature of school leadership etc.

That the feedback should provide a basis for *self-evaluation* implies that the feedback should not simply be used for self-assessment, but that once such judgements have been made, they ideally lead to some kind of action, e.g. the closer investigation where and why the school under-performs, and the development of a school improvement policy.

3.   REASONS FOR SCHOOL PERFORMANCE FEEDBACK SYSTEMS

A number of factors seem to have contributed to the growth of formal school performance feedback systems in many countries over the last twenty or so years.

In many western countries in the 1980s and 90s the rise of a political climate of public sector accountability can be observed. The pressure to evaluate and report on the performance of publicly funded educational institutions did not really lead to SPFSs, however helped to create a climate in which school performance feedback is seen as more salient than previously.

Related to the accountability trend is the trend towards decentralisation in the administration of educational systems. As a result schools are more likely to seek information they can utilise for school quality control, i.e. some sort of SPFS.

There is moreover some evidence (e.g. Murdoch & Coe, 1997) that in some countries schools' perceptions of the unfairness of the public judgements of their effectiveness (cf. Visscher, 2001, for an overview of the drawbacks of public school performance indicators) were a factor in their choice to implement a confidential value added school monitoring system. The published school performance information included average raw achievement of a school's students which did not adjust for relevant features of the student intake (e.g. achievement levels of a school's intake). Schools wanted more accurate and fairer data on their own performance - among other things, to be sure about their performance and about whether improvement was really needed or not.

Next, the progress made in research in the twin fields of school effectiveness and school improvement. The former line of research has resulted in a knowledge base (Scheerens & Bosker, 1997) that can be utilised in developing systems to monitor the quality of schools (e.g. the ZEBO feedback system which will be described below).

School improvement research may have influenced the development of SPFSs too, as scientific activity there showed that educational change initiatives imposed upon schools were often not very successful. Innovation and success are considered much more probable if schools themselves are convinced that something needs to be changed ('ownership'). Receiving information on how your school is doing in comparison with similar schools may be a powerful way to make you aware and determined that something needs to be changed in your organisation.

Dalin (1998), McLaughlin (1998) and Miles (1998) stress the local variability of schools, implying that general, centrally developed policies and reform strategies will not lead to educational change in all schools. Schools are considered to differ so much with respect to their performance levels (and the underlying reasons for them), their innovation capacities and contextual characteristics, that change efforts should take much more account of what is called the 'power of site or place'. Smith (1998) goes a step further. He states that as practitioners know their educational practice best they should state the goals and changes to be worked on and, after extensive training, try to accomplish those. Adaptation to the user-context can then be achieved. A SPFS may a valuable tool within this perspective on school improvement, providing timely, high-quality information on how a school 'is doing' as a basis for practitioner-led improvement actions. That may help practitioners in finding problems in their schools as well as in solving them, before it is too late. An important additional effect may be that practitioners gain a better insight into how their school works (enlightenment) and which interventions work best in their situation.

Related to the pessimism of the school improvement authors is the view of Glass (1979) who regards 'education' as a very complex, highly uncertain and unpredictable system on which we possess only incomplete knowledge. We should not try to find eternal truths about which of several things works well in particular circumstances, as a basis for planning and manipulating education at a large distance from the teaching-learning process in schools. What should be done is the diligent monitoring of the system while the services are highly decentralised, the actors are flexible, and can choose from options what they consider best instead of precisely implementing a universal approach that has been developed somewhere at a higher level.

The increase in feedback information to schools has also been influenced by the development of multi-level and value-added data-analysis models which enable the computation of more reliable and valid information on school functioning. The availability of computerised systems for information processing has made a significant contribution to the logistics of school performance feedback (cf. Visscher, Wild & Fung, 2001).

Last but not least, research results indicate that feedback can be beneficial to future performance. The most comprehensive synthesis of research on feedback effects is Kluger and DeNisi's (1996) meta-analysis. Overall, they found an effect size of 0.41 (0.38 after various exclusions), which they interpret as "suggesting that, on average, feedback intervention has a moderate positive effect on performance" (p. 258). However, the wide range of effects found suggested that various features of the feedback, the task to be performed, or its context were significant moderators of the effect. In other words, we should attempt to clarify under what conditions feedback can optimally enhance performance.

4.   AN EXAMPLE: THE DUTCH ZEBO SCHOOL PERFORMANCE FEEDBACK SYSTEM

ZEBO is an instrument for primary education of which the development took five years. Thirteen school process and classroom process variables (for example, the extent of educational leadership, the achievement orientation of teachers, the way student performance is evaluated, students' time on task, the classroom climate) which had been found in school effectiveness research as correlates of high student performance were selected for the development of ZEBO (Scheerens & Bosker, 1997). In other words, for each of these variables a scale has been developed to measure the variable and to feed back information on this variable in terms of how the school is doing in comparison with the average Dutch primary school.

After two pilots (in 1997 and 1998), a final field test took place in 1999 in a representative sample of 123 schools in the Netherlands. In 2002, the final market version of ZEBO was released in a computerized form. This format allows schools to use ZEBO whenever they need the information, and they can obtain feedback immediately.

The process variables are measured by means of questionnaires for school management, for teachers and for grade 3-8 pupils. After completing the questionnaires in the schools, schools can generate two kinds of feedback:

- *A school report*: One can download graphic and written represen-
  tations of the results of the school under study in comparison with
  schools from a national sample on each scale in the school report.
  Furthermore, the scores of the teachers are compared to the school
  management scores.
- *A classroom report*: This report is based on information from the
  pupil and teacher questionnaires. The results from the students of the
  school in a certain grade are compared to the results of students in
  the national sample from that same grade. The responses of the
  students are also compared to the responses of the teachers.

5. THE FACTORS SUPPOSED TO MATTER FOR THE SUCCESSFUL IMPLEMENTATION OF SPFSs

Figure 1 below presents a model depicting the assumed relationships
between four groups of factors (Blocks A - D) on the one hand, and the use
(Block E) and impact (Block F) of SPFSs on the other. The model is based
on a review of the relevant literature (Visscher, 2002).

The Figure shows that the nature and intensity of SPFS use is supposed
to be influenced by the SPFS features, which result from its design process.
The nature of the implementation process and the organizational
characteristics of schools are also supposed to influence SPFS use. The
implementation process can promote SPFS use directly (e.g. by supporting
schools in accomplishing the innovation), or indirectly (e.g. via training
school staff in the required SPFS skills). Finally, the degree of SPFS use,
and the way in which it is used, is expected to lead to intended and
unintended effects.

It is important to stress that Figure 1 is meant to clarify which factors
influence SPFS use and the resultant effects (so Blocks E and F are crucial).
In other words, the Figure neither shows how all factors contribute to the
effects in Block F nor how other blocks in the Figure are related. If the latter
would have been the case, arrows between other blocks could also have been
drawn.

Figure 1 also indicates that the school environment plays a role. For
example, the extent to which the school board, district and the community
play an active role in running schools and demand high school quality may
influence to what degree schools use a SPFS to improve performance. If the
quality of school functioning is a hot issue, for instance shown by published
league tables and 'punishments' for under-performing schools, then schools
may be more inclined to improve than when external quality control is only
weak, and parents are unable to choose the school of their choice. The
educational system can also play a more supporting role by providing
schools with the resources required for change and improvement.

The variables in each of the Blocks in Figure 1 cannot be discussed more in detail here, instead we will focus on reporting the results of a study into the implementation and utilization of the Dutch SPFS called ZEBO (for more details on the backgrounds of the factors the reader can refer to Visscher & Coe, chapter 5, 2002).

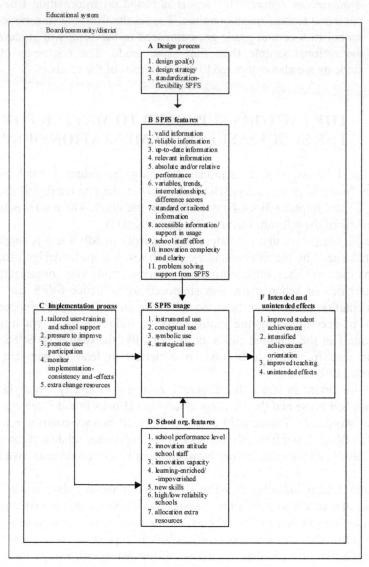

Figure 1: The assumed relationships between the factors influencing SPFS use and effects

6. LONGITUDINAL DATA ON THE IMPLEMENTATION OF ZEBO

From 2003 to 2006 the use of ZEBO has been studied in a group of Dutch project schools (in 2003 the group included 64 primary schools which used ZEBO; in 2006 this number had decreased to 43 schools). School staff filled out questionnaires and interviews were held in a selection of schools; moreover student achievement was measured by means of standardized tests for spelling and mathematics.

The research findings show that the so-called instrumental use (using feedback for improvement-oriented actions) and conceptual use (the feedback influences recipients' ideas but no visible actions) of ZEBO-output are limited especially at the teacher level. About 30 % of the schools use the ZEBO output in the period 2003-2006. In 2003 about 40% of the teachers did not study the ZEBO output. It was encouraging however that some positive effects of the introduction of ZEBO were observed: better consultation and communication between school staff, and staff paid more attention to quality care and school improvement. Student achievement did not improve in the schools using ZEBO more intensively. Negative effects were not found. Figure 2 below shows which factors especially promoted the use of ZEBO:

- several *characteristics of the ZEBO system*, e.g. relevant information, ease of use, the time ZEBO use takes, the clarity of the innovation;
- two aspects of the *implementation process*: training for ZEBO use, and extra resources to use ZEBO;
- four *school features*: staff's attitudes towards ZEBO, the encouragement to use ZEBO from principal, innovation capacity, and the ZEBO scores in 2003.

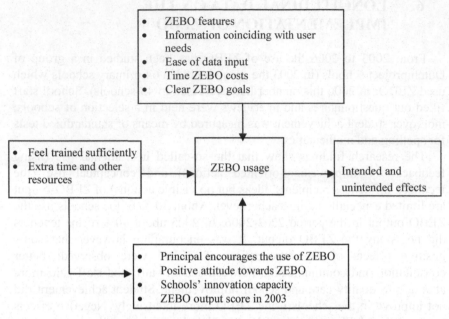

Figure 2: Factors influencing ZEBO use and effects

7.   THE COMPLEXITY OF THE UTILIZATION OF RELEVANT FEEDBACK

Overall, the level of ZEBO use was still limited in 2006. This finding is not unique as the under-utilization of valuable evaluative data has been observed in many other contexts. Weiss (1998) is one of the most well-known of the scholars who have written on this topic and based on her long experience she points to several potential problems that may occur when organizations or individuals are provided with evaluative information (like feedback) of which the content is relevant to them as a basis for improving performance.

First of all evaluation results (in our case feedback) may not be disseminated fully among all target users. We saw examples of this in the ZEBO schools: principals who did not distribute the ZEBO feedback to their teachers because the principals did not appreciate the content of the feedback.

Target users also may not understand (e.g. because of the statistics involved in feeding back student achievement data), or believe the feedback and therefore reject or ignore it.

If the feedback is accepted and understood, and it points to underperformance the recipient (the individual teacher, or the school as a whole) may not have an idea of how to improve. However, even if the recipient(s) know how to tackle underperformance, other prerequisites for improvement may not be fulfilled: the required skills and resources may be lacking.

One other potential barrier for transforming feedback into performance improvement should be mentioned: the political aspects of performance and improvement. It may, for example, be difficult to openly discuss the poor performance of a colleague, and therefore not be the preferred way to do this.

Reflecting on the utilization of the feedback schools are provided with in many countries nowadays clarifies that instrumental use (the type of information use we expect when we feed back performance information to schools) presupposes a rather complicated set of skills. Schools need to be able to work with ZEBO in terms of entering data and retrieving output. Next they need to posses the skills to interpret the feedback correctly which is not always easy as usually statistics is involved.

If the data has been interpreted and underperformance has been observed somewhere in the school, then the challenge is to find out the cause(s) of the problem and to design and successfully implement a potential remedy. These prerequisites for success will not be fulfilled in many schools.

Moreover, feedback research tells us that the effects of feedback quite heavily depend on the features of the individual who receives the feedback. To what extent is the recipient for example motivated for the goals the feedback refers to (feedback usually shows whether there is a gap between a goal and actual performance), and how motivated is (s)he for using the feedback? The latter will be dependent on the perceived feedback credibility and on the recipient's view on his/her self-efficacy (I can (or cannot) improve performance).

In our view *the* levers for furthering the use of SPFSs within schools are the provision of the resources required for working with ZEBO (as working with SPFS is time consuming) and the training and support of those who are supposed to benefit from the introduction of SPFSs. If we manage to combine the provision of feedback with the required resources and with tailored training activities (training for the skills to analyse data, diagnose problems, and to design, implement and evaluate remedies), and the support (motivate staff, social support and encouragement form school management) of school staff for working with SPFSs, then we may be able to make a difference. We may then be able to establish a basis for the improvement of processes at school and at classroom level, and via that line it may also be possible, where necessary, to improve the performance of students, teachers and schools.

8.   REFERENCES

Brophy, J., & Good, T. (1974). *Teacher-pupil relationships*. New York: Holt, Rinehart & Winston.

Dalin, P. (1998). Developing the twenty-first century school, a challenge to reformers. In A. Hargreaves, A. Lieberman, M. Fullan & D. Hopkins (Eds.), *International Handbook of Educational Change* (vol. 5, pp. 1059-1073). Dordrecht/Boston/London: Kluwer Academic Publishers.

Ehren, M.C.M. (2007). *Toezicht en schoolverbetering.* [Supervision and school improvement]. Doctoral dissertation. Delft: Eburon.

Fitz-Gibbon, C.T. (2002). A typology of Indicators. In A.J. Visscher. & R. Coe (Eds.). *School improvement through performance feedback.* Lisse/Abingdon/Exton/ Tokyo: Swets and Zeitlinger.

Glass, G.V. (1979). Policy for the Unpredictable (Uncertainty Research and Policy). *Educational Researcher, 8*(9), 12-14.

Huberman, M. (1987). Steps towards an integrated model of research utilization. *Knowledge: Creation, Diffusion, Utilization, 8*(4), 586-611.

Kluger, A.N., & DeNisi, A. (1996). The effects of Feedback Interventions on performance: a historical review, a meta-analysis, and a preliminary Feedback Intervention Theory. *Psychological Bulletin, 119*(2), 254-284.

Maslowski, R., & Visscher, A.J. (1999a). The potential of formative evaluation in program design models. In J. van den Akker, R.M. Branch, K. Gustafson N. Nieveen, & Tj. Plomp (Eds.), *Design Methodology and Development Research in Education and Training.* Dordrecht: Kluwer Academic Publishers.

McLaughlin, M.W. (1998). Listening and learning from the field: tales of policy implementation and situated practice. In A. Hargreaves, A. Lieberman, M. Fullan & D. Hopkins (Eds.), *International Handbook of Educational Change* (vol. 5, pp. 70-84). Dordrecht/Boston/London: Kluwer Academic Publishers.

McLaughlin, M.W. (1990). The Rand change agent study revisited; macro perspectives and micro realities, *Educational Researcher, 19*(9), 11-16.

McPherson, R.B., Crowson, R., & Pitner, N.J. (1986). *Managing Uncertainty: administrative theory and practice in education.* Columbus: C.E. Merril Publishing Company.

Miles, M.B. (1998). Finding Keys to School Change: A 40-year Odyssey. In A. Hargreaves, A. Lieberman, M. Fullan & D. Hopkins (Eds.), *International Handbook of Educational Change* (vol. 5, pp. 37-39). Dordrecht/ Boston/London: Kluwer Academic Publishers.

Murdoch, K., & Coe, R. (1997). *Working with ALIS: a study of how schools and colleges are using a value added and attitude indicator system.* Durham: School of Education, University of Durham, United Kingdom.

Rossi, P.H., & Freeman, H.E. (1993). *Evaluation; a systematic approach.* Newbury Park/London/New Delhi: Sage.

Scheerens, J., & Bosker, R.J. (1997). *The foundations of educational effectiveness.* Oxford: Elsevier Science Ltd.

Schildkamp, K. (2007). *The utilisation of a self-evaluation instrument for primary education.* Doctoral dissertation. Enschede: Print Partners Ipskamp.

Smith, P. (1995). On the Unintended Consequences of Publishing Performance Data in the Public Sector. *International Journal of Public Administration, 18*(2&3), 277-310.

Smith, L.M. (1998). A kind of educational idealism: integrating realism and reform. In A. Hargreaves, A. Lieberman, M. Fullan & D. Hopkins (Eds.), *International Handbook of Educational Change* (vol. 5, pp. 100-120). Dordrecht/Boston/ London: Kluwer Academic Publishers.

Van Vilsteren, C.A., & Visscher, A.J. (1987). Schoolwerkplanning: mogelijk in schoolorganisaties? [School work planning: possible in school organisations?] In B. Creemers, J. Giesbers, C. van Vilsteren & C. van der Perre (Eds.), *Handboek Schoolorganisatie en onderwijsmanagement* (pp. 6120-6124). Alphen aan den Rijn: Samson.

Visscher, A.J. (2001). Public School Performance Indicators: problems and recommendations. *Studies in Educational Evaluation, 27*(3), 199-214.

Visscher, A.J. (2002). A framework for studying school performance feedback systems. In A.J. Visscher & R. Coe (Eds.). *School improvement through performance feedback*. Lisse/Abingdon/Exton/Tokyo: Swets and Zeitlinger.

Visscher, A.J. & Coe, R. (2002). Drawing up the balance sheet for school performance feedback systems. In A.J. Visscher & R. Coe (Eds.). *School improvement through performance feedback*. Lisse/Abingdon/Exton /Tokyo: Swets and Zeitlinger.

Visscher, A.J., Wild, P., & Fung, A. (Eds.) (2001). *Information Technology in Educational Management; synthesis of experience, research and future perspectives on computer-assisted school information systems*. Dordrecht/ Boston/London: Kluwer Academic Publishers.

Weiss, C.H. (1998). Improving the use of evaluations: whose job is it anyway? In A.J. Reynolds & H.J. Walberg (Eds.), *Advances in Educational Productivity*, volume 7, pp. 263-276. Greenwich/London: JAI Press.

Whitford, B.L., & Jones, K. (1998). Assessment and accountability in Kentucky: how high stakes affects teaching and learning. In A. Hargreaves, A. Lieberman, M. Fullan & D. Hopkins (Eds.), *International Handbook of Educational Change* (vol. 5, pp. 1163-1178). Dordrecht/Boston/London: Kluwer Academic Publishers.

First no Choice, then Some Choice, and Finally Overload
A Reasonable Data Management Evolution?

Don Passey

Department of Educational Research, Lancaster University, UK

Abstract: Data management has moved in evolutionary ways in the education system in England. Although some might say that the current evolution has moved from a situation where there was no choice (20 and more years ago), to one where there was some choice (up to 20 years ago), to a position where there is now overload, this paper will argue that that is not the case when the position is viewed from certain perspectives. The paper will contend that data itself has changed little over a period of 20 years, but that data analyses, forms of data presentation, and access to data handling facilities have all changed a great deal. The paper argues that this has led to 'data complexity' rather than 'data overload'. Indeed, as the paper will show, when concerns about current national policies are considered, it is inevitable that the evolution will continue. It is argued that in this period of future evolution, 'smarter' systems will be needed if increasing numbers of facilities are to be used effectively and efficiently.

Keywords: Data management; data handling; data in schools; features of data systems; educational management and data; future of data systems

1. INTRODUCTION

It is sometimes said that the educational system in England suffers from overload in terms of quantities of data available and in terms of provision for its access. Whether this is a recent phenomenon is one question that could be asked, but whether this is a phenomenon at all is another that is perhaps more important. If the questions are viewed from the perspective of what is available and accessible, then different answers will arise from those answered from a perspective concerned with those who use or access the data and data facilities. A review of facilities that are accessible (Passey, 2008) suggests a much greater level of potential than that described when users are asked about their levels of use (indicated, for example, in Kirkup et al., 2005).

Please use the following format when citing this chapter:

Passey, D., 2009, in IFIP International Federation for Information Processing, Volume 292; *Evolution of Information Technology in Educational Management*; Eds. Tatnall, A., Visscher, A., Finegan, A., O'Mahony, C., (Boston: Springer), pp. 69–82.

So, there is clearly some truth in a statement about future wider potential of uses of data for curriculum management purposes, but the extent might well depend upon perspective. However, some forms of data have always been accessible to teachers and practitioners. There are basically, over a period of 20 or more years, three dimensions that have changed: one dimension is the flow of data within the educational system (more people have access to other people's sources of data than they had ten years ago, for instance); a second dimension is the ways in which data are analysed (added value analyses, and estimates of outcomes based on previous results have become accessible widely in the last ten years), and a third dimension is the ways that data are presented (they are accessible now in on-line format, with sophisticated graphical interfaces, which were not accessible ten years ago). So, a key question is not whether levels or forms of data have changed and evolved, but actually whether it is the ways in which they have been handled that have changed (at least, changed more than the levels and forms of data themselves). Indeed, this paper will argue that there are, in spite of claims that England has too much data, some forms of data that are still not accessible readily to teachers, and that potentially limit what practitioners can do to support young people in classrooms (which is surely where a main focus of intention of data uses should be). Current and emerging policy in England is calling for access to further forms of data, so the period of evolution is not yet at a standstill.

2.   AN EVOLUTIONARY OVERVIEW

Is it possible to plot what has happened over time with regard to data, their flow, the ways in which they are analysed, and the ways they can be accessed? Have certain features and factors remained unchanged, and what sort of pattern of evolution has there been? It is certainly possible to identify three key phases at a fairly simplistic level.

Some twenty years ago and more, there was no real choice available. Data that was easily accessible was data generated locally (teacher marks, and teacher records), and that generated nationally (external test and examination results). The amount of flow of those data was likely to be limited; school records were retained, but the data were not necessarily shared even with teachers in the same school. Analysis of data was very localised, and numbers of grades were sometimes the most sophisticated measures used in schools as value indicators.

As Selwood (1995) indicates, a turning point arose with the advent of the inspection system (suddenly schools were interested in how others would and could judge them on the basis of certain data), and of school management information systems introduced to support local management of schools (allowing data to be held as records, retained over periods of time, and reviewed to indicate shifts or trends). Both features were coincident with the advent of the National Curriculum in 1989. A range of measures to identify performance at a pupil level were developed at that time, some of them at a national level (the Standard Assessment Tasks - SATs), but others at a research level (such as those in the Centre for Educational Management - CEM, at Durham University).

By the year 2000, there was already a greater focus on school improvement, in part supported by the fact that data was more accessible to those concerned with both policy and local authority support. Ofsted (the inspection service) was in a position to chart measures and outcomes of performance, and the government department at that time was concerned with how to bring about school improvement using data (discussed in Coe, 2002). The concepts of school improvement and data feedback resulted in a range of forms of ways of reviewing data, fed back to schools to support positive development. Local authorities became interested in concepts of estimating future likely outcomes of pupils on the basis of prior results. The interest of schools in showing that their performance should account for background factors, including prior attainment and socio-economic groupings, was one element that fuelled the development of a range of measures referred to as 'added value'. This range of additional elements and analyses has led to what is sometimes referred to as 'overload'.

3. IS THE CURRENT STATE OF PLAY A MATTER OF OVERLOAD OR A LACK OF FOCUSED USE?

So, having moved through perhaps three periods of evolution, what forms of data handling facilities now exist, and for whom? A wide range of possible systems is available to teachers, schools and policy makers. Is there good reason to have them all, or do they all do the same thing? What makes them different? Is it the types of data they focus on? Or is it how the facilities handle and analyse data? Or indeed, is the difference a matter of when data is used?

As a secondary school teacher or manager, or someone supporting a secondary school, a number of facilities might be suggested as data handling tools that could be of value. For the purposes of this paper a range of twelve of the most popular data handling facilities are considered (although it should be noted that other data handling tools exist that have not been included here, including the Pearson Phoenix, the RM Integris and the Bromcom school management information systems, the Essex Target Tracker, question level analysis facilities such as that provided by Alfiesoft.com, and bespoke school facilities that have often been created using spreadsheets). The twelve facilities selected here can be categorised according to source:

- Government department and agency facilities (Key to Success, Pupil Achievement Tracker, and RAISEonline, although an additional facility, Achievement and Attainment Tables, allowing schools to login and see their data due to be published in the form of a spreadsheet of individual contextual value added scores and all coefficients used in calculations, and to calculate contextual value added analyses for groups additional to those given in RAISEonline, is not included).

- Commercial company facilities within a much wider school management information system (SIMS Assessment, Facility CMIS, and Edix Live).
- Commercial company facilities with a specific range of data handling functions (Cognitive Abilities Tests - CATs, 4Matrix, and Track to Success).
- Research and charitable status support groups (CEM, Fischer Family Trust - FFT, and Data Enabler Toolkit).

To review what these facilities offer, a first port of call might be to look at what is stated on provider web sites. The relevant provider describes each facility on-line as follows:

- Key to Success provides: "2007/08 Gifted and Talented Year 7-11 pupil data, 2007 KS3 e-results, 2007 KS2 e-results, 2007 KS3 e-results including 2007 question level data, 2007 KS2 validated e-results, 2006 KS1 PAT compatible files, 2007 KS2 e-results, KS3 PAT compatible files based on the data published in the 2006 Achieve-ment and Attainment tables (these files contain the prior attainment and pupil characteristics data used in the Contextual Value Added, CVA, model), KS4 PAT compatible files based on the data published in the 2006 Achievement and Attainment tables (the import of these files into PAT will produce CVA, Contextual Value Added, analyses)" (Department for Children, Schools and Families - DCSF, n.d.).
- Pupil Achievement Tracker can be used by teachers to: "ask questions about the effectiveness of their classroom practice looking at graphical data on the progress made by their pupils; set pupil targets informed by the progress made by similar pupils nationally; and understand fully what pupils can achieve by the diagnostic analysis of test papers. Headteachers and senior managers can view recent performance against other similar schools to help set development priorities; ask questions about the achievement of different groups within the school; and review the success of different initiatives, particularly through the ability to group pupils and look at their achievement and progress. The Pupil Achievement Tracker includes all the national data and brings it to life on screen, but takes it into the classroom by adding: pupil target setting, allowing schools to set targets informed by the progress made by similar pupils nationally; question level analysis, bringing to life what pupils can achieve in National Curriculum and Optional Tests from Years 2 through to 9. The PAT fully incorporates the functionality of the 2003 QCA diagnostic software; analysis of value-added data by different cohorts within the school, including the ability to create groups of pupils" (DCSF, n.d.).

- RAISEonline: "aims to enable schools to analyse performance data in greater depth as part of the self-evaluation process, provide a common set of analyses for schools, Local authorities, inspectors and School Improvement Partners, better support teaching and learning. Features include reports and analysis covering the attainment and progress of pupils in Key Stage 1, 2, 3 & 4, with interactive features allowing exploration of hypotheses about pupil performance, contextual information about the school including comparisons to schools nationally, question level analysis, allowing schools to investigate the performance of pupils in specific curriculum areas, target Setting, supporting schools in the process of monitoring, challenging and supporting pupil performance, data management facility providing the ability to import and edit pupil level data and create school-defined fields and teaching groups" (Ofsted and Department for Education and Skills, n.d.).
- SIMS Assessment: "helps raise pupil achievement by giving school leaders, teachers, pupils and parents the information needed to make the right decisions about pupils' learning … gives you the freedom to focus on what really matters in your school … can help you personalise learning for pupils and ease the burden of lesson planning and paperwork … can ensure leadership teams focus on school improvement and target the issues that need addressing; whether that is to raise achievement, reduce administration or target truancy … provides a means of recording a pupil's marks, grades and other scores to meet the school's day-to-day assessment needs and the statutory assessment requirements of the National Curriculum … parents can be given online access to information about how their child is doing on a daily basis so they can provide better support at home" (Capita Children's Services, 2007).
- Facility CMIS: "is the only totally integrated management information system available to schools. The program was specially designed to reduce paperwork by operating from a central data store. Data is entered once and is available immediately for all management functions, ensuring that the stored information is always up-to-date and accurate. Changes can be made through various associated programs so there are no delays or time lags. Whenever data is called up it is extracted from live figures and so produces an accurate picture of the school at the time it is needed" (Facility, 2005).
- Edix Live: "brings together all the information held in schools, local authorities and central government departments so that you can move from ad-hoc data to a knowledge based system" (Edix Live, 2007).
- CATs measure: "the three principal areas of reasoning - verbal, non-verbal and numerical - as well as an element of spatial ability, allowing you to test the full range within an entire class or year. CAT 3: provides indicators of outcomes at Key Stages 2, 3 and 4, including 29 GCSE and 24 Scottish Standard Grade subjects;

identifies individuals' strengths and weaknesses; standardised scores allow you to compare your pupils' results with the national average; results inform target-setting and the development of individual learning plans; a sound basis for year-on-year comparisons and a measure of the added value that your school creates for its pupils; generates information that helps you to build and maintain standards of achievement" (GL Assessment, 2007).

- 4Matrix allows: "schools to analyse the comparative performance of pupils across groups, providing the key measures of Within School Variation needed to support a school improvement strategy" (4Matrix, n.d.).
- Track to Success: "provides data management, online analysis, progress tracking solutions and consultancy to schools. In building a relationship with your school, Track To Success will become an essential partner in your drive for improvement" (Track to Success, 2007).
- CEM provides: "information by developing, producing and providing tests and questionnaires to be completed by students under standardised conditions. We analyse these and provide clear graphical feedback and comparisons with many hundreds of other schools and colleges. Data on pupil progress (value added) is provided when outcome measures become available. At each stage we try to measure what matters, be it attitudes, safety, relationships, learning and teaching processes etc." (CEM Centre, 2007).
- Fischer Family Trust: "Online reports are now available for Primary as well as Secondary schools (England & Wales) and can be accessed at FFT Online. Secondary schools have three main reports: (a) Subject value-added for KS4 and KS5, (b) Segmentation/ Significant Areas Grid., (c) Estimates by categories of pupils. Primary schools have two main reports: (a) Significant Areas Grid, (b) Estimates by categories of pupils" (Fischer Family Trust, n.d.).
- Data Enabler Toolkit: "supports schools in making better use of examination data. The toolkit includes the Jesson framework tutorial with personalised results alongside FFT, Raise on-line and a range of resources" (Specialist Schools and Academies Trust, 2007).

A key question that might be asked (and which is not necessarily answered by the information provided on the web sites) is whether each of the facilities provides data (raw data that is not sourced from any other data base or bank) as an element of the facility, whether they source raw data from other places, whether they analyse raw data in particular ways, or whether they present analyses of raw or transformed data. Table 1 provides an overview of these levels of functionality for each of the twelve data handling facilities.

Table 1: Categorising data handling facilities according to a range of user features

Source of data handling facility	Name of data handling facility	Whether raw data is provided	Whether raw data can be entered or sourced from elsewhere	Whether raw data is analysed within the system	Whether raw or transformed data is presented in non-tabular visual forms
Government department and agency	Key to Success	✓	✗	✗	✗
	Pupil Achievement Tracker (original)	✗	Manual transfer (copy and paste) or by import	✓	✓
	RAISEonline	✓	Transfer by import	✓	✓
Commercial company facilities within a wider school management information system	SIMS Assessment	✗	Input and transfer by imports, wizards, or copy and paste	✓	✓
	Facility CMIS	✗	Input and transfer by imports or copy and paste	✓	✓
	Edix Live	✗	Electronic transfer	✓	✓
Commercial company facilities with a specific range of data handling functions	CATs	✓	✗	✓	✓
	4Matrix	✗	Transfer by import routines or copy and paste	✓	✓
	Track to Success	✗	Transfer by import routines or copy and paste	✓	✓
Research and charity support facilities	CEM	✓	✗	✓	✓
	Fischer Family Trust	✓	✗	✓	✓
	Data Enabler Toolkit	✓	Manual transfer (copy and paste)	✓	✓

(The author would like to acknowledge the kind support of key providers who checked features in Tables 1 and 2 so that they are, to the best of knowledge, correct at the time the paper was written, but may change as features are added in the future.)

It is clear from Table 1 that choice of data handling facilities can be a difficult task for users. Some users may well wish to select facilities according to specific features. However, without this form of tabular categorisation, making such a choice might well be a quite daunting task in itself. Indeed, selecting just on this basis could well mean that certain important features concerned with more precise or fundamental curriculum uses are overlooked.

To explore issues concerned with more precise curriculum use, it is necessary to look at a second form of categorisation of data management facilities. The categorisation used (described in Passey, 2007), distinguishes eight different forms of data facility. These relate to specific uses of the data, and are much more concerned with data analysis and presentation features:

- Background results (these are prior national attainment results in each subject at the end of each Key Stage, both test paper and teacher assessment results, and they may be presented in forms for teachers to compare results in their subject with those in other subjects).
- Estimated likely outcomes for the end of the next Key Stage (are statistically produced, based on different statistical calculations, on the basis of prior results).
- Target summaries (these are set by teachers, and indicate the results that pupils should aim for in the future).
- Target histories (show changes in targets that are set by teachers over time, so it is possible to see whether aspirations are shifting up, down, or remain unchanged over time).
- Teacher assessments (these are marks that are recorded by teachers in each subject, across a year, and these might be for behaviour, attendance, effort, or homework as well as subject attainment), rather than SAT records of teacher assessments of end of Key Stage attainment.
- Monitoring displays (these records allow teachers to see whether their assessments match an expected progression, between pupils' prior attainment results and the future targets that the teacher sets).
- Added value measures (these measures are calculated at the end of certain periods of time, to show how a pupil or pupil group has performed in comparison to an expectation, which would indicate whether an added value has been gained or not).
- Measures that inform classroom practice (are measures that show details about pupil learning approaches, that offer data that go beyond those provided by monitoring displays of comparative levels of subject attainment performance, to allow teachers to make decisions about learning approaches and choices in classrooms).

Table 2 shows whether each of the twelve selected data handling facilities analyses and displays these forms of curriculum features in a visual (which could be tabular or graphical) way (irrespective of whether the data is entered into or sourced by the facility). In some cases, it will be seen that differences arise because of specific forms of analyses that underlie certain features.

Table 2: User features identifiable within the range of data handling facilities

Source of data handling facility	Name of data handling facility	Background results	Estimated likely outcomes	Target summaries	Target histories	Teacher assessments	Monitoring displays	Added value measures	Measures informing classroom practice
Government department and agency	Key to Success	✓	✗	✗	✗	✗	✗	✗	✓ (Question level analyses of SATs and gifted and talented list)
	Pupil Achievement Tracker (original)	✓	✓ (Based on DCSF calculations)	✗	✗	✗	✗	✓ (Based on DCSF calculations)	✓
	RAISEonline	✓	✓ (Based on DCSF calculations)	✓	✗	✗	✓	✓ (Based on DCSF calculations)	✓ (Question level analyses of SATs)
Commercial company facilities within a wider school management information system	SIMS Assessment	✓	✓ (If calculated, entered or imported)	✓	✓	✓ (If entered or imported)	✓	✓	✓ (If calculated, entered or imported)
	Facility CMIS	✓	✓ (If entered or imported)	✓ (If entered or imported)	✓	✓ (If entered or imported)	✓	✓	✓ (If calculated, entered or imported)
	Edix Live	✓	✓ (If entered or imported)	✓ (If entered or imported)	✓	✓ (If entered or imported)	✓	✓ (Based on system calculations, and if imported)	✓ (Based on identification of common attributes)
Commercial company facilities with a specific range of data handling functions	CATs	✗	✓ (Based on CATs calculations)	✗	✗	✗	✗	✗	✓ (Based on CATs tests)
	4Matrix	✓	✓ (Based on WSV calculations)	✓	✗	✗	✗	✓ (Based on WSV calculations)	✗
	Track to Success	✓	✓ (If entered or imported, and based on system calculation for Years 7 and 8)	✓	✓	✓	✓	✓ (Based on system calculations for any year group and groups with common attributes at any time)	✗
Research and charity support facilities	CEM	✓	✓ (Based on CEM calculations)	✗	✗	✗	✗	✓ (Based on CEM calculations)	✓ (Based on CEM tests)
	Fischer Family Trust	✓	✓ (Based on FFT calculations)	✓	✗	✗	✗	✓ (Based on FFT calculations)	✗
	Data Enabler Toolkit	✓	✓ (Based on DCSF, FFT, and Jesson calculations)	✗	✗	✗	✗	✓ (Based on DCSF, FFT, and Jesson calculations)	✗

(Note on an abbreviation not previously used: WSV = within school variation)

It is clear from Table 2 that there is no single data handling facility that might provide all of the functionality that a teacher or school might want. Indeed, the array of different forms of underlying techniques (particularly those concerned with calculations for estimated likely outcomes and added value) may well be bewildering for some teachers and schools. Although web sites, for example, sometimes indicate differences, the implications for those differences are not necessarily discussed in places that can be easily accessed. Data Enabler Toolkit, in this respect, is a potentially useful addition to the data handling facility armoury, as it offers a 'triangulation', allowing schools to compare estimated likely outcomes and added value measures on the basis of DCSF, FFT and Jesson analyses. The benefits and advantages of each can be seen and considered in the context of school need.

The analysis presented through Table 2 indicates that forms of data accessible to teachers are largely those that have been accessible in the past: national test and examination data; results from specific tests available from commercial or research groups; and teacher assessments. What the table shows is that the overload arises because of the differences that exist across the different forms of data handling facilities, and the differences that underpin the range of analytical techniques employed. It would be more correct to say that teachers and schools are confronted with 'data complexity' rather than with 'data overload'.

4.   EVOLUTION FROM THIS POINT IN TIME

So, where does the evolution go from this point on? There are clearly a number of different features where evolution might move in the future. One feature would be concerned with the flow of data. This has been a major concern of the government agency focusing on technological infrastructure (and reported on by Becta, 2005; 2007). The issue of flow of data still remains an issue, for a wide range of reasons (including the fact that virtual learning environments are being seen as a potential 'solution' to this issue in the future, even though data flow through interoperability has not been implemented successfully to date by all providers of virtual learning environments). The direction of evolution of data flow, however, appears to be now more clearly identified, since Becta (2008) have stated that they: "are clear that [the Schools Interoperability Framework] SIF has proven potential to deliver a wide range of benefits at the front line and at local and national levels, and now recommends SIF as a preferred solution ... the expectation is that the SIF standard will be adopted by local authorities and system suppliers to meet specific local business needs over the next 18 months or so".

A second feature would be concerned with the forms of underlying analyses being used, and whether there will be greater rationalisation of these, or whether they will be widened further. It is certainly not clear at this time that rationalisation will happen, but there is a clear need to explain the analyses that exist in a way that teachers and schools can understand more, and as a consequence, make better informed choices. Although not an aspect for major discussion within this paper, it should be pointed out, for example, that with regard to just one of the data handling areas that schools have access to, value added measures, at least seven different measures currently exist: raw percentages of grades; unadjusted value added; contextual value added (adjusted by DCSF for a range of background factors); within school variation; CEM measures; FFT measures; and Jesson measures. There is no known document to show clearly the distinctions between these, the benefits of each, and the ways they have or could be used to support specific school improvement needs.

A third feature would be concerned with forms of presentational access. There has been a great deal of development in this area over the past 8 years or so, and visual forms of presentation have been developed that now show traffic lighting, and the highlighting of exceptions or potential issues shown up in data sets. Presentational access is certainly an area where evolutionary developments could help a great deal more; the creation of a single portal, allowing access to key information, for example, would be a potential asset to teachers and schools. This aspect is also clearly related to the issue of what teachers or managers want or expect from a system. Many who guide schools indicate that a range of features of systems are not being used currently, and that this situation is coupled with requests from teachers or managers for information about how to get a system to offer a particular outcome (arising sometimes because of a lack of expertise in certain areas within a school, often from an information and communication technology perspective).

A fourth, and potentially important area of possible development, is concerned with a much finer grain of detail that allows different pupil groups to be considered more. A number of the measures which have been commonly used by teachers and schools to inform classroom practice (such as the use of CATs to identify whether a class has a larger number of concrete and visual learners, or abstract and textual learners, or the use of RAISEonline to look at the analysis of test data at a question subject topic level) is not yet built into a framework that meets the ways that teachers talk about or think about groups of learners or individual learners. Some new systems are being developed that attempt to provide ease of access to question level results (for example, an online system created and available from Alfiesoft.com, 2008). At the moment, data handling facilities do not allow the teacher or the school to look at the evidence that might help with questions such as: How can you find out how to help quiet pupils? How can you support those who do not have broadband at home? How can you help those who are in one-parent families? Basically, this form of evolution calls for different forms of raw data to be available, and different forms of analyses. So, rather than being concerned about data overload, we should perhaps be concerned about being 'smarter' with data.

5. DIRECTIONS AND POLICIES

The analysis presented suggests that the next stages of evolution, to satisfy some of the issues and needs of the present, should focus on four main areas:

- A wider consideration should be given to benefits of data flow, involving key stakeholders, and enabling innovative approaches to be developed.
- A wider awareness of the underlying analyses and techniques used, described in terms of benefits and uses in different curriculum situations.
- A bringing together of facilities available at a level whereby teachers and schools can see the width, and how they can make informed choices.
- A diversification of access to additional raw data, to enable different analyses to be undertaken, so that teachers can explore questions about learner groups and potential ways to support them.

This form of evolutionary development would certainly seem to be consistent with features of current national educational policies in England. The concern identified within the last point in the list above, that there is a diversification of raw data to support a wider understanding at pupil group and individual level, is clearly apparent within policies such as that described in the Government White Paper focusing on personalised learning (DfES, 2005). This policy document stated that: "Central to personalised learning is schools' use of data to provide structured feedback to pupils and their parents on progress. The National Strategies have helped over three quarters of secondary schools, last year with assessment for learning, but Ofsted tell us that assessment is still one of the weakest aspects of teaching. We will, therefore, redouble the support and challenge through the National Strategies, especially where there is danger of teachers underestimating the potential of pupils. We will also use the new School Improvement Partners to scrutinise the progress that different groups of pupils are making, so that success with some groups does not hide failure with others". A second policy document, the Government e-strategy (DfES, 2005), stated that an e-strategy should seek: "to transform teaching, learning and help to improve outcomes for children and young people, through shared ideas, more exciting lessons and online help for professionals; to engage 'hard to reach' learners, with special needs support, more motivating ways of learning, and more choice about how and where to learn; to build an open accessible system, with more information and services online for parents and carers, children, young people, adult learners and employers; and more cross-organisation collaboration to improve personalised support and choice; and achieve greater efficiency and effectiveness, with online research, access to shared ideas and lesson plans, improved systems and processes in children's services, shared procurement and easier administration". Becta (2006) in their e-strategy delivery plan, stated that: "There is a clear and simple goal: that children's services, schools, colleges, higher education and all learning providers should get the best out of the current and future technologies to improve the quality of learning and to help raise standards. We want all institutions and providers to regard using technology for learning as an essential but normal and integrated aspect of their teaching, learning, assessment and management practice. We want all children and learners to harness technology to have more choice and chances to learn in a way that suits them, which leads to greater opportunities to learn inside and outside formal education".

It is clear that the evolution of data management in education, through the use of data handling facilities, is not at an end. Indeed, some might say that it is at a mere beginning; in the past data have been focused for administrative purpose, and then for management purpose, but our current concerns are that data are focused on teacher purposes, yet policy demands that data are focused in the future on learner and carer purposes. To achieve these needs, it appears that we need to move away from perceptions of data overload, address issues of data complexity, and move towards planning for 'data smartness'.

6. ACKNOWLEDGEMENTS

The author would like to thank the representatives of the companies and agencies who kindly provided supportive feedback and checked details for the purposes of the presentation of this paper.

7. REFERENCES

4Matrix. (n.d.). *4Matrix 'Within School Variation' Toolkit.* Retrieved February 25, 2008, from http://www.4matrix.org/

Alfiesoft.com. (2008). *Assessment for learning made easy.* Retrieved August 14, 2008, from http://www.alfiesoft.com/index.php

Becta. (2005). School Management Information Systems and Value for Money: A review with recommendations for addressing the sub-optimal features of the current arrangements. Coventry: Becta.

Becta. (2006). Harnessing Technology Delivery Plan. Coventry: Becta.

Becta. (2007). *The Schools Interoperability Framework (SIF).* Retrieved July 13, 2007, from http://industry.becta.org.uk/display.cfm?resID= 28188

Becta. (2008). *Statement of intent on interoperability from DCSF, DIUS and Becta.* Retrieved August 14, 2008, from http://news.becta.org.uk/ display. cfm?resID=37481

Capita Children's Services. (2007). *SIMS - Schools Information Management System.* Retrieved February 25, 2008, from http://www. capitaes.co.uk/ SIMS/index.asp

CEM Centre. (2007). *The CEM Centre.* Retrieved February 25, 2008, from http://www.cemcentre.org/

Coe, R. (2002). Evidence on the role and impact of performance feedback in schools. In A.J. Visscher and R. Coe (Eds.). *School improvement through performance feedback.* Routledge: Abingdon.

Department for Children, Schools and Families. (n.d.). *Key to Success.* Retrieved February 25, 2008, from https://www.keytosuccess.dfes. gov.uk/

Department for Children, Schools and Families. (n.d.). *Pupil Achievement Tracker.* Retrieved February 25, 2008, from http://www.standards. dfes.gov.uk/performance/pat/

Department for Education and Skills. (2005). Harnessing technology: transforming learning and children's services. Norwich: HMSO.

Edix Live. (2007). *Edix Live 2008 – this time it's personal.* Retrieved February 25, 2008, from http://edixlive.com/

Facility. (2005). *Facility CMIS.* Retrieved February 25, 2008, from http://www.serco.com/others/facility/independent/facilityproducts/facilit ycmis/index.asp

Fischer Family Trust. (n.d.). *Data Analysis Project.* Retrieved February 25, 2008, from http://www.fischertrust.org/

GL Assessment (2007). *Cognitive Abilities Test: Third Edition.* Retrieved February 25, 2008, from http://shop.nfer-nelson.co.uk/icat/7916204main

Her Majesty's Government Department for Education and Skills (2005). White Paper: *Higher Standards, Better Schools For All - More choice for parents and pupils.* Norwich: HMSO.

Kirkup, C., Sizmur, J., Sturman, L. and Lewis, K. (2005) *Research Report No 671: Schools' Use of Data in Teaching and Learning.* Department for Education and Skills: Nottingham

Ofsted and Department for Education and Skills. (n.d.). *Welcome to RAISEonline.* Retrieved February 26, 2008, from https://www. raiseonline.org/login.aspx?ReturnUrl=%2findex.aspx

Passey, D. (2007). Technology enhancing learning: Limited data handling facilities limit educational management potential. In A. Tatnall, T. Okamoto and A. Visscher (Eds.). *Knowledge Management for Educational Innovation.* Springer: New York.

Passey, D. (2008). Data integration and school management systems in the United Kingdom. In A. Breiter, A. Lange and E. Stauke (eds.). *School Information Systems and Data-based Decision-making.* Peter Lang: Frankfurt-am-Main.

Selwood, I. (1995). The Development of ITEM in England and Wales. In B.Z. Barta, M. Telem and Y. Gev (Eds.). *Information Technology in Educational Management.* Chapman Hall: London.

Specialist Schools and Academies Trust. (2007). *Toolkits.* Retrieved February 26, 2008, from https://secure.ssatrust.org.uk/eshop/default. aspx?mcid=22&scid=34&productid=627

Track to Success. (2007). *Welcome to Track to Success.* Retrieved February 26, 2008, from http://www.tracktosuccess.co.uk/

Information Technology for Educational Management at a Ugandan Public University

Ronald Bisaso

Department of Management Studies, University of Tampere, Finland

Abstract: This article discusses the introduction of information and communication technology in educational management (ITEM) into the academic and financial administrative activities of Uganda's oldest and largest university. This university has seen the relevance of ITEM especially in enhancing its efficiency and effectiveness in view of increased enrolment. Data used were collected through documentary analysis and thematic interviews. The interviews involved 17 respondents comprising two top managers, eleven deans and directors of faculties, schools or institutes and four administrative personnel knowledgeable about the academic and financial ITEM systems. Data were transcribed and emergent themes identified. The findings illuminate a mixture of optimistic expectations and lamentations to the ITEM systems that have been aimed at integrating the highly decentralized administrative structure in the university. These comprehensive ITEM systems have been a vendor-developed and donor-funded venture. Consequently, adopting the systems has in some instances been compounded by incompatibility to the existing administrative practices. In light of these findings, it is suggested that ITEM systems ought to be first piloted in a few units prior to university-wide deployment in this developing setting with its peculiarities. Besides, on-site ITEM development would more likely remedy the mismatch between ITEM systems and the administrative processes it is meant to support even though they are projects and time-bound.

Keywords: Information technology in educational management (ITEM), information systems, management, university

1. INTRODUCTION

Universities as organizations are increasingly embracing information communication technology in educational management (ITEM) for their managerial accuracy, efficiency and effectiveness. This is premised on the changing requirements for more accountability since universities have become responsible to a variety of stakeholders for instance; students,

Please use the following format when citing this chapter:

Bisaso, R., 2009, in IFIP International Federation for Information Processing, Volume 292; *Evolution of Information Technology in Educational Management*; Eds. Tatnall, A., Visscher, A., Finegan, A., O'Mahony, C., (Boston: Springer), pp. 83–94.

governments, the private sector, funding bodies, and standards agencies. Yet, at the same time, universities are just actors in the environments in which they operate, influencing and being influenced by other actors (Amaral, Jones, & Karseth, 2002 p. 281; Maassen & van Vught, 2002 p. 225). So, the usually timely and errorless information that computerization can provide is an essential aspect for the universities' systemic and systematic responsiveness. Moreover, '[university] organizations with an inferior [information technology] IT infrastructure will be at a competitive disadvantage and will find it difficult to stay in business' (McCredie, 2003 p. 22).

Research on ITEM in universities has been reported for example; case studies on ITEM usage in workload planning in the United Kingdom (Burgess, 1996) and in Finland (Höltta & Karjalainen, 1997), and students' admission in the United States (McClea & Yen, 2005). Besides, anecdotal evidence reveals some studies on ITEM in universities in the developing regions e.g. Rodrigues & Govinda (2003) highlight advantages accruing from onsite ITEM development at a university in Mauritius. In addition, previous findings from Ugandan universities show that initial automation has been ad hoc (Magara, 1999), with low computer use among deans, heads of department and secretaries who manage students' information (see also Wakanyasi, 2002; Zziwa, 2001). Also, Inyaga (2002) reveals that there is more information technology usage in students' records management compared to research and library functions. A recent study has further proposed a strategy for an information management system for Uganda's higher education sector (Magara, 2006).

Even then, research on ITEM utilization in universities has remained generally scanty with few case studies (Tatnall & Davey, 2005 p.212), practitioner-oriented and theoretically deficient (Allen, Kern, & Mattison, 2002 p.160). Additionally, little attention has been paid to the dynamics of the higher education environment in Uganda and its linkages to the intensifying utilization of ITEM in universities hence this paper. Whether a vendor-evolved ITEM system fits into the prevailing financial and academic administrative circumstances at a developing country premier institution is another intention of this paper. The rest of this paper is structured as follows. First, the subsections on the changing context of institutional management and the evolution of ITEM at Makerere University are presented. The research question and the conceptual framework follow. The method used is given followed by the findings, and finally, the discussion and conclusions.

1.1 The Changing Context of Institutional Management at Makerere University

Makerere University was established in 1922 and is the largest university comprising 22 academic units including; eleven faculties, five schools and six institutes. The total student enrolment was 33,488 as at July 2007 (Makerere University, 2007). Makerere University has both centralized and decentralized management. There are a number of hierarchical positions including; the vice chancellor as the executive head, with two deputies (one for academic affairs and the other for finance and administration), university secretary, university bursar, academic registrar among others, all comprising top management. The deans or directors of schools or faculties or institutes are the middle managers responsible for academic, administrative and financial matters in their faculties, schools or institutes whereas the heads of departments are in-charge of academic matters at the lowest academic unit.

Institutional leadership is supported by management bodies like the university council – the highest decision-making organ, and senate responsible for all academic affairs of the university. Furthermore, the university also operates a committee structure at faculty level such as faculty boards, research and higher degrees committees, faculty finance committees, and the new faculty quality assurance committees all aimed at collective decision-making. The coordination of academic and financial activities is the responsibility of the academic registrar and university bursar respectively. The bursar authorizes all payments made by any unit of the university while the academic registrar ensures the authenticity of academic enrolment, progression and graduation. Following administrative decentralization, each faculty has either a deputy registrar and one faculty registrar or at least a faculty registrar depending on its size. These personnel are responsible for academic coordination at faculty level on behalf of the central academic registrar's department. Similarly, each faculty or school or institute has an accountant responsible for the financial procedures and transactions at that level on behalf of the bursar's office or finance department.

The present nature of management at Makerere University has been a result of recent changes in Uganda's higher education sector, a consequence of public sector reforms. These reforms have culminated into new legislation, decline in funding from government amidst increasing demand for higher education, and hence the entry of market approaches in public universities. For instance in 1992 private higher education became government policy marking the beginning of private sponsorship or fee paying programs (Court, 1999; Mayanja, 2001) with students enrolling on either day or evening programs. There was also semesterization of all academic provisions (Court, 1999; Mayanja, 2001; Musisi & Muwanga, 2003). Because faculties, schools, institutes and departments had been asked to become entrepreneurial – designing courses that the market would be willing to pay for, student enrolments have increased from 7000 students in the academic year 1993/1994 (Musisi & Muwanga, 2003 p. 33) to 33,488 students as at July 2007 (Makerere University, 2007).

These increasing enrolments coupled with diversity in funding alternatives especially private sponsorship, have seen the devolution of the financial (Mamdani, 2007 p. 175), academic and administrative structures (Court, 1999; Epelu-Opio, 2002). However, this extensive devolution has not only made financial management complex but has also put to question the allocation and monitoring of the academic and financial resources (see also Visitation Committee to Public Universities 2006, 2007). Yet with the prevailing private sector practices, Ugandan public universities ought to step up their accuracy, efficiency and effectiveness. Hence, Makerere University has started strengthening its administrative operations through ITEM systems utilization for management reporting and basic evidence-based planning and decision-making.

1.2   Evolution of ITEM at Makerere University

While computers were introduced in Uganda in 1967, adoption has been at snail-pace (Mulira, 1995). It was not until the early 1980s that systematic introduction of information and communication technology (ICT) in Makerere University commenced with funding from the African Development Bank (ADB), as an initiative of an individual university professor (Tusubira, 2005 p.89). In 1991, the university introduced e-mail usage with support from the International Development Research Council (IDRC). This project was short-lived especially with departure of an individual change agent who managed the network (Musisi & Muwanga, 2003 p.28). Over the years various units have made efforts to continue operating in a 'connected' environment e.g. in 1998 the faculty of law embarked on the use of ICT in teaching, research and administration by hiring a consultant, and with support from United States Agency for International Development (USAID), a legal information centre was established. In 1999, the newly established faculty of forestry was also fully networked with funding from the Norwegian Development Agency (NORAD). The faculty of technology has also been furnished with large functional computer laboratories (Musisi & Muwanga, 2003 p.28).

Attempts at university-wide ICT initiatives have been reported to start in 1999 after envisioning ICT as integral component in rebuilding the university (Makerere University, 2000 p. 12-13). This has provided a basis for the evolution of an ICT Policy and Master Plan, with the vice chancellor as chair of the ICT implementation committee. In the same way, the Directorate of ICT Support (DICTS), a service unit under the vice chancellor's office has been established (Musisi & Muwanga, 2003 p.29). The university has become a networked campus with total connectivity and access to electronic research journals has been facilitated through Makerere Library Information System (MakLIBIS). These initiatives have been extensively funded by the Swedish International Development Cooperation Agency (SIDA) (see Greenberg & Versluis, 2005). It should be noted that the urgency of a Financial Information System (FINIS), Academic Records Information System (ARIS) and the Human Resource Information System (HURIS) to augment the administrative processes has been addressed through funding from NORAD. Whereas the anticipated 'formal commissioning' and full production had been scheduled for May 12, 2005 (Greenberg & Versluis, 2005 p.20), it was not until January 12, 2007 that the

FINIS, ARIS, and HURIS systems were commissioned (Luboobi, 2007 p.5). It is argued that the plans for implementation of these systems have been rather unrealistic hence the delays in complete utilization. For example, 'the need to customize the systems [has] not [been] fully understood or analyzed, and this has caused some additional delay' (Greenberg & Versluis, 2005 p.20). However, in the opinion of Greenberg and Versluis, the project has been quite on time if based on a realistic timeline, and the anticipation that the ITEM systems would be in production in the 'foreseeable future, and should meet expectations'.

2. RESEARCH QUESTION AND CONCEPTUAL FRAMEWORK

The following research question and research framework guided this study.

What is the current nature of academic and financial information systems utilization in the changing context of institutional management at Makerere University?

Universities as open systems are in a perpetual state of instability. Whereas universities affect and are affected by their environments, the interaction is as unpredictable as it is nonlinear eliciting equally indeterminable consequences (Birnbaum, 1988 p. 34-35). This is further compounded by the highly fragmented nature of universities according to disciplines (Clark, 1983), yet universities also have several hierarchical levels (Hölttä, 1995 p. 235). Within this complexity, universities have opted for various tools to maintain equilibrium in their subsystems for instance departments and faculties as they operate in or respond to their increasingly unstable internal and external environments. The tools have been either 'soft' – taking the form of sanctions of committees in the decentralized management structures or 'hard' tools – in the form of computerized management information systems. Hierarchical management of complex subunits can solve the information problem (Hölttä & Karjalainen, 1997 p. 231; McClea & Yen, 2005 p. 89-91) due to the reduced amount of information on each particular unit. The higher hierarchical level then monitors output and regulates input through 'feedback information on output variables, without any need to understand the internal mechanisms of the [decentralized] subsystems' (Hölttä & Karjalainen, 1997 p.231). This would then keep the university and its units in relative equilibrium as it can stabilize or accelerate its operations basing on the prevailing environmental conditions.

3.   METHODS AND DATA ANALYSIS

This study is an exploratory case study investigating the utilization of academic and financial information systems in a changing context of institution management at Makerere University. Data were collected from 17 respondents through face to face thematic interviews on the relevance and the nature of academic and financial information systems utilization in this context. The study explored each of these participant's opinions on this guiding theme. The respondents included; the deputy vice chancellor – in charge of finance and administration and the academic registrar who represented the opinions of top university management with respect to financial monitoring and academic coordination. The director of the graduate school was included in the study on ground of being a coordinator of graduate research in the university. The deans and directors participating in the study were representative of Makerere University's 22 academic units consisting of 11 faculties, five schools and six institutes (Makerere University, 2007).

Using stratified sampling, nine deans and one director were selected from the physical sciences (computing and information technology, technology, library and information sciences, science), biological sciences (veterinary medicine, agriculture and medicine) and the social sciences (social sciences, law and education). Stratification was preferred because the sample drawn reflected the proportions of individuals with certain characteristics of the population (Creswell, 2003). In addition, the researcher sought the opinions of four administrative personnel courtesy of the deputy vice chancellor and the academic registrar as they regarded them practically knowledgeable about the ITEM systems. The researcher also purposively selected the accountant at the school of education basing on the respondent's knowledge of actual utilization of the finance information system. All interviews were recorded. Transcriptions were made according to the respondents' opinions and emergent themes were identified from the data as they provided inroads to answering the research question.

4.   FINDINGS

The data from this study suggests that the top university managers, deans or directors and administrative personnel participating in the study have seen the relevance of the ITEM systems in the efficient and effective operation of the university. The general picture of the utilization is diverse and fragmented in the case of the academic records system (ARIS). On the other hand, the finance information system (FINIS) is relatively homogeneous and consolidated. These ITEM systems are part of an integrated system procured from a vendor through donor support and installed in the first half of this decade. The system runs on a relational database and operates on a network. The procured integrated system comprises ARIS, FINIS, HURIS and

MakLIBIS. The discussion in this paper concentrates on ARIS and FINIS because these are supposedly the most widely used systems in academic units and at all administrative levels in the academic and financial operations of the university. The urgency of ARIS and FINIS is premised on the opportunity for centralized coordination of the highly decentralized nature of the university. In the same way, the increased enrolment and the devolution of financial and academic responsibilities renders manual operations ineffective and inefficient hence the need for ITEM systems.

While the university has opted for a comprehensive system that would bring together all the academic units, the incompatibilities of the system with the administrative practices has impeded complete utilization. Besides, faculties have either opted for supplementary systems or used generic software packages for their administrative support especially in students' examination results management. The interviews have further revealed that even at the centre – the academic registrar's department who are the custodians of ARIS, customization of this vendor-evolved ITEM system has been elusive hence the evolution of a supplementary system – the 'results system'. It thus appears that the centre and faculties have both found the vendor-evolved ARIS incompatible to all the university academic administrative processes hence improvisation. Moreover, the ITEM system cannot meet certain peculiar requirements of the university's school of graduate studies for instance; there is completely a mismatch between ARIS and the administration of graduate programs and tracking of graduate students' progress. As a remedy, the graduate school has opted for a home grown system from the faculty of computing and information technology at this case university.

The actual process of using ARIS starts when undergraduate students manually fill in forms and these are handed over to the deputy registrar or faculty registrar. Depending on the skill level of the registrar and the secretaries at a given faculty, the student data is either entered into the system at the faculty or the filled-in hard copies are carried to the academic registrar's department at centre where student data is then captured. It is evident that even with the decentralized administrative personnel from the academic registrar's department; the advantages that would accrue from ARIS in decentralized arrangements are yet to be fully exploited. Some modules in ARIS such as time-tabling and other managerial components are not yet used. Although the ITEM system would be presumably aimed at reducing information at the centre, the current nature of utilization serves to pile information at the centre that this may blur its performance monitoring and evaluation role.

Nevertheless, the apparent interface between ARIS and FINIS is likely to enhance concerted utilization at the faculty level. For instance, after a student has paid tuition fees, the FINIS will reflect the credit on the university account but this money cannot be disbursed to any faculty[5]. It is not until a student has been registered in ARIS, and the bank slip number obtained on payment recorded, that the system would now recognize the identity of the payee and what is due to their faculty. On that basis, the utilization of ARIS could be relatively enhanced otherwise the faculty would not receive its percentage of the tuition hence curtailing its operations.

As already noted, the FINIS has been widely adopted. This is partly because it supports the distribution of income accruing from privately sponsored academic programs to faculties basing on the existing sharing ratios. Additionally, success in the utilization of FINIS has been partly due to the technical, financial and managerial support from the University of Bergen, Norway. The now more extensive utilization of FINIS has enabled the university to avoid being defrauded through inept manual verification processes at a time of increased students' numbers. A respondent from the finance department noted thus:

> '... I will tell you, there are certain functions we had failed to do in finance. For example, it was never possible to find out how much a student had paid and what the balance is. It would take us to call a student and say bring your receipts and the student brings their receipts we add them up, we say now you were supposed to pay this, you have paid this [and] the balance is this, looking at the receipts from students. And the students used to forge right, left and centre. I am very sure that very many students studied without paying any tuition!'

The consequences of liability in case of financial errors possibly explain why the university has found it critical to solicit external support so that FINIS is fully utilized. Apparently, the university bursar can also issue monthly financial statements on the exact revenue and even the likely disbursements to the respective faculties because of the interface between FINIS and electronic bank statements from the respective banks on one hand, and FINIS and ARIS on the other.

However, the extent of FINIS utilization to disburse funds to faculties is still not as automatic as it ought to be. After the computations have been made as to what is due to which faculty or unit, cheques are then written to the respective faculties or units. This is because of the unsystematic flows of revenues from government for the payment of staff salaries, students' welfare, utilities like water, electricity, telephone bills etc. Hence there can be inadequacy of funds that if the central university administration is not keen, it may possibly transfer the figures when the money is actually not available. This finding shows that there is a mixture of 'soft' and 'hard' tools as the university maintains equilibrium. A faculty would not fully get what the central administration owes it but rather the bursar may make adjustments depending on the prevailing fiscal circumstances or requirements.

---

[5]   The central administration and the academic unit at which a privately sponsored student is registered have sharing ratios or percentages of the tuition fees paid by the student.

5. DISCUSSION AND CONCLUSIONS

The study set out to investigate the question: what is the current nature of academic and financial information systems utilization in the changing context of institutional management at Makerere University?

Like in earlier studies on the evolution of ITEM in schools (Nolan, Brown, & Graves, 2001; Wild & Walker, 2001), prior attempts at Makerere University were individual efforts of a university professor. This may possibly explain why documented efforts at ITEM utilization spanning close to three decades have been slow and are yet to be entrenched at Makerere University even though the findings show that the relevance of ITEM is underscored by all the university personnel participating in this study.

Equally important is that universities are by nature decentralized according to disciplinary bounds but also integrated by institutional management through various means. In the case of Makerere University, faculties as subunits have become power centres perhaps even justifying their decisions to evolve or procure supplementary systems to become more responsive. The current university-wide ARIS and FINIS was centrally conceived as can be seen in the ICT Policy and Master Plan, the implementation committee under the chair of the vice chancellor, DICTS – a centralized service unit under the vice chancellor's office etc. It is noticeable that this approach to the infusion of ICT into the university administrative process has been rather incongruent to the prevailing dynamics of shifts in academic, administrative and financial decentralized responsibility. Earlier ITEM ventures at Makerere University have transitioned from individual to specific faculty initiatives (Musisi & Muwanga, 2003 p.28) yet this university-wide initiative has been somewhat centralized even after the introduction of decentralization reforms. Within this changing context of institutional management, it is argued that possibly piloting ARIS and FINIS at faculty level to full utilization would have created ownership of the venture among the pilot faculties and that the other faculties would have systematically followed.

Besides, it has also been noted that instead of the centre concentrating on only 'reduced' information from faculties for performance monitoring and evaluation, it is overwhelmed with bulks of information from the decentralized academic units. This is at variance with what Höltt & Karjalainen (1997 p.231) have expressed and may have a negative effect on the institutional monitoring mechanisms. This prevailing condition could be a result of time-bound ITEM projects that are misaligned to the dynamics of institutional management. An alternative to the ITEM systems in facilitating institutional integration has been the softer mechanisms of committee structures and minutes from meetings against which academic and financial decisions have in most cases been made.

As an open system (see Birnbaum, 1988), Makerere University has seen the implementation of its ITEM systems affected by the environment from which it has been initiated and supported. In this same vein, it is clear that ITEM systems at Makerere University have had a history of donor-funding (Greenberg & Versluis, 2005 p.20; Musisi & Muwanga, 2003 p.28; Tusubira, 2005 p.89). Whereas this is an indicator of successful institutional partnerships, the timelines at times associated with these projects may not permit assimilation and even the preparedness of the university to carry on the ventures is often curtailed by the availability of finances. This has also had its effect on cultivating a sense of ownership that only surfaces when projects are fazing out, for example, the recently introduced technology fee as part of the students' tuition fees. Against this backdrop, vendor-evolved products have been the option since they would not presumably require a lot of time in proffering requirements analyses hence suiting the donor's project timelines. Moreover the vendor products have adequate documentation for reference in case of technical difficulty (Gorr & Hossler, 2006 p.14). On the other hand, legacy or homegrown systems have been found inseparable from the institutions where the vendor products have been introduced because they are easily adjustable in case of a change in the processes it is meant to support (Gorr & Hossler, 2006 p.18). This is similar to the findings in this study where a vendor product was installed but traditional or supplementary systems have been evolved in the different faculties and also the academic registrar's department. At the same time, Rodrigues & Govinda (2003 p.46) highlight the benefits that an onsite ITEM system has provided for the University of Mauritius enabling the project to address the peculiar processes in the university. It is argued that the current mismatch in the utilization of ARIS and FINIS e.g. in the academic activities of the school of graduate studies would have been probably minimized or avoided through a similar approach.

6.   REFERENCES

Allen, D., Kern, T., & Mattison, D. (2002). Culture, power and politics in ICT outsourcing in higher education institutions. *European Journal of Information Systems, 11*, 159-173.

Amaral, A., Jones, G. A., & Karseth, B. (2002). Governing higher education: Comparing national perspectives. In A. Amaral, G. A. Jones & B. Karseth (Eds.), *Governing higher education: National perspectives on institutional governance.* (pp. 279-298). Dordrecht: Kluwer Academic Publishers.

Birnbaum, R. (1988). *How colleges work. the cybernetics of academic organization and leadership.* San Francisco: Jossey-Bass.

Burgess, T. G. (1996). Planning the academic's workload: Different appro-aches to allocating work to university academics. *Higher Education, 32,* 63-75.

Clark, B. R. (1983). *The higher education system. academic organization in cross-national perspective.* Los Angeles: University of California Press.

Court, D. (1999). *Financing higher education in Africa: Makerere, the quiet Revolution* . Washington D.C.: The World Bank and The Rockefeller Foundation.

Creswell, J. W. (2003). *Research design qualitative, quantitative and mixed methods approaches*. London: Sage.

Epelu-Opio, J. (2002). Higher education reform at system and institutional level. the case of Makerere university. *British Council International Seminar,* Barnet Hill Conference Centre, London.

Gorr, W., & Hossler, D. (2006). Why all the fuss about information systems? or information systems as golden anchors in higher education. *New Directions for Higher Education,* (136), 7-20.

Greenberg, A., & Versluis, G. (2005). *Sida supported ICT project at Makerere University in Uganda* No. Sida Evaluation 05/17). Stockholm: Swedish International Development Cooperation Agency, Department for Research Cooperation.

Hölttä, S. (1995). Towards the self-regulative university. University of Joensuu. *University of Joensuu Publication in Social Sciences, 23*

Hölttä, S., & Karjalainen, K. (1997). Cybernetic institutional management theory and practice: A system of flexible workload for university teachers. *Tertiary Education and Management, 3*(3), 229-236.

Inyaga, A. (2002). The utilisation of information and communication technology (ICT) in the management of Uganda Martyrs University, Nkozi. Unpublished Masters thesis, Makerere University.

Luboobi, L. S. (2007). *Address by the vice chancellor on occasion of the 54th and 55th graduation ceremonies.* Freedom Square, Makerere University:

Maassen, P. A. M., & van Vught, F. A. (2002). Strategic planning. In I. Jenniskens (Ed.), *Management and decision-making in higher education institutions* (pp. 225-240). The Hague: Lemma Publishers.

Magara, E. (1999). Automation of students records system at Makerere University: An analytical approach. Unpublished Masters thesis, Makerere University.

Magara, E. (2006). *A framework for an integrated student information management system for higher education in Uganda.* Unpublished PhD dissertation, University of South Africa.

Makerere University. (2000). *Makerere university strategic plan 2000/01 - 2004/05.* Kampala-Uganda: Planning and Development Department Makerere University.

Makerere University. (2007). *Makerere university. "we build for the future".* Retrieved September, 28th, 2007, from http://mak.ac.ug/makerere/

Mamdani, M. (2007). *Scholars in the marketplace. the dilemmas of neoliberal reform at Makerere University, 1989-2005.* Kampala: Fountain Publishers Ltd.

Mayanja, M. K. (2001). Makerere University and the private students scheme. *International Higher Education, 25,* 11-13.

McClea, M., & Yen, D. C. (2005). A framework for the utilization of information technology in higher education admission department. *International Journal of Educational Management, 19*(2), 87-101.

McCredie, J. (2003). Does IT matter to higher education? *Educause Review,* , 15-22.

Mulira, N. K. (1995). Managing information technology in Uganda: Strategies and policy formulation. *Information Technology for Development, 6,* 95-105.

Musisi, N. B., & Muwanga, N. K. (2003). *Makerere university in transition, 1993-2000.* Oxford and Kampala: James Currey and Fountain publishers.

Nolan, P. C. J., Brown, M. A., & Graves, B. (2001). MUSAC in New Zealand from grass roots to system-wide in a decade. In A. J. Visscher, P. Wild & A. C. W. Fung (Eds.), *Information technology in educational management: Synthesis of experience, research and future perspectives on computer-assisted school information systems* (pp. 55-75). Dordrecht: Kluwer.

Rodrigues, A. J., & Govinda, S. (2003). Towards an integrated management information system: A case of the University of Mauritius. *Information Technology for Development, 10,* 41-56.

Tatnall, A., & Davey, B. (2005). Future directions in ITEM research. In A. Tatnall, J. Osorio & A. Visscher (Eds.), *Information technology and educational management in the knowledge society* (pp. 209-217). New York: Springer.

Tusubira, F. F. (2005). Supporting university ICT developments: The Makerere university experience. *African Development, XXX*(1 & 2), 86-97.

Visitation Committee to Public Universities 2006. (2007). *Report of the visitation committee to public universities.* Kampala: Author.

Wakanyasi, N. (2002). Capacity utilization of information technology in organizations: A case study of Nkumba University. Unpublished Masters Thesis, Nkumba University.

Wild, P., & Walker, J. (2001). The commercially developed SIMS from a humble beginning. In A. J. Visscher, P. Wild & A. C. W. Fung (Eds.), *Information technology in educational management: Synthesis of experience, research and future perspectives on computer-assisted school information systems* (pp. 19-38). Dordrecht: Kluwer.

Zziwa, G. (2001). *Computer utilization in the management of students' information at Makerere University.* Unpublished Masters Thesis, Makerere University, Kampala.

A New Perspective on Competency Management
Implemented Through Effective Human-Computer Interaction

Elspeth McKay and Kathy Henschke
School of Business Information Technology, RMIT University, Australia

Abstract: Making an informed decision on whether an individual is suited to undertake an educational course or industry training programme can be very frustrating. When dealing with young adults at different cognitive skill levels, it is important to be able to identify and distinguish between their knowledge/competency levels, mostly on the basis of the evidence gathered from test-items. The current absence of appropriate measurement tools to determine skill/competency/knowledge levels remains a practical issue. The main aim of this paper is to discuss the management of this important differentiation in cognitive skill performance. One of the dilemmas surrounding this type of competency evaluation is the time it takes to test an individual. Insisting for instance, that a novice undergoes a long and arduous test, including many difficult testing items, results in lowered self-esteem, reduced motivation for learning something new, may induce stress related disorders. Similarly, expecting a more competent individual to undergo numerous simple test-items can generate the same negative result. A Competency Management System (CMS) is presented to initiate effective human-computer interaction (HCI) for cognitive skills assessment.

Keywords: Effective HCI, ICT, eLearning, instructional design, workplace training, experiential learning, knowledge navigation, competency management system

1. BACKGROUND

Today's large business entities need to employ a wide range of people with diverse skills across their organizational network. The development of high level skills across the workforce is expensive and requires major investment. The cost to employers of vocational education and structured training *(even 10 years ago)* has been estimated by the *Australian National Training Authority* in 1996 as $6.186 billion, which reflects 57% of the total training cost of $10.845 billion (Richardson 2004).

Traditionally, employers view training as an expensive solution that is implemented to fix problems. In the current climate of changing work practices, every time a new *information and communications technology*

Please use the following format when citing this chapter:

McKay, E. and Henschke, K., 2009, in IFIP International Federation for Information Processing, Volume 292; *Evolution of Information Technology in Educational Management;* Eds. Tatnall, A., Visscher, A., Finegan, A., O'Mahony, C., (Boston: Springer), pp. 95–106.

(ICT) tool enters the work-environment employers seem to pour endless amounts of money into upgrading their employees' skill base (McKay, Axmann, Banjanin & Howat, 2007). The difficulty of this continual invest-ment in workplace learning begs the question of what we know about the impact of these emerging ICT tools on institutional effectiveness. Furthermore, a large number of the eLearning solutions that have been implemented recently have been poorly designed and inadequately tested. Much of the paper-based training materials are simply loaded into a learning management system or courseware shell (McKay et al. 2007); without including adequate knowledge navigation or consideration for the principles of instructional design. eLearning implementations frequently fail to check whether learning actually occurs (as demonstrated by increased proficiency of the participants). In cases where checks are made, most attempts fail to use valid measures of the *changes* in proficiency (Fahy 2004). Within the corporate sector, it is no wonder that current eLearning solutions are poorly regarded by management and often remain unused by employees (McKay et al. 2007); thereby making them ineffective and an expensive waste of limited resources. There are similarities within the education sector, where there is further concern for upgrading higher-education graduates' employability skills.

2.   EMPLOYABILITY SKILLS FOR PROFESSIONAL PRACTICE

A recent report from the ICT Skills Foresighting Working Group highlighted an increasing demand for ICT professionals with a broader skill set that includes technical and non-technical skills (DCITA, 2006). Yet a report funded by the Department of Education, Training and Youth Affairs (DETYA), notes the predicament of *"... a large proportion of applicants for positions are considered unsuitable"* (DETYA, 2000:vii). They identify key skill deficiencies of graduates in the areas of oral business communication; creativity and flair; problem solving; independent and critical thinking; and understanding of business practice.

Beckett & Hager (2002) propose employability skills are acquired through completing a variety of tasks in a range of novel workplace contexts. However, providing the variety of classroom contexts for experiential learning/training is limited. So too are the scope of tasks that can be offered for execution. For example, there is an assumption that learning the theory of teamwork and then working on a team assignment within a university setting provides students with the teamwork skills that transfer into the workplace setting. Research evidence suggests that knowledge and skills gained in the classroom does not become usable at work without further learning in the workplace (Eraut 2002). Eraut explains why managing this type of skills' transfer is problematic by adding that acquired knowledge only has meaning once used; and its meaning is strongly influenced by previous contexts of use.

Professional competencies are developed through the experience of professional practice (Hager 2001 in Gonczi 2004). Over time professional practitioners develop expertise in their field of specialty. They acquire the ability to read situations on how to behave, how to communicate and act at work; and the capacity to make judgments. The Dreyfus Model of Skill Acquisition (DMSA) charts the incremental changes of a professional's cognitive skill development over five levels of proficiency: novice, advanced beginner, competent, proficient and expert. Benner (1982) and Smith & Sadler-Smith (2006) found that learning needs of professionals varied according to their stage of professional development. Individuals in the early stages of professional development require more learning support in the form of guided instructions, feedback and affirmation; while learning approaches and materials required for the final stages of professional development should support holistic thinking and formation of abstract concepts to develop practice-based theory.

Learning/training practitioners responsible for planning the professional development of workplace personnel are required to recognise and accommodate the different stages of professional development. To manage this process, a clear knowledge of the differentiation of humans' information processing is vital. Competency management is now discussed using the DMSA as a means to appreciate the complexities of cognitive skill acquisition.

3. UNDERSTANDING COGNITIVE SKILL ACQUISITION

In any instructional/training event it is important to identify the learning domain (Clark et al. 1983), and to specify the tasks that are essential for developing the skills and knowledge to achieve the expected learning outcomes (the instructional goals). While DMSA shows incremental changes in cognitive skill acquisition, in this paper our use of the same term however divides cognitive skill development into two clear sets. As such, the first refers to the set of cognitive skills associated with declarative (knowing what); the second relates to the procedural knowledge (knowing how) (McKay & Merrill 2003). This type of cognitive skill acquisition can be analysed in four discrete categories (van Dongen 1996):

1. *Verbal information* (knowing basic terms)
2. *Intellectual skill development* (basic rules, discriminating and understanding concepts and principles)
3. *Intellectual skill* (higher-order-rules, problem solving, the ability to apply concepts and principles in new situations)
4. Two different types of *cognitive strategies* (a) to identify sub-tasks, recognize un-stated assumptions, and (b) to recall simple prerequisite

rules and concepts, integrating learning from different areas into a plan for solving a problem.

In some instances, these categories of skill can be embedded within the learning content (hierarchical skill development). However, this type of framework is unsuitable for some other training environments (building skills for a specific task). Instead, according to McKay (2007), the learning domain should concentrate on the intellectual skills associated with a particular problem solving issue (like deciding which form of public transport to catch to work).

3.1   Identify Cognitive Style Preference

It is not sufficient to categorize human information processing as neat DMSA skill categories (McKay, 2000). To fully understand the complexities of cognitive skill acquisition, one first needs to explore the various ways human-beings gather up their new information. The literature reveals research which distinguishes the human ability to process information, as a combination of mode of processing information, and the way people represent information during thinking (see Figure-1) (Riding & Mathais 1991). There are two fundamental cognitive dimensions, *'Wholist-Analytic'* and *'Verbal-Imagery'* that affect human performance in two ways. The first relates to how information is perceived and interpreted, while the second relates to how already memorised related information is conceptualised (Riding 1993). Cognitive style is therefore understood to be an individual's preferred and habitual approach to organizing and representing information.

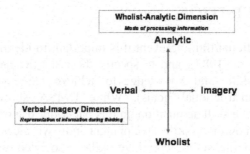

Figure-1: Cognitive style construct

Measurement of an individual's relative right/left hemisphere performance and cognitive style dominance has been a target of researchers from several disciplines over the last decade (Riding & Rayner 1998). Different theorists make their own distinctions about cognitive differences (Riding & Cheema 1991). According to Riding and Cheema, for example, the *Wholist-Analytic* continuum maps to the cognitive categories used by other researchers (see Table 1). These well known terms are used frequently throughout the literature in a number of different research disciplines.

Table-1: Researchers' terms for processing information – mapped to Riding's WA continuum

Terms describing cognitive differences	Researchers
Levellers-sharpeners	(Holzman & Klein 1954)
Field dependence-field independence	(Witkin et al. 1962)
Impulsive-reflective	(Kagan 1965)
Divergers-convergers	(Guilford 1967)
Holists-serialists	(Pask & Scott 1972)
Wholist-analytic	(Riding & Cheema 1991)

The *Wholist-Analytic* dimension (or continuum) defines that learners tending towards the Wholist side of the continuum are able to understand a concept as a whole, but may find difficulty in disembedding its separate components (McKay 1999). On the other hand, learners who are identified towards the Analytic end of the scale, analyse material into parts, but find difficulty in understanding the whole concept.

The *Verbal-Imagery* continuum measures whether an individual is inclined to represent information verbally or in mental pictures during thinking (Riding & Rayner 1998). Verbalisers prefer and perform best on verbal tasks, while Imagers are superior on concrete, descriptive and imaginal ones. When there is a mismatch between cognitive style and instructional material or mode of presentation, performance is deemed to be reduced (Riding & Caine 1993).

The difficulty in the past for competency management has been in knowing how to initiate effective instructional strategies to suit a wide range of cognitive styles. An answer to this problem lies in knowing how to manage the interactivity of instructional format and cognitive style preferences. An effective tool is discussed next, which provides a means to operationalize cognitive style preference and instructional format has been used to initiate competency skill development (McKay, 2007).

3.2   Meta-Knowledge Process Model

Previous research has shown this variation in cognitive style, with participants demonstrating preference for verbal (textual) or visual (pictorial) representation (McKay 2007). For this reason, it is critical to create an instructional environment which caters for the full range of cognitive style preference with delivery options for users to choose from. To this end, the *Meta-Knowledge Processing Model* shown below represents an effective and robust learning systems' design tool (Figure-2). This Model articulates an adaptive courseware designing tool, which reflects the user's preference for thinking mode (*Verbal- Imagery*), while also providing both

Wholist-Analytic instructional strategies to capture the user's inherent information processing mode. Moreover this Model can also be used to broker the DMSA proficiency levels.

Drawing on the *Meta-Knowledge Processing Model*, every component of the learning/training environment can be described fully to provide detailed learning system specifications. This is especially important with the production of the visual resources. Each picture should be logged with the associated interactions for audio and access arrangements. To reduce (users') stress, it is also important to keep track of the inter-relating eResources. This ensures a seamless access path to the learning/training resources. Contemporary approaches to instructional design repeatedly lack an ability to recognise and accommodate the dynamics of cognitive processes necessary for online learning (see Figure-2). This systems' design modelling tool identifies interactive relationships between cognitive style and instructional format, and the need to adapt the instructional format dynamically. It requires a concurrent acquisition of meta-knowledge relating to the learner's cognitive performance with a knowledge-level-analysis of task difficulty (McKay 2000).

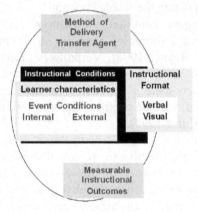

Figure-2: Meta-knowledge processing model

The instructional environment can be described in detail using this *Meta-Knowledge Processing Model* to define each facet of the system. Consequently, the method of delivery that is to be chosen to achieve the measurable instructional outcomes, for instance: for each of the DMSA proficiency levels with graded expectations for novice, advanced beginner, competent, proficient and expert. This Model can also be used to determine readiness for study or skills development, when using computer keyboard is difficult. In cases such as this the delivery method (or transfer Agent as shown in Figure 2) could be identify replacing the keyboard with touch screen technology. This is where a systems designer may wish to keep track of specific learning system essentials: like ensuring that the learning systems are always fun to use, and the (knowledge) navigation is kept simple

(Duchastel, 1991-2). For instance: instead of using a keyboard and mouse, users are to press the touch screen to navigate forward, backward and exit the learning programme.

To demonstrate how using a design tool such as the Meta-Knowledge Processing Model, can improve competency management through effective HCI a competency measurement pilot system is discussed next.

4. COMPETENCY MANAGEMENT STRATEGIES

The reasons why people need to develop new skills or retrain for the workplace are countless. In some cases the individual is merely committed to life-long-learning; while in others the choice to develop new skills may be due to unforseen circumstances: like responding to new management in an organizational change, or needing to find a different job because of an accident, or enduring long-term unemployment. Managing the decisions that are made concerning appropriate training/education/reskilling programmes for people after some type of traumatized event, it is important to differentiate what an individual knows, from what they do not. This paper describes a skills/competency measurement technique that is efficient, reliable, and safe to administer. Competency evaluation for both education and corporate training sectors is necessary to determine remedial intervention for youthful individuals, and adults requiring vocational re-training/ rehabilitation. Knowing an individuals cognitive style preference is critical (McKay 2000), because not all individuals respond to text and visual instructions in the same manner. Thereby incorporating features of the DMSA to determine skill level proficiency.

A new approach will therefore depend upon competency assessment that enables: differentiated teaching, provide adaptive cognitive skills measurement, correctly identify different levels of competency, promote self-confidence and enhance motivation towards learning abilities. Benefits of such a competency management system (Anderson et al. 2007) increase opportunities for people to participate in appropriate learning/retraining programmes. In turn, this targeted reskilling enhances the socio-economic fabric of an economy by reducing wasteful welfare support, and promoting personal growth.

Motivation for a *'competency management system (CMS)'* follows the successful Australian 2003 research project funded by the Telematics Trust: *'Automated Educational/Academic Skills Evaluation: Enhanced opportunities for young people returning to study or vocational training'* (McKay 2007). The EASY project team developed a simple computerized cognitive skills testing instrument which showed clear differentiation of competency levels between participants. The Meta-Cognitive Process Model was used by the developer to customize the instructional conditions, which identified the users' attitude towards using a keyboard in a test-environment. A distinctive feature of the CMS is the innovative use of touch screen technology.

Touch-screens offer a non-threatening mechanism to alleviate computer-phobia (Fisher 1991). However, the EASY pilot had several instructional design issues which need to be improved. Firstly, the EASY test-items were grouped into subject categories, not in order of competency requirement. By using the pilot results, it was possible to reorder the test-items from simple to more difficult, adding more test-items at each competency level. This initiates the development of a reliable competency measurement tool to identify individual cognitive performance. This customized cognitive performance test instrument identified where appropriate intervention, based on existing cognitive skill level, and assisted an EASY user select appropriate entry level for courses/training programmes (McKay, Martin & Izard 2005).

Once the competency hierarchy has been developed, an '*Adaptive Instructional Differentiation (AID)*' measurement tool will be built to enhance the reliability of EASY. In simple terms, the AID competency measurement tool captures the user's response time and scoring (right/wrong) to logically modify the sequence of test-items. If a user has quickly and correctly answered 2 or 3 simple level test-items, then the EASY-AID will move transparently into the next skill/competency level. Conversely, if the user is having difficulty within a competency skill level, the test-items offered will remain within that level or even revert to the previous lower skill level. Once the user's skill/competency level has been determined, EASY-AID will acknowledge their participation and terminate the test. In addition, to respond to the popularity of the moving image expressed by the EASY Mk-2 users in the 2003 project (McKay 2007), video clips will be used to stimulate elevated attitudinal/motivational outcomes. The fundamentals of instructional design strongly suggest absolute necessity for *"show-me"* visual examples (Merrill 2003).

EASY-AID will be implemented within community welfare services, government agencies and places of learning (including the secondary school system); where differentiated teaching strategies are a necessity for dealing with the wide range of skills and competency levels of people wishing to take up retraining programmes and/or return to study.

5. EASY-AID FEATURES

The first enhancement will be the empirical reordering and expansion of the original screening test-items (identified in the 2003 Telematics Final Report); thereby filling in the gaps in cognitive performance, identified from the 2003 data analysis with newly designed test-items.

The next step will be to design, test and build adaptive assessment instrumentation using ICT tools, which determine an individual's success on individual cognitive skills' test-items, while monitoring the overall time an individual takes to complete the whole skills' test. The EASY-AID system will test for competency with:

- Literacy skills – written, oral comprehension, expression
- Numeracy skills
- Problem solving and organization
- Memory and concentration levels

To satisfy the instructional conditions/learner characteristics identified in the Meta-Knowledge Processing Model, the electronic content for the EASY-AID system will involve everyday activities including: identification of familiar objects, decisions on magnitude (basic maths), health and safety, food preparation, and knowledge of consumer awareness issues. These life-skills examples will be implemented through graphical metaphors involving objects that may include: pictures, textual paragraphs and diagrams, and video vignettes (including audio). The input device implemented for the EASY-AID system will be through touch screen devices (human tactile response/stylus-pen).

Success rate and completion times will be logged by EASY-AID, and as such will be transparent to the participant. Personal details of the EASY-AID user will not be stored electronically by the system. These confidential data will be the responsibility of the facilitator.

6. EASY-AID APPLICATION

It is expected that EASY-AID will facilitate the following outcomes:
1. **Enable differentiated teaching:** Correctly targeted learning/training programmes that facilitate appropriate instructional/training strategies are prescribed on the basis of an appropriate skill diagnosis.
2. **Provide adaptive cognitive skills measurement:** Tailoring the competency skills' assessment session increases self-worth/confidence/ motivation through: (a) reducing the time to take a test, and by providing a more efficient measurement level of skill/competency/ knowledge levels, (b) giving credit for more rapid completion of task.
3. **Correctly identify different levels of competency:** A widely dispersed skills monitoring device that tracks progress is especially important for locating cognitive skill deficiencies following some kind of traumatized life-event.
4. **Promote inclusive learning environments through assistive technology:** When touch screen technologies are utilized as the sole input device, this increases accessibility to cognitive assessment for a wide range of physical disabilities, including the recovery from spinal cord injuries, stroke, or amputees, removing the need to interact with the EASY-AID system through a computer keyboard and mouse device (McKay, 2007).

7.   CONCLUSIONS

The development of professional practitioner skills is an on-going priority for organisations and educational institutions. The use of adaptive assessment instrumentation in computer-based training materials not only promotes learning by catering to individuals at different skills levels with different learning requirements; but also has the potential to track the progress of professional skills' development. Once the CMS is fully developed it will be trialled by students at the start and end of their 12-month industry placement. This is an experiential workplace programme that occurs in the third year of their 4-year undergraduate Business Information Systems degree. Results of these trials will track the contribution of workplace learning in the development of the students' professional skills.

The findings will highlight complications that are amplified when assessing people who are entering vocational rehabilitation, looking for work after a long absence. The significance of this competency management technique is highlighted by the range of educational/training programmes that would benefit from such a tool. For instance, proactive skills/knowledge testing of young children can reveal where remedial instructional activities should best begin to correct a literacy problem. Differentiating competency in older people means there can be more effective decisions made for their re-entry to study or re-skilling for a new job.

8.   REFERENCES

Anderson, N., Lankshear, C., Courtney, L. & Timms, C. (2007). Girls and ICT survey: Initial findings, *Curriculum Leadership Journal*, Retrieved 29/02/07 from Http://Cmslive.Curriculum.Edu.Au/Leader/Default.Asp?Id=13812

Beckett, D. & Hager, P. (2002). Life, *Work and Learning: Practice in postmodernity*, London & NY, Routledge.

Benner, P. (1982) From Novice to Expert. *The American Journal of Nursing,* 82, 402-407.

Clark, R. C., Elam, R. J. & Merrill, M. D. (1983). Training Content Experts to Design Instruction: An Adaptation of Component Display Theory. *Performance & Instruction Journal*. September: 10-15.

DCITA (2006). Building Australian ICT skills: Report of the ICT Skills Foresighting Working Group. In Australia, C. O. (Ed.) Barton, ACT.

DETYA (2000). Employer satisfaction with graduate skills: Research Report 99/7, Feb 2000 Evaluations and Investigations Program. In Division, H. E. (Ed.) Canberra.

Duchastel, P. (1991-1992). Towards methodologies for building knowledge-based instructional systems. *Instructional Science* 20(5-6): 349-358.

Eraut, M. (2002) The interaction between qualifications and work-based learning. in K. Evans, P. H., L. Unwin (Eds.) Work to Learn. London, Kogan Page.

Fahy, J. F. (2004). *Media Characteristics and Online Learning Technology. Theory and Practice of Online Learning.* T. A. F. Elloumi (Ed.) Canada, Athabasca University. Available through http://cde.athabascau.ca/online_book/copyright.html ISBN: 0-919737-59-5

Fisher, M. (1991). Computerphobia in Adult Learners. *Computer Education*: 14-19.

Gonczi, A. (2004). The new professional and vocational education. In Foley, G. (Ed.) *Dimensions of Adult Learning: Adult education and training in a global era.* Crows Nest, NSW, Allen & Unwin.

Guilford, J. (1967). *The Nature of Human Intelligence.* NY, McGraw-Hill.

Holzman, P. & Klein, G. (1954). Cognitive-system principles of levelling and sharpening: Individual differences in visual time-error assimilation effects. *Journal of Psychology* 37: 105-122.

Kagan, J. (1965). Individual differences in the resolution of response uncertainty. *Journal of Personality and Social Psychology 2*: 154-160.

McKay, E. (1999). An investigation of text-based instructional materials enhanced with graphics. *Educational Psychology* 19(3): 323-335.

McKay, E. (2000). *Instructional Strategies Integrating the Cognitive Style Construct: A Meta-Knowledge Processing Model (Contextual Components That Facilitate Spatial/Logical Task Performance): An Investigation of Instructional Strategies That Facilitate the Learning of Complex Abstract Programming Concepts through Visual Representation.* Applied Science (Computing and Mathematics Department). Waurn Ponds, Geelong, Australia, Deakin University, Available online from http://tux.lib. deakin.edu.au/adt-VDU/public/adt-VDU20061011.122556/

McKay, E. (2007). Planning effective HCI to enhance access to educational applications, *International Journal Universal Access in the Information Society.* Springer Berlin / Heidelberg(6:1). ISSN:1615-5289(200706)6:1; 1:0. 77-85.

McKay, E., Axmann, M., Banjanin, N., & Howat, A. (2007). Towards web-mediated learning reinforcement: Rewards for online mentoring through effective human-computer interaction. Paper presented at the 6th IASTED International Conference on Web-Based Education. Held March 14-16, Chamonix, France, p:210-215, ISBN:978-0-88986-650-8, Retrieved 15/04/07 http://www.iasted.org/conferences/pastinfo-557.html.

McKay, E., Martin, J., & Izard, J. (2005). Cognitive awareness in vocational training programmes: Targeting successful outcomes for young people and those wishing to undertake vocational training. Paper presented at the 3rd International Conference on Universal Access in Human-Computer Interaction, held at the 11th International Conference on Human-Computer Interaction (AC, UAHCI, HIMI, OCSC, VR, U&I, EPCE):, Las Vegas.

McKay, E. & Merrill, M. D. (2003), E. McKay (Ed.) Cognitive skill and Web-based educational systems. *eLearning Conference on Design and Development: Instructional Design - Applying first principles of instruction.* Informit Library: Australasian Publications On-Line: [Online] Available 25.1.07 (http://www.informit.com.au/library/) from http://search.informit. com.au/browsePublication;isbn=0864592841;res=E-LIBRARY. 96-108.

Merrill, M. D. (2003), E. McKay, Ed. Keynote Address: Does your instruction rate 5 Stars? *eLearning Conference on Design and Development: Instructional Design - Applying first principles of instruction*, Melbourne, Informit Library: Australasian Publications On-Line: [Online] Available 25.1.07 (http://www.informit.com.au/library/) from http://search.informit.com.au/browsePublication; isbn=0864592841; res=E-LIBRARY 13-14.

Pask, G. & Scott, B. C. E. (1972). Learning strategies and individual competence. *International Journal Man-Machine Studies* 4: 217-253.

Richardson, S. (2004). Employers' contribution to training, *Formal Report: National Centre for Vocational Education Research (NCVER)*. ISBN 1 92086 00 7. 2006.

Riding, R. (1993). A trainer's guide to learning design : *Learning Methods Project Report*. Birmingham, Assessment Research Unit, University of Birmingham, UK: 47.

Riding, R. & Cheema, I. (1991). Cognitive styles - an overview and integration. *Educational Psychology* 11(3&4): 193-215.

Riding, R. J. & Caine, R. (1993). Cognitive style and GCSE performance in mathematics, English language and French. *Educational Psychology* 13(1): 59-67.

Riding, R. J. & Mathais, D. (1991). Cognitive styles and preferred learning mode, reading attainment and cognitive ability in 11-year-old children. *Educational Psychology* 11(3 & 4): 383-393.

Riding, R. J. & Rayner, S. (1998). *Cognitive Styles and Learning Strategies*. UK, Fulton.

Smith, P. J. & Sadler-Smith, E. (2006). *Learning in Organizations: Complexities and diversities*, London & NY, Routledge.

van Dongen, C. (1996). Quality of life and self-esteem in working and non-working persons with mental illness. *Community Mental Health* 32(6): 535-549.

Witkin, H. A., Dyke, R. B., Patterson, H. F., Goodman, D. R. & Kemp, D. R. (1962). *Psychological Differentiation*. NY, Wiley.

Students' Inquiry Learning in the Web 2.0 Age

Jacky W.C. Pow, Sandy C. Li and Alex C.W. Fung
Department of Education Studies, Hong Kong Baptist University, Hong Kong, China

Abstract: The information proliferation in the Web 2.0 age has led to several emerging issues, namely, the authenticity of information, disorientation, and information searching and citation issues in the academic field. Students often find themselves in a difficult situation when they are doing Web-based inquiry learning when the usefulness and truthfulness of the Web information are doubtful. Based on the study of pre-reading activity and Web searching behaviour of Lawless, Schrader, and Mayall (2007), and the Web information evaluation work of Eagleton and Dobler (2007), this paper proposes a guiding framework to help students determine the usefulness and truthfulness of information in their inquiry process. This framework also provides guidance on how to store and cite Web 2.0 information. However, the effectiveness of the guiding framework has not been empirically tested and further study regarding its applicability is called upon.

Keywords: Web 2.0, Inquiry Learning, guidance framework

1. BACKGROUND

Over the past couple of years, the development of Asynchronous Javascript and XML (AJAX) has provided us not just a browsing tool but a Web-based platform where we can *participate* and *publish*. The concept of 'the Web as a platform' is one of the key principles of Web 2.0 (O'Reilly, 2005). Because of this the amount of information on the Web has expanded in an exponential scale. This augmentation of Web information may mean more resources for our students, on the one hand, but also an impediment in their learning on the other. In Web-based inquiry learning, students need to manage their inquiry processes such as searching, categorizing, prioritizing, and rearranging of information; and they should also learn to differentiate facts from opinions. Besides having a skeptical mind to examine the information they have collected on the Web in the inquiry process, they need to have a systematic way to store, retrieve and cite the collected information.

Please use the following format when citing this chapter:

Pow, J.W.C., Li, S.C. and Fung, A.C.W., 2009, in IFIP International Federation for Information Processing, Volume 292; *Evolution of Information Technology in Educational Management*; Eds. Tatnall, A., Visscher, A., Finegan, A., O'Mahony, C., (Boston: Springer), pp. 107–116.

These tasks are becoming more challenging to students as a result of the blooming Web 2.0 and this paper is an attempt to put forward a guiding framework for them to address these issues.

2.   WEB 2.0 AND THE INQUIRY PROCESS

While there is seemingly no agreed definition of Web 2.0, some preliminary principles were outlined in the first Web 2.0 Conference in 2004 (O'Reilly, 2005). Among the principles, 'Web as a platform' and 'Harnessing Collective Intelligence' were the most eye-catching ones. In simple terms, Web 2.0 is the second generation of the World Wide Web where colla-boration of participants' efforts in building up social, business, or other communities has been made possible; in contrast to the traditional surfing on WWW sites merely for browsing information. Thus Weblog and Wiki have become common terms that are illustrative of Web platforms where users can publish their views or share their experience. In Web 2.0, users can now have more freedom to "add, remove, or otherwise edit and change all content very quickly and easily, sometimes without the need for registration" (Wikipedia, as cited in Edmonds, 2006). This new and efficient mode of knowledge-building for anybody with any background to contribute has in some ways played down the role of *expert* knowledge. However, it is also exactly this 'collective intelligence' (The New Media Consortium and the EDUCAUSE Learning Initiative, 2008) that the proponents of Web 2.0 treasure.

In the early days of the information age, educational institutions simply had to provide facilities for students to access the needed informational resources in support of their inquiry learning initiatives. Access to information on the internet was not as easy and widespread as today, and students needed only training in information searching skills. Apparently students of today need something more. On top of facilities and surfing skills in cyberspace, their habits of mind is also an important concern. Students need to have not only an inquiry mind but also a critical mind. There is so much deceptive information on the Web nowadays that makes us hard to judge what is authentic. Hence, the problems associated with accessibility to information have now evolved into problems related to identifying trustworthy, relevant and quality information. Convenience in accessing information is no longer a priority in the inquiry process. The success of ICT now depends on whether one can get useful and truthful Web information (Eagleton and Dobler, 2007) rather than on the ability to just get access to information. As a result, we need to develop students' critical thinking and evaluation skills in order to assist them to evaluate the usefulness and truthfulness of the information collected on the Web. As pointed out by Richardson (2006, p.77), "given the fact that the amount of information going online shows no sign of slowing, if they (the students) are unable to consistently collect potentially relevant information for their lives and careers and quickly discern what of that information is most useful, they will be at a disadvantage. And, as with the rest of these changes, it's our job to model and teach these skills."

3. THE EMERGING ISSUES

3.1 The Authenticity of Information

The emergence of Web 2.0 technology seems to have led us from an information age to a *misinformation* age. The flooding of blogs, social networking and social video-streaming platforms (e.g., YouTube and Yahoo!Video) may well only mean more opinions but not facts and knowledge. Through the Internet, spreading a piece of rumour is as simple as a mouse click. It would be really difficult not only for our students but even for us to tell what is *real* on the Web. In this respect, we have to find a way to help our students learn to distinguish the *good* from the *poor* information. Thus Wikipedia, for instance, has recognized the potential problems of 'everyone can contribute' in providing information, and has already strengthened its monitoring or quality assurance mechanism so as to regain the confidence of its readers to make reference to it as a reliable source (Wikipedia:Verifiability, accessed 2007). This is not something trivial as more and more people are using Wikipedia as a reference source.

Authenticity and authoritativeness of information thus has become an important issue in today's world since information is so easily accessible and distributed over the internet. In this Web 2.0 age, virtually everyone can *participate* and *publish* online. Publishing on the Web is so popular nowadays because the production cost is much lower than its print counterpart as a result of the shortened production cycle of a publication. People can publish and enter the e-publishing industry much more easily than in the old days. The question is – who would gatekeep the quality so that the information or knowledge on the Web is accurate and trustworthy?

For long we have trusted academic publishing (e.g. journal and books) because of the peer review or editorial refereeing. Publishers especially the established ones would be very conscientious in what they are publishing. The editors of the publishers are the *gatekeepers* and this quality checking mechanism has been functioning well. Many of us may agree that information on the Web is profuse, updated, easily accessible, useful, etc. This impression might have been implanted in the minds of our students and it is now time to do something in remedy. We tend to assume that most of the print text are credible and take for granted that we are not "the first stop in the evaluation chain, which initially begins with authors, editors, and publishers, all of whom have provided additional layers of evaluation before the printed text reaches his hands." (Eagleton and Dobler, 2007, p.163.) However, we have to educate our students that most of websites do not automatically have this built-in evaluation mechanism. This has been contrasting to the established evaluation mechanism mentioned above. There is thus a need to have some good guidelines for our students in evaluating Web information.

3.2 Disorientation issue

Another problem that many of us might not handle well in using the Web is *when to pause*. The vast information on the Web makes one easily disoriented in an ocean of knowledge. Searching on the Web is much more complicated than reading a book, with different websites organizing different contents of different levels in various ways. The Web is not a well organized information depository and students would have difficulties in encountering this issue of breadth versus depth when surfing on it. This is especially so for young students who may not have much Web or hypertext experience. The spaghetti-like hyperlinks embedded in a hypertext environment often exacerbate this disorientation problem, and students can easily get lost in the cyberspace. As Kehoe puts it, "access to vast amounts of information is not the whole answer. The power to discover the right info quickly and easily, to separate nice to know from need to know info is essential if superhighway users do not drown in electronic junk info....An info flood does not necessarily mean that people become informed." (cited in Eagleton and Dobler, 2007, p.163.) Too often, unfortunately, the responsibility of getting the appropriate level of information is solely put on the students.

3.3 Information searching and citation issues

Another emerging issue with Web 2.0 is one's inability to make reference to the exact location of dynamic webpages written with AJAX. Web content written with AJAX will update automatically without the need to reload the whole webpage. This means that the links which we once cited would likely be constantly updated. This dynamic nature of AJAX webpages creates problems for the existing search engines. The search results of most existing search engines provide links that contained the keywords. With AJAX webpages, although links are provided, they may not necessarily bring us back to the previously identified webpages by the search engines since the page content might have been changed a number of times already. This has made proper citation of Web2.0 information problematic.

Web 2.0 may be doing something good to the business or communication industry such as word-of-mouth advertising and staying in touch with the customers through *social networking* (Skul, 2008). In education, the benefits are not so eminent yet. Web 2.0 does provide more opportunities for us to communicate and collaborate but it may not have direct benefits to teaching and learning. On the contrary, Web 2.0 seems to *dilute* the truthfulness of information on the Web as the authoritativeness of a piece of information on the Web cannot be easily established. This is because there is usually no quality assurance or peer review of what is posted on the websites (Sandars, 2006). This is especially the case when anonymous users (some wiki websites do not require the users to register or identified themselves) can edit the content of wiki quickly and easily (Edmonds, 2006).

So getting back to inquiry learning, Internet resources are said to be useful when students can search for suitable information to complete their project and teachers can find useful information to support their teaching. But how could we effectively locate useful and truthful information in Web 2.0 environment? How could the information on AJAX webpages be cited? How can we square this circle? These are the obstacles that needed to be surmounted.

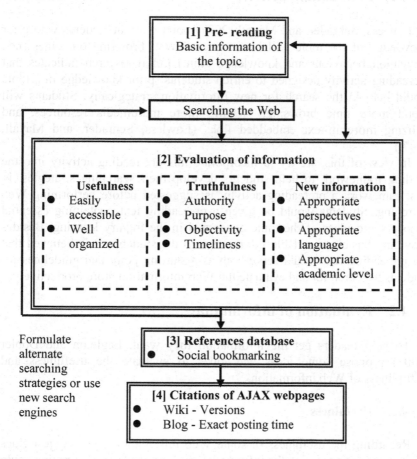

Figure 1: The proposed guiding framework in managing inquiry process in Web 2.0 age

4.   A PROPOSED GUIDING FRAMEWORK

Our proposed guiding framework consists of four parts, with each part focusing on different stages in the inquiry learning processes. They are [1] pre-reading activity which focuses on information searching strategies and behaviours, [2] Evaluation of information which highlights the evaluation of usefulness and truthfulness of information, [3] References database which refers to organizing the information, and [4] Citations of AJAX Webpages which emphasizes the need to give additional information in citing Web 2.0 materials (see Figure 1 above).

4.1   Pre-reading activity

Lawless, Schrader, and Mayall (2007) point out that students with prior knowledge of the topic will have better WWW browsing outcomes (i.e., navigation behaviour and knowledge gain.) Initial research indicates that prereading activity designed to enrich students' prior knowledge in a topic would help in the search for new information strategically. Students will spend more time browsing, viewing more multimedia resources, and utilizing more in-text embedded links (Lawless, Schrader, and Mayall, 2007.)

In view of this, we try to incorporate this pre-reading activity into the guiding framework to help students develop their searching strategies. In this framework a prereading activity is suggested before performing Web searching. Students would be given a prereading text containing essential concepts and ideas of the topic concerned in the inquiry learning. Besides providing basic and reliable information to the students, it is believed that the prereading text would serve both as a starting point and guidelines for students to search for and evaluate the Web information more productively.

4.2   Evaluation of information

To help readers get the information they want, Eagleton and Dobler (2007) propose some ideas and clues to evaluate the usefulness and truthfulness of Web information.

4.2.1 Usefulness

Regarding the usefulness of some Web information, they suggest clues like the ease of accessing the information and whether the information could help them to answer the questions on hand. Usually graphics, diagrams, figures or multimedia within the website are helpful for users to understand the topic concerned. If the information is not systematically organized or the supporting materials are not helpful, then the usability of the information of that website would be low.

4.2.2 Truthfulness

Regarding the evaluation of trustfulness of Web information, they propose an array of clues to be used, viz. authority, purpose, objectivity, and timeliness. *Authority* refers to who wrote the information. Assess the credential of the author (personal, company or organization). If possible look for the qualifications of the website author and his/her email address. The *purpose* of the website also guides the type of information available and the way information is shown. The *objectivity* of web information requires a fair description of all sides involved without bias and opinion. Users should try their best to detect bias or opinions versus truth and facts. *Timeliness* refers to whether the Web information is current and up-to-date. Most credible websites contain a footer to show the dates of creation and last update. Users can then decide whether or not to use the information in these websites. With all these clues, users may have a better chance to get more reliable Web information.

4.2.3 New Information

The evaluation of new information will work with the prereading text. In this part, students would assess the Web information from three aspects: appropriate perspectives; appropriate language; and appropriate academic level. With the basic information provided by the prereading text (or a detailed mind-map), students may be able to search for information from the orientation set out in the text. Moreover, the language used in the prereading text may serve as guidance for students to search for information of similar level of language use. With the level of details provided in the prereading text, students may be able to compare the academic levels of the Web information and hence to facilitate the evaluation process.

4.2.4 References database

After the evaluation, there will be two possible outcomes. One is that the search did not contain the needed information and it is necessary to formulate alternate searching strategies or use a new search engines (Eagleton and Dobler (2007). Another possibility is that the needed information had been identified. In this case, the students would need a way to store and retrieve their information. In this respect, we consider social bookmarking (a Web 2.0 service) to be fitting for this purpose. Simply put, social bookmarking (e.g., del.icio.us) is a public and online service for Web users to "save links, annotate them with unique keywords or 'tags' to organize them, and then share them with the world." (Richardson, 2006, p.91) Through this find-tag-share process, students can then create a community of researchers that have the same interests or endeavours, gathering relevant information together with other Web users (Richardson, 2006). Most importantly, teachers can also participate in this social bookmarking, helping the students to gather more quality websites for inquiry learning.

4.2.5 Citations of AJAX Webpages

As for the issue of citation of AJAX webpages, we do not have a simple and direct solution. Although more and more scholarly publishers begun assigning Digital Object Identifier (DOI) to journal articles and documents (APA Style, 2007), this can only solve part of the problem. As the content of blogs and wikis is prone to be updated, revised, moved and restructured without an overarching body to supervise all these resources, the chances to be assigned a persistent link (or DOI) are thin. Therefore even though a link was cited, it would still be unable to direct the readers to the source that used. Nevertheless, we need to edify our students to recognize the importance of proper referencing, in the least. Perhaps the addition of some extra information, such as the *version* of a Wiki and the *exact posting time* of a Blog, should be included in the citations; so that readers are provided with the paths as far as possible if they are interested to re-locate the information.

5.   IMPLICATIONS ON MANAGING STUDENTS' INQUIRY LEARNING

Managing a class of students to use technology-based inquiry learning is demanding because it would require the provision of extensive scaffolding and guidance to facilitate student learning by the teachers (Hmelo-Silver, 2006; Quintana, 2004). As Hmelo-Silver *et al.* have said, the teachers would need to assume "a key role in facilitating the learning process and may provide content knowledge on a just-in-time basis." (Hmelo-Silver, Duncan, and Chinn, 2007, p. 100.) This is a challenging and demanding role for teachers as inquiry learning is a process with multi-stages of Planning, Retrieving, Processing, Creating, Sharing and Evaluating (Alberta Learning, 2004). Generic information literacy skills are required on students' part in the various stages to identify possible information sources, to choose and record pertinent information, and to organize the information. In this regard, our proposed framework can provide guidance to students to construct meaningful linkages between various stages in the inquiry model. At the same time, teachers can use the framework as a road-map to help manage and monitor students' progress at the different stages in the inquiry learning process. With terminologies and a common language based on the framework, the provision of just-in-time input and feedback by teachers to students would be much facilitated.

Moreover, teachers would also have a clearer picture on the quality of the Web information collected by the students. As suggested in the framework, a references database could be developed on a social bookmarking platform (e.g., Del.icio.us), so that both students and teachers can refer to a common central source of references for the issue(s) being inquired. While students can thus learn collaboratively by cross-checking the truthfulness and usefulness of the Web information collected by peers, teachers can assess the ability of their students in evaluating and organizing the Web information. This centralised repository is also useful for teachers to verify what the students have referenced in order to provide timely feedback; or to input subject knowledge as necessary to fill in any gaps identified.

6.   CONCLUDING REMARKS

While inquiry learning is gaining its popularity as a learning approach, we have to let our students know the important question – where does this piece of information come from (Cafolla, 2006)? We all agreed that referencing system is essential in academic community. Therefore, it is natural for us to nurture our students to have a skeptical view towards Web information. This is important. The Web may bring us convenience in accessing information but at the same time may also bring us troubles in digging out useful information when there are too much. A little more effort to verify the information is better than using a piece of misinformation or acquiring some wrong concepts. This essential academic practice should be fostered in our basic education.

This paper is an attempt to propose a guiding framework for students and teachers undertaking inquiry learning. The proposed framework is intended, on the one hand, to help students learn to categorize and manage the information they collect on the Web; and on the other hand, to help teachers to better manage students' inquiry learning process. However, this guiding framework is still in a conceptual stage and its effectiveness is yet to be empirically tested and further study regarding its applicability is called upon.

7.   REFERENCES

Alberta Learning (2004) *Focus on inquiry*, Alberta, Canada: the Minister of Learning.

APA Style (2007) Electronic Media and URLs, *APA Style Guide to Electronic References*. Retrieved 2 Feb 2008, from http://www. apastyle.org/elecmedia.html

British Computer Society (2007) *The Web: Looking back, looking forward.* Retrieved 3 June 2007, from http://www.bcs.org/server.php?show= conWebDoc.10773

Cafolla, R. (2006) Project MERLOT: Bringing Peer Review to Web-Based Educational Resources. *Journal of Technology and Teacher Education*, 14(2), p. 313-323.

Eagleton, M.B. and Dobler, E. (2007) *Reading the Web*. New York: The Guilford Press.

Edmonds, R. (2006) Up from the grassroots. *E.learning Age*, October, p.14–16.

Hmelo-Silver, C. E. (2006). Design principles for scaffolding technology-based inquiry. In A. M. O'Donnell, C. E. Hmelo-Silver, & G. Erkens (Eds.), *Collaborative reasoning, learning and technology* (pp. 147–170). Mahwah, NJ: Erlbaum.

Hmelo-Silver, C.E., Duncan, R.G. and Chinn, C.A. (2007) Scaffolding and Achievement in Problem-Based and Inquiry Learning: A Response to Kirschner, Sweller, and Clark (2006). *Educational Psychologist*, 42(2), p. 99–107.

Lawless, K.A., Schrader, P.G., and Mayall, H.J. (2007) Acquisition of Information Online: Knowledge, Navigation and Learning Outcomes, *Journal of Literacy Research*. 39(3), p. 289-306.

The New Media Consortium and the EDUCAUSE Learning Initiative (2008) *The Horizon Report 2008 Edition*. CA: Author.

O'Reilly, T (2005) What Is Web 2.0? *O'Reilly*. Retrieved 25 December 2007, from http://www.oreillynet.com/pub/a/oreilly/tim/news /2005/09/30/what-is-web-20.html

Quintana, C., Reiser, B. J., Davis, E. A., Krajcik, J., Fretz, E., Duncan, R.G., et al. (2004) A scaffolding design framework for software to support science inquiry. Journal of the Learning Sciences, Vol.13, p. 337–386.

Richardson, W. (2006) *Blogs, WiKis, Podcasts, and Other Powerful Web Tools for Classroom*. Thousand Oaks, CA: Corwin Press.

Sandars, J. (2006) Twelve tips for using blogs and wikis in medical education. *Medical Teacher*. Vol. 28, Iss. 8; p. 680–682.

Skul, D. (2008) Web 2.0 – Advertising Advantages. *Article Alley*. Retrieved 30 Jan 2008, from http://www.articlealley.com/article_463605_81.html

Wikipedia:Verifiability, Retrieved 8 December 2007 from, http://en.wikipedia.org/wiki/Wikipedia:Verifiability

How and Why Finnish Universities of Applied Sciences Defined a New Approach to Build a Next Generation Student and Study Management System

Tuulikki Paturi

HAAGA-HELIA University of Applied Sciences, Finland

Abstract: This paper reports a project where Finnish Universities of Applied Sciences (UAS) defined a new approach to build a next generation Student and Study Management System (SSMS). The project identified, defined and described the key processes in a future SSMS. The definition based on business processes described by expert users. The project developed tools and rules to draw and read the process charts.

Keywords: Student and Study Management System (SSMS), business process definition, process description.

1.   BACKGROUND

The Finnish Universities of Applied Sciences, UAS, (former polytechnics) have operated from the mid-1990's. Each UAS introduced an own SSMS at that time. The systems have been developed continuously but they are based on client-server architecture and their operational logic has its origin in the outdated techniques of that time. They do not satisfy in all respects the information needs of universities any more and few or none educational planning processes are supported. The present systems register the transactions well but do not support resource planning nor are the present systems in accordance with the linings of the information management strategy of the Finnish Ministry of Education.

The Ministry of Education has published a strategy for information management in years 2006 – 2015 (2006). The strategy has a vision:

As a result of cooperation in information management the administrative sector has well defined concepts, business processes and interfaces which have helped to build innovative integrated and dedicated services for the sector. This leads to efficient operation and

Please use the following format when citing this chapter:

Paturi, T., 2009, in IFIP International Federation for Information Processing, Volume 292; *Evolution of Information Technology in Educational Management*; Eds. Tatnall, A., Visscher, A., Finegan, A., O'Mahony, C., (Boston: Springer), pp. 117–128.

services in education, research and culture are available in a uniform and easy way.

The strategy has two significant linings that met the needs of UAS:

1. Strengthening of the common basic information about teaching, research and culture and electronic services.
    The objective is to improve the information support of studying, teaching, research and culture, to increase the integrated use of the information and to reduce the number of separate systems. For this, the core concepts and basic processes concerning the students, study records and teaching are unified and they serve as a basis for the common information processing systems which include the whole process from application up to the completion of studies. All the new services are carried out with electronic services.

2. The common architecture of information management and services
    In the services of the administrative sector, the architectural linings of the public administration, defined standards and open interfaces are carried out. The basis for the system development is service oriented architecture (SOA) which makes the effective use of core functions and databases possible also in unconnected applications.

These reasons led to the fact that ARENE (the Rectors' Conference of Finnish Universities of Applied Sciences) established the project ProAMK (Pro UAS) to specify the functionality of the student and study management system for Finnish Universities of Applied Sciences. The project started in the autumn of 2005 and ended December 2007. The project was financed by the Ministry of Education and by the UAS equally, and the costs were 60000 Euro.

2.   ORGANISATION OF THE PROJECT PROAMK

Based on preliminary work ARENE named a steering group for the project and a project group of eight experts as well. Each expert represented a certain field in educational management within UAS. They were nominated by ARENE after a survey of willingness to participate. The project group was supported by five expert groups in different fields in educational management. The project had a full-time project manager. A total of 29 UAS were represented in the expert groups by 250 experts in educational and administrative management. The project used Moodle learning environment as working space and all documents were published there for those interested to follow the proceedings (Project ProAMK 2007).

3.   THE PROJECT OBJECTIVES

The future information system will be used as the most central infor-mation system of the educational management. All the information which is necessary for the planning, operating, reporting and evaluating a university in action is registered in it. The project has three main objectives

1. To identify and define the processes which are common to all the actors and are described on the basis of the present state. On the basis of these the core level of the system is defined.
2. To identify and describe the processes which are common to every UAS and which are the key processes to be supported by the new SSMS.
3. To define the models, types of functionalities and interfaces for UAS to enable other information systems to operate as a part of the new SSMS. These can be for instance payroll systems or do-it-yourself systems for specialized needs.

(Project ProAMK 2007)

What kind of a future does the new SSMS serve? (Stenlund 2007)

*   From a registration system to a resource planning system.
*   Versatile (funding bodies, administrator(s), customers, students, management).
*   Time conscious; changes in the structures are possible and expected.
*   It always supports the objectivity; from the individual level to ministry level.
*   Supports evaluation and prognoses; from objective definition to the outcomes.
*   Both the social mission and the financing model place the students' success to realize their own plans at the core of the matter.

4.   OPERATIONAL ENVIRONMENT

The project group first identified all the actors involved in the UAS and what kind of functionality they represent in the year around life of the UAS. The result is depicted in Figure 1 (Ruuskanen, Hyttinen 2007).

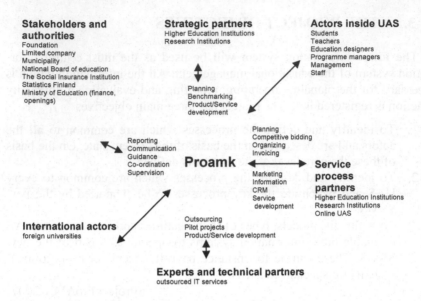

Figure 1: The UAS operational environment

5.   WHAT PROCESSES SHOULD AN SSMS INCLUDE?

At first the project group gathered together in order to define the most essential core processes and supporting processes in SSMS. After many sessions, the result is depicted in the following Figure 2 (Ruuskanen, Hyttinen 2007).

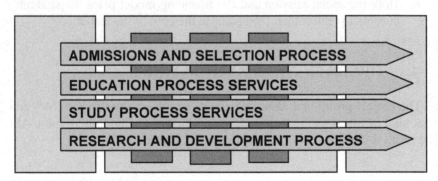

Figure 2: Core processes and supporting processes in SSMS

The core processes of an SSMS are service processes which support both the core processes and the supporting processes of a University of Applied Sciences. The core processes are the following: Admissions and selection process, Education process, Study process and Research and development process. The supporting processes are User services, Student services and Report services.

This approach is at so high a level that every UAS could accept it. While defining the sub processes we found the difficulty of speaking the same language. All the core concepts did not have the same content and the processes were managed differently in every UAS. The actors in the processes differed in their organisational status and this was a common fact to confuse the mutual understanding about the process content. Soon we found out that we need tools to success in the SSMS definition. The tools were the selection of a standard notation for process descriptions and the definition of the concepts.

6. HOW TO ACHIEVE JOINT UNDERSTANDING IN PROCESS DESCRIPTIONS?

One of the most significant tasks of the definition phase was to describe the processes of the basic operation of UAS so that they give a good base to continue to the system specification. Each member of the project group was responsible for one big process and together with the expert groups they divided the processes into sub processes.

The project group studied earlier implementations of process definitions by users and learned the need for easy tools to draw the processes and the need for well-specified notations. The project group chose MS Visio to be the drawing tool mainly because every UAS had MS Visio due to the contract between Microsoft and Finnish higher education institutions. The processes were described using BPMN (Business Plan Model Notation) Swim lane charts and the project group guided the drawing by defining a template, choosing a stencil and making rules for process elements. The stencil included all the necessary and the only allowed symbols. The rules were simple:

- The actor at the end of the swim lane is universal and reveals only the role of the actor, not the organisational position. Each UAS can conjure up their professionals as actors.
- The process proceeds with the model **input - process – output**. Every activity is followed by an output which serves as an input to the next activity. This was the key success factor in managing the thinking of several people in several organisations with different backgrounds.

After describing the processes, each project group member demonstrated the charts to his/her expert group. The discussion in expert groups was stormy and revealed the need for concept definitions. The project group decided not to define every concept within a UAS (= never ending task). Instead the concept definition was strictly restricted to those concepts needed within the SSMS. These concepts were found in the process descriptions as data objects and were defined from the point of view of the information system. Every process description has a user story to help the decoding of the chart. The next Figure (3) depicts one example of 45 produced process descriptions.

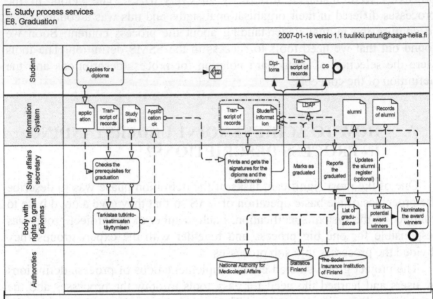

User story

- The student applies for a diploma by submitting a form when he/she has passed all the studies required.
- The study affairs secretary (or comparable) gets the message and checks that all the documents needed for graduation are available and marks the application ready for the next step.
- The body with the right to grant diplomas verifies that the student has met all the prerequisites for graduation and marks the application as accepted.
- The study affairs secretary
  - o   prints out the diploma, diploma supplement and transcript of records and asks for all signatures needed,
  - o   marks the student as graduated in the SSMS and
  - o   updates the alumni register if applicable
- The SSMS produces
  - o   a report of graduates in the order of superiority between a given time to the body who decides scholarships
  - o   reports of graduations to all in need and
  - o   data extractions to be delivered to authorities.

Figure 3: Example of a process description (Project ProAmk 2007)

The project manager organized a wide road show (7 meetings) to introduce the processes to about 250 experts in UAS. Afterwards the descriptions were circulated for official expert comments to the UAS at the end of 2006. The first round generated so many comments that the steering group decided to have a second circulation for comments at the beginning of

2007. The process descriptions were updated according to all relevant comments.

7.   DEFINING THE CONCEPTS

The terminology work was begun after the production of the first versions of the process descriptions. The project group produced a lexicon of about 180 terms, their concepts and with references to other lexicons. All terms used in the process descriptions were restricted to be in the scope of the SSMS to be defined. The project group did not try to define all the terms within the sector of educational administration and management because the specified definitions are related to the context they are used in. This fact was very important to realize and it clarified the discussions and definitions.

8.   FOREIGN REFERENCES

The project group decided to take as foreign references the extensive cooperation projects that have been carried out in other Nordic countries and Germany. These systems were LADOK in Sweden, Felles Studentsystem in Norway, STADS in Denmark, SAP and HIS in German. The German system HISinOne is currently under heavy development and it proved to be the only one to meet the strategic linings of Finnish Ministry of Education.

9.   THE RESULTS

The project succeeded well in identifying, defining and describing the key processes in a Student and Study Management System for Universities of Applied Sciences. These are a good starting point to develop a new SSMS of the future university.

The key processes and their sub processes to be included in the future SSMS are the following:

1. Education process services
   - Planning of the coming education
   - Planning of the coming courses
   - Planning of teachers workloads and timetables
2. User Services
   - Students
   - Staff
   - Student union
   - Alumni
3. Student admission and selection services
   - Making public the programmes and their entrant places

- Managing the applications
- Student selection
4. Student services
   - Managing the right to study
   - Managing changes in the right to study
   - Student self-service
   - Student financial aid
5. Study process services
   - Career planning
   - Participating in courses
   - Finding a way to enrol for courses in partner HEI's
   - Enrolling for exams
   - International mobility
   - Work placement
   - Thesis
   - Graduation
6. Reporting services
   - Support for quality management (course feedback, programme feedback)
   - Reports of all activities inside SSMS
   - Data transfers to other information systems
7. Research and development services
   - R&D activities with results
   - R&D reporting
   - Project management

(Project ProAMK 2007)

These processes are common to all Universities of Applied Sciences. Other processes like facility management, human resource management and financial management were left out because they depend on the status of the UAS ownership. Municipal UAS use the municipality's information systems and private UAS have their own systems for resources, finance and payrolls.

The vision of the information technology in educational management within higher education is presented in Figure 4. It is based on the ideas of electronic services and service oriented architecture.

The operational system has core functions that may have been implemented with IT systems from different software producers. The only requirement is that these systems can change data by integrating them together via open interfaces. A layer of service process applications (in one portal) provide process oriented web services to the user.

The interface to the system is so well designed to support the business process that no special training is needed for the users. The users have role dependent views to the system which define the rights to see and update the stored data. User self service is available 24/7.

A data warehouse is attached to the operational system to gather all the relevant information for managing the university. The data warehouse includes business intelligence tools (for reporting and analysing), tools to extract, transform, and load data into the repository, and tools to manage and retrieve metadata. The whole repository is used to by the university management and some statistical parts of it can even be used by authorities.

The performance feedback system includes the tools for quality assurance to provide confidence of the effectiveness of the universities functions.

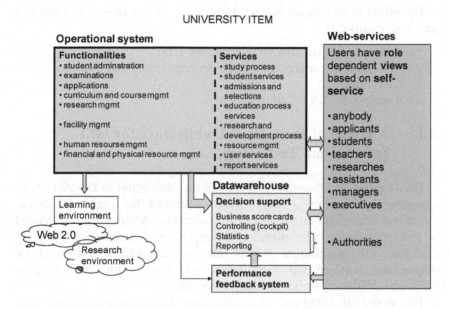

Figure 4: University Information Technology in Educational Management

The project did not succeed in defining the models, types of action and interfaces connecting other information systems to operate as a part of the new SSMS. This definition required a vision of the technical realization of the system and the project group did not reach consensus in this matter. The interest groups and comparison of alternatives were too many and the amount of work needed to reach a consensus did not meet the deadline. The open questions were among others the way to organize the building of the system, should the database be centralized or decentralized, should the system be built from a scratch or is there a ready made system that fulfills the objectives, what is the role of UAS and its DIY-systems connected to the current SSMS an so on.

During the project period the traditional universities realized that they have same kind of problems and they showed some interest to start a similar project. In a country of 5 million people it is neither wise nor cost-effective to build two separate SSMS in higher education. The steering group decided not to give more time to the ProAMK project. Instead they outlined a new approach to the problem area and a new project is starting to continue the work together with the traditional universities, Ministry of Education and

CSC. (CSC is the Finnish IT center for science, a non-profit company administered by the Ministry of Education providing IT support and resources for academia, research institutes and companies).

10. THE FUTURE

The Ministry of Education started in March 2008 a project to carry out three master projects:

1. A model of Enterprise Architecture for HEI
2. Definition of concepts, common concept model and a common data warehouse
3. A generic SSMS for all HEIs.

10.1   A model of Enterprise Architecture for HEI Information Technology

The Ministry of Education proposes that a description of functions with supporting information systems to be developed for higher education institutions according to the model of Enterprise Architecture developed for Finland's public administration. Enterprise architecture is a tool for developing the organisation and its information systems. It is used for collaboration between top management and chief information officers (Pulkkinen, Valtonen, Heikkilä, Liimatainen 2007).

The model of enterprise IT architecture defines responsibilities and common functional models at the following levels:

- **Functional architecture**
  The services and processes from the point of view of the life cycle of the users and objects and from the point of view of administrative structures and the social role.
- **Information architecture**
  The concepts which are related to functionalities, the production of services and processes, the data elements corresponding to the concepts, the structures of the concepts and data relations between them and the relations to the processes and services.
- **IT-system architecture**
  The services produced by the information systems and the information processing support for functionality and the relations between the information systems and data.
- **Technology architecture**
  The technology related solutions for IT-systems and IT-infrastructure and the structure of IT-systems.

10.2   Definition of concepts, common concept model and a data warehouse

This project will produce a data warehouse to be shared within all HEIs and the project will take into account the outcomes of the ProAMK-project and other releated previous projects and data warehouse solutions as well. The Ministry of Education reserves the right to define the concepts needed for governing HEIs.

10.3   A generic SSMS for all HEIs

A cooperative project between the traditional universities and universities of applied sciences will be started with following actions:

- Define and implement a generic SSMS (uniform knowledge and uniform basic processes).
- The University of Kuopio started a project to report the essential functional similarities and differences in current SSMS.
- The applicability for Finnish circumstances and the quality of the HISinOne system currently under development by German non-profit organization Hochschule-Informations-System GmbH will be evaluated.

    HISinOne is web-based integrated software system that covers all business processes of universities of any size and form of organization and supports the requirements of the Bologna process. It uses service-oriented architecture with interconnected components. Interoperability with existing environments is possible with webservices, integration of databases and import/export functions. HIS is an open source developing community.

- The definition of study administrative processes will continue based on the ProAMK project.
- The existing admission and student selection systems within HEI will be recognized.

CSC, the Finnish IT center for science, will coordinate these projects and the next checkpoint will be on November 2008 with further decisions.

During the ProAMK period the surrounding world changed so that the project can now be considered as the first step to realize a new SSMS for Finnish HEI. All the agreements of objectives and results for the year 2009 between the Ministry of Education and universities (traditional and UAS) include the commitment to participate in these three master projects explained above.

11. REFERENCES

HISinOne Die neue Software-Generation 2008 http://www.his.de/pdf/01/
HISinOneInformationsbroschuere.pdf. (with English summary) HIS
Hochschule-Informations-System GmbH: http://www.his.de/english/
organization, Date accessed 30.5.2008

Ministry of Education (2006): The strategy for information management in
years 2006 – 2015 in the administrative sector of Ministry of
Education, Helsinki Finland, ISBN 952-485-260-8

Project ProAMK (2007) documentation on web-page https://www.ProAMK.
fi/ (in Finnish), Date accessed 30.5.2008

Pulkkinen, Valtonen, Heikkilä, Liimatainen 2007: Enterprise architecture
models, Finnish Enterprise Architecture Research, Project Research
and studies 3/2007, Ministry of Finance, June 2007 ISBN 978-951-804-
713-4

Ruuskanen, Hyttinen (2007) Proamk – loppuraportin tiivistelmä 17.1.2007
WM-data Oy, https://www.proamk.fi/raportit/Proamk-v1.0.pdf, *part of
Project ProAMK documentation,* Date accessed 30.5.2008

Stenlund Thomas (2007) Tietoperusteinen johtaminen ammattikorkea-
koulukontekstissa, Ineo Corporate Performance Management, *part of
Project ProAMK documentation,* Date accessed 30.5.2008

The Role of the School MIS in Pupil Transfer Within England

Alan Strickley and Sue Allen
Birmingham City Council, UK

Abstract: Transfer is a stage at which the education of pupils can be detrimentally affected if continuity of the curriculum and programmes of learning are not seamless and appropriate to the learner. As such the movement of the pupil profile is key. This paper looks at the current data transfer model and considers its strengths and weaknesses in the context of primary, secondary and in year admissions. It considers solutions that would optimise the availability, quality and accessibility of the process and the viability of each. It concludes that an improvement would be best facilitated by an investment in the technological infrastructure and hence recommends a shared database with web-enabled access to all appropriate parties.

Keywords: Management information systems; common transfer file; pupil transfer; curriculum continuity; admissions

1.   BACKGROUND

The transfer of pupils from one school to another was identified by the Department for Education and Science (DES, 1987) as a time at which curriculum continuity and progression of individual pupils is most at risk. As Capel, Zwozdiak-Myers & Lawrence (2007) suggest whilst the introduction of the National Curriculum (NC) has helped to create more continuity in schools in England it is not promoted consistently during transfer, particularly from primary to secondary schools (secondary admissions).

The report 'Changing Schools' (OFSTED. 2002) found, amongst its conclusions, that whilst there was a recognition that good arrangements for transfer were important, that there was variation in the quality of information generally leading to additional testing in year 7. While the report accepted that the Common Transfer Form as it was then and more currently Common Transfer File or CTF (DCSF, 2007a) for Key Stage 2 (KS2) information was

Please use the following format when citing this chapter:

Strickley, A. and Allen, S., 2009, in IFIP International Federation for Information Processing, Volume 292; *Evolution of Information Technology in Educational Management*; Eds. Tatnall, A., Visscher, A., Finegan, A., O'Mahony, C., (Boston: Springer), pp. 129–142.

an improvement, they also found that very few primary schools provided
information over and above the KS levels and test scores. At this time they
commented that there was a lack of non-core subject records, curricular targets
and exemplar work and that very few used electronic transfer mechanisms.

School Management Information Systems (MISs), although lacking in
some of the more knowledge-based information, do contain a large amount
of data about the pupil within the school. In addition most of the information
is structured for easy access and analysis. The transfer of this data would
seem a logical step as an agent to improve this critical transitional stage as
well as at any other stage of transfer for the pupil.

However the way that the MISs are structured in the current educational
setting causes some problems in this respect. In most other MISs once data
is input it remains in that source database for the duration of its useful life.
As such it is always available for informed decision making to those with
appropriate access.

The situation for school MISs is different in so much as the information
about the pupil is held at the school currently attended and the pupil will
change schools at least once in their educational life. This change will be at
admission to secondary school and may occur at several other times within a
single phase as an in year (or casual) transfer. In an area with high mobility,
such as is increasingly being observed in urban settings, the in-year change
can happen many times during a pupil's education.

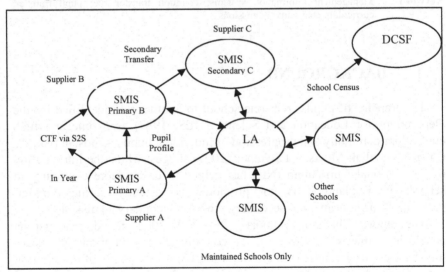

Figure 1

Figure 1 attempts to illustrate this complex arrangement. The outer
circles represent Local Authority (LA) maintained schools. These may be of
any type including nursery, primary and secondary. Each school has its own
self-contained schools management information system (SMIS) which may
be from any of a number of commercial suppliers or a system bespoke to the

school or the whole LA. Secure data transfer will occur between the schools and the LA on a regular basis for a variety of purposes including School Census (DCSF, 2008c) and the population of the central LA children's database (see section 4).

Transfer of validated school data from school census will occur from the LA to the Department for Children Schools and Families (DCSF) on a termly basis. DCSF will return data to the LAs and schools but this will generally be via portals such as RAISEOnline (OFSTED, 2008) and Key to Success websites (DCSF, 2007e) hence the arrow is one way only.

Each school in the LA will build up a profile of the pupils within in its care and much of this data will be entered into the MIS. Such data items are discussed later in this section.

The figure shows the transfer of a pupil from a primary school A to a different primary school B as an in year transfer possibly as a result of the parents moving home. Data about the pupil is transferred from school A to B via the secure DCSF School To School (S2S) web portal (DCSF 2007d) as a CTF (see sections 5 & 6).

A subsequent transfer from primary school B to a secondary school C as a secondary transfer will generally be via the LA and is described in Section 3.

With an increase in statutory returns and as a result of more strategic MIS modules (e.g. assessment, attendance, Special Educational Needs Coordinator (SENCO) etc.) the schools' MISs are containing more and more vital information about the pupils' programmes of learning, pastoral issues and other related data. As such the transfer of this data with the pupil as they move from school to school is vital to enable a seamless transition from one learning environment to the next. This is a system of data transfer envisaged by Smith & Wild (2001) and Nicholls & Gardner (1999).

Such a transfer of data will enable learning programmes and resources within the school to be tailored more specifically to the needs of the pupil. As the quotation below, from the recently published governmental children's plan (DCSF, 2007f), illustrates:

"Personalised learning will ensure that information about the child's academic progress and their personal development at primary school will be passed on to the secondary school to ensure continuity." (p.57)

Therefore we have a position in which the data appertaining to a pupil needs to move from the existing school (sender) to the school to which the pupil is moving to (recipient). This creates several problems and opportunities as this paper attempts to investigate.

As a tool for evaluating the effectiveness of the transfer of pupil data we will focus on the three Cs of the process. These are; the consistency (how uniformly is it applied?); the conduit (how effectively is it transferred?); and the content (what is transferred?) of the data transfer process.

For the purposes of this paper we will be considering the transfers of pupils to primary school (primary admissions), from primary to secondary

(secondary admissions) and in year. Whilst some LAs in England have a system with first, middle and high schools the situation is similar although the ages of the pupils are different.

2.   PRIMARY ADMISSIONS

In many cases the admission of pupils to primary school will be the first point of entry for the pupil into the educational system. As such there will be no previous learning programmes available to transfer. In some cases the child may have attended nursery school, however many of these do not have a school MIS. Many primary schools have nursery classes attached to their main primary school and share a single MIS so transfer is not an issue. In any case most pupils will only have received one year of education prior to transfer (and at a very early age) hence the amount of detailed information regarding the child will be less than for secondary transfer. As such whilst the basic premise regarding data transfer applies the effects on the pupils are likely to be less significant.

3.   SECONDARY ADMISSIONS

The transfer of pupils from primary to secondary school constitutes the major movement of pupils in an LA and consequently is a well researched area from the perspective of the effects on the transferring pupils. For example, Derricott (1985); Galton & Willcocks (1983); Gorwood (1991); Schagen & Kerr (1999); Galton Morrison & Pell (2000). All of them suggest that transfer has an effect on the pupil.

Currently in England, since the introduction of the admissions code of practice (DfES 2002 & 2007) secondary admissions is coordinated by the LA that the pupil resides in.

Briefly the process involves the LA collecting school preference information from the parents either on a paper form or online and allocating schools to the highest available preference on a formula-based criteria, as defined by the admitting authority, where schools are oversubscribed.

The importance of the process is that on allocation day (March 1st of the year of admission to the new school) the LA holds data appertaining to all of the pupils allocated to its secondary schools for the following September. As a minimum this will be the information supplied by the parent i.e. name, address, date of birth etc. but with the advent of the children's database, held at the LA, it may contain considerably more. As such the children's database requires further discussion.

4.   CHILDREN'S DATABASE

Since the implementation of the Department for Education and Skills' (DfES') Information Management Strategy (IMS) in 1998 (DCSF, 2008a) and more recently the Every Child Matters legislation (HMSO, 2003) together with the reducing the bureaucratic burden on schools (Implementation Review Unit (IRU), 2003; 2005) most LAs will have a central database of all of the pupils within its maintained schools (although not those in the independent sector).

These databases are normally populated from the schools' MISs via weekly, monthly or termly data feeds and will contain a subset of the pupil data within the schools. Precisely what will be held will depend on the LA requirements and the systems being used.

As such after allocation day the LA has the capacity to send electronically information about each pupil to its new school. Exactly what it sends and how is the focus of the next section.

5.   THE COMMON TRANSFER FILE (CTF)

The CTF was introduced by the DfES in 2000 (DCSF, 2007a) originally as a paper form and subsequently in 2002 as an electronic xml file. It is a statutory requirement, within the pupil regulations (HMSO, 2005; DCSF, 2007b) for the governing body of the sender school to create this file and send it on to the recipient school within 15 days of the pupil leaving.

The CTF has been through several updates during its existence and is currently in version 7 i.e. CTF7. The full specification for the CTF may be found at the Department for Children, Schools and Families Teachernet website (DCSF, 2007a). The key data items held are: sending and receiving school names; basic pupil information (Date of Birth (DOB), name, ethnicity, NC year group etc.); SEN information including previous history (level, need, supplementary information), contact address information, contact information, (telephone, responsibility etc.), school KS information (Foundation Stage, KS1, KS2 and KS3 down to component level); school history, am-pm level attendance data and aggregate attendance information. This list is a subset of the data which can be usefully stored against a pupil in even the most basic MIS. However it should be noted that most of the above data items are not mandatory.

With the information the LA has in its children's database and the list of allocated schools within its admissions system the LA is able to send a CTF for each of the pupils that will be attending their new secondary school in September. In fact most do this soon after allocation day in addition, or as a replacement, to electronic or paper lists.

For the purposes of this particular transfer the DCSF developed the Admission Transfer File (ATF). The ATF is equivalent to CTF with regards to basic pupil data except that it does not require a Unique Pupil Number

(UPN) (DCSF, 2007g) as a mandatory field as this may not be available within the LA admissions system. Since 2007 the ATF (DCSF, 2007c) has had all non-core pupil data elements removed and as such the CTF will be the predominant file discussed in this paper. The onus is now on the primary school or secondary school to obtain these non-core elements from the Key to Success (DCSF, 2007e) website.

What the LA actually sends will depend upon what it has in its children's database. Some LAs have all of the data that the CTF can hold including assessments and attendance whilst others only have basic pupil data. The CTF can be sent as many times as required as an update file and hence KS2 assessments can be sent after the tests have been marked in the July before the pupils' entry to the secondary school.

6.   THE SCHOOL TO SCHOOL SECURE WEB SITE (S2S)

The original paper-based CTF could be transferred from school to school via surface mail, by internal LA post or even in an envelope via the transferring pupil. With the advent of the electronic version there was a tendency by some schools to attach the CTF to an email via a public server or send on a diskette through the mail. Neither of these methods are secure and are in breach of the Data Protection Act (HMSO, 1998) and the Pupil Information Regulations (HMSO, 2005).

As a response to this issue the DFES set up a secure web site with the primary purpose of facilitating the transfer of the CTF (although since its inception it has been developed to service the transfer of other files).

Basically the process required for a school to send or receive a CTF is as follows. Firstly the school will need to register itself or a specified user with a password and user name to log into the site (DCSF, 2007d). This registration process will ask for basic details including a contact email address.

For each recipient school a CTF will need to be created, through the MIS, by the sender school for the pupil(s) moving to that school. If the recipient school is unknown a special CTF can be created which indicates this.

To transfer the CTF the school user will need to log onto the S2S web site and upload the CTFs through a simple menu driven system. The file name of the CTF contains information about the sending and recipient school based on a unique combination of the LA number and school establishment numbers and will be stored in the S2S database for downloading by the appropriate school.

An email message will be sent to the appropriate registered users of the recipient school should a CTF be uploaded onto the S2S site based on the registration information given above. To download the file the school will perform a logon process similar to the above, download the appropriate file(s) and then import them into their MIS.

CTFs that have no recipient school will be uploaded into the 'lost pupils database'. These will normally be the responsibility of the LAs to check on a regular basis in an attempt to resolve the issues of missing pupils.

The site works well in technical terms. However as can be seen from the above it does involve considerable interaction from the schools in terms of producing the CTFs in the first place to logging onto the system and then uploading the files. A similar process for downloading is then required for accessing and importing the CTFs. Any process that relies on such high interactivity is likely to be used less frequently than a seamless one particularly when the uploading process generates no immediate net gains for the school involved and the download process relies on an accurate and up to date email contact address which may not always be the case.

As such the process is subject to the adoption by the schools who by their very nature are busy places with such tasks often seen as lower priority. The result is that when a new pupil arrives the CTF has not always been sent by the sender school and the recipient has to type in the data manually. Hence faith is lost in the system which results in less CTFs being uploaded and the effect is a loss of faith in the process.

7. IN-YEAR ADMISSIONS

Many LAs do not coordinate admissions in year and as such the transfer of information about the child via the CTF takes on even greater importance. Basically parent/carers will liaise with the school directly, either via advice from the LA, if new to the area, or completely independently if locally based.

Upon admission to the new school the transfer of the pupil information from the old school should be via the CTF. Whilst there is a statutory obligation for this to occur it is known that it does not always happen. Basically there are six possible reasons for this:

1. The LA may not have a secure school to school transfer system and the sending school may not be aware of, or wish to use, the National S2S secure data transfer system (DCSF, 2007d).
2. Even if a secure inter-LA system exists and is used, if the child is transferring to a school outside of the LA such a system will be ineffective. The issues in 1 above will apply to the use of the S2S site which does allow inter-LA transfer.
3. In some cases the new school that the pupil is transferring to is not known. Therefore unless the S2S system is used to place the record in the 'lost pupils area' the transfer will not take place.
4. It may be a period of time before the school is notified that the pupil has left and by the time the CTF has been created and sent by

the sender school the recipient school will have collected and entered the data manually.

5. Schools in the independent sector are not included in any statutory regulations and hence transfer between themselves and the maintained sector is unstructured.

6. The transfer to schools outside of England, whilst currently covered by the regulations (DfES, 2005) from 2005/6, is not currently commonplace via the CTF and S2S website.

Whilst in year admissions affects less pupils than primary and secondary transfer for those that it does affect the availability of data from their previous school is important. Clearly a pupil moving on their own to a new school needs to settle in quickly to enable their learning to proceed with as little disruption as possible. For this to occur the school needs information about the pupil's prior education at their time of admission or ideally beforehand.

8. ISSUES

The transfer of pupil data via the CTF is a step in the right direction but is limited in several areas:

1. Whilst CTF7 contains considerably more information than the original file or form (CTF1) it still lacks the rich data that is required to plan the pupils' education from day one at the new school.

2. Although most LAs will transfer a CTF to the secondary school as part of the allocation process the children's database may only contain limited information about the child with which to populate it.

3. LAs generally only transfer the data once even though the CTF allows partial files for update purposes. This will generally be before KS2 results are known.

4. Some schools do not use the CTF, for the reasons given earlier in section 6, even though it is a statutory requirement (Keane, 2005).

With reference to the three C approach discussed in section 1 we can see that the process is not consistent and that the existing conduit is user-intensive requiring actions at both the sender and recipient schools. This is particularly true for pupils changing schools as an in year transfer. In all cases the content is a small subset of the data that may be potentially held within a school's MIS appertaining to the pupil's profile.

9.   SOLUTIONS

There are a number of possible solutions to these issues each with its own advantages and disadvantages as discussed below:

9.1   Increasing the data items transferred in the CTF

These could include items which are contained in many schools' MISs but are not in the current CTF: positive and negative behaviour records including all types of exclusions; the Qualifications and Curriculum Authority or National Foundation for Educational Research optional test results (where administered); medical and social issues; more detailed SEN information such as Individual Education Plans, interventions etc.; pupil end of term reports; other free text fields.

However even if the CTF were to contain everything in a school MIS it would still be lacking schemes of work, preferred learning style etc. together with some of the more tacit data generally not held on the school MIS.

Whilst it could be argued that much of the above is transferred as hard copy from school to school this is not always the case as observed by Schagen & Kerr (1999) in which one in three of the secondary schools surveyed did not receive even the basic information from their feeder schools. Also the unstructured format of this paper-based information often means that it is not looked at or used by the receiving school (Brown et al. 1996; OFSTED 1998).

The electronic transfer of data in a structured format would help in the development of learning plans for the new intake as Capel, Zworzdiak-Myers & Lawrence (2007) found in their study into transfer from primary to secondary school.

Whilst there are some clear advantages to extending the facilities of the existing CTF infrastructure with its statutory status, this solution still suffers from the inherent problems of schools not transferring the file (particularly for in year) and the lack of KS2 data from the LA at secondary transfer.

9.2   A central shared database

The creation of a single LA database, which is accessed by the schools through a web-enabled ePortal, would facilitate the removal of the process of physical file transfer. Such a system would ensure that the data at both school and LA was concurrent by essentially creating a single LA-wide database.

A local copy of the data at the schools would ensure processor-dependent tasks such as timetabling and analysis were not affected by bandwidth and downtime.

Regional groups of LAs could be connected through regional portals connected together to create a national system. This would create a model similar to that to be introduced by Contact Point (HMSO, 2007).

The resultant system could support the sharing of tacit knowledges across school communities in a Community of Practice type approach (Skyrme, 2002).

Additional advantages would be that files would not need to be physically transferred, unless moving outside of the LA and local and central government audits could be carried out remotely (IRU, 2005).

Unfortunately with the onus on school autonomy, supplier commercial interests and less LA intervention there is not currently the political will for such a model. In addition a lack of confidence in the technical infrastructure to implement such an arrangement makes it unlikely in the short term. However a pilot in Scotland (Capita, 2007) utilising just such a method for small schools and the more recent national intranet GLOW (GLOW, 2008) will be monitored with interest.

9.3   The regular update from schools' MISs

Some LAs do implement a similar model to the above in which they exchange data on a regular basis. For LAs and schools that use the same supplier systems this can be done seamlessly and with a large number of data items. For others the CTF is often the transfer vehicle with the same inherent problems as in 8 above, limiting the data items transferable.

Such an option enables the LA to deliver better information at secondary transfer but still does not improve the in year situation as this is outside of the LA coordination process. Problems with reconciliation between school files and the LA database, particularly with address information, also constrain its effectiveness.

9.4   Software Interoperability Framework (SIF)

The implementation of an automatic, interoperability data structure could remove many of the problems identified above. The SIF Association (SIFA UK, 2007) provides the detail of this process. However it basically specifies the data to be transferred and the agents to transfer them with, via a zone integration server or ZIS, to the appropriate recipient.

Such a method may still only offer the transfer of defined data items leaving some of the important textual items to be transferred by hard copy as with the current situation.

10.   ACCESS

Whatever solution is selected there still remains the issue of access. Assuming that information about the pupils is transferred to the new school, how easily will the staff at the school have access to that data? Strickley (2004; 2007) would suggest that, particularly in primary schools, access is severely restricted. This lack of access will affect not just the information retrieval but also the recording of pupil data in the first place.

Such restrictions would also inhibit the use of data from within the school i.e. transition from one year to the next, an area less widely researched but according to Galton, Gray & Ruddick (1999 & 2003) still having a significant impact.

11. SUMMARY AND CONCLUSIONS

The movement of pupil data between schools is important for the continuity of education at all stages of transfer. The content and method of transfer are of particular interest.

Whilst the CTF has made a significant improvement there is a lack of uniformity in the transfer of this file as well as a serious deficiency in content that is needed to assist continuity of learning for the transferring pupils. The lack of transfer of anything at all by some schools is of particular concern.

There are a number of options available each realising benefits as well as having some constraints.

Whilst it is unlikely that it is possible to have too much information on the pupils previous learning, much of this information needs to be structured so that it can be easily analysed by the receiving school.

Once received it is important that the correct staff have the required access to the information for both input and retrieval.

The web-enabled central database provides the preferred option as it not only gives concurrent and representative data but also allows seamless data transfer at point of entry as well as the option to share tacit information. However even this model will need a change in central policy if independent schools and those outside of England are to be fully integrated into the system.

This model in which structured data can be used to give a thumbnail sketch of the pupils' learning together with an ability to drill down into more detailed and rich information, perhaps interacting electronically with relevant teachers, would support the continuity of learning for the pupil.

The Admissions Code of Practice (DfES, 2007) having been revised in 2007 is currently in the consultation phase for changes (DCSF, 2008b) which would affect the 2010/2011 admissions round. The inclusion of in year coordination for LAs in these draft regulations could potentially address some of the issues regarding the consistent and improved transfer of the CTF for these pupils but not the content of the CTF itself.

As a result of the British Educational Communications and Technology Agency (BECTA, 2005) value for money document and resultant memorandum of understanding with software suppliers, the SIF proof of concept stages 1 and 2 have been commissioned (SIFA UK, 2007). In particular one of the objectives of the stage 2 in Northern Ireland is 'to

establish SIF as a possible solution for data interoperability for assessment'
which is of particular relevance to the transfer of the pupil profile as
discussed in this paper.

Strickley (2007) reports, from his case study of Birmingham primary
schools, a quotation from an office administrator which sums up the
situation with regards to the original paper-based CTF and equally to the
more recent electronic file concisely:

"The transfer form doesn't give enough information either."(p. 253)

If we are to move to a situation where we are effectively using the MIS
to support the transfer of pupils the next few years will be crucial.

12.   REFERENCES

Brown, J. M., Taggart, B. McCallum, B & Gipps, C. (1996). The impact of
key stage 2 results. In *Education 3 to 13*, Volume 24, No. 3, (pp. 3-7).

BECTA (2005). *School management systems and value for money.*
Coventry: BECTA.

Capel, S., Zwozdiak-Myers, P. & Lawrence, J. (2007). *The transfer of pupils
from primary to secondary school: a case study of a foundation subject:
physical education.* Research in education. 77: (pp. 14-30). Manchester:
Manchester University press.

Capita. (2007). *ONE in Scotland.* [Online] http://www.capitaes.co.uk
/EMS/Scotland.asp [Accessed 18 December 2007].

DCSF (2007a). *CTF Definition.* [Online]. http://www.teachernet.gov.uk/
management/ims/datatransfers/CTF/ctf7/ [Accessed 18 December 2007].

DCSF (2007b). *Information on the transfer of CTF.* [Online] http://
www.everychildmatters.gov.uk/resources/ig00202/ [Accessed 18 December
2007].

DCSF (2007c). *ATF Definition (2007).* [Online] http://www.teachernet.
gov.uk/management/ims/datatransfers/coordadmissions/CoorAdmin2008
/ [Accessed 18 December 2007].

DCSF (2007d). *S2S File transfer site.* [Online] http://www.teachernet.
gov.uk/management/ims/datatransfers/s2s/ [Accessed 19 December
2007].

DCSF (2007e). *Key to Success website.* [Online] https://www.keytosuccess.
dfes.gov.uk/ [Accessed 19 December 2007].

DCSF (2007f). *The children's plan.* Norwich: The Stationery Office.

DCSF (2007g). *Unique pupil numbers; policy and guidance practice for
schools and Las.* [Online] http://www.teachernet.gov.uk/management/
ims/datamanagement/UPN/ [Accessed 23 November 2007].

DCSF (2008a). *Information management strategy.* [Online] http://www.
teachernet.gov.uk/management/ims/ [Accessed 27 March 2008].

DCSF (2008b). *School Admissions Consultation 2008.* [Online] http://www. dcsf.gov.uk/consultations/conDetails.cfm?consultationId=1561 [Accessed 3 July 2008].

DCSF (2008c). *School Admissions Consultation 2008.* [Online] http://www. teachernet.gov.uk/management/ims/datacollections/sc2009/ [Accessed 5 August 2008].

DES (1987). *The curriculum from 5 to 16: Curriculum matters 2.* London: HMSO.DfES (2002). *Admissions Code of Practice (2002).* London: TSO.

DfES (2005). *Explanatory memorandum to the education (pupil information) (England) regulations 2005; 2005 No. 1437.* London: HMSO

DfES (2007). *Admissions Code of Practice (2007).* London: TSO.

Derricott, R. (1985). *Curriculum continuity: primary to secondary.* Windsor: NFER-Nelson.

Galton, M. & Willcocks, J. (Eds.) (1983). *Moving from the primary classroom.* London: Routledge & Kegan.

Galton, M., Gray, J. & Ruddick, J. (1999). *The impact of school transitions and transfers on pupils' progress and attainment.* London: DfEE.

Galton, M., Gray, J. & Ruddick, J. (2003). *Transfer and transition in the middle years of schooling (7-14).* London: DfES.

Galton, M., Morrison & Pell. (2000). Transfer and transition in English schools: reviewing the evidence. *International Journal of Educational Research.* 33: (pp.341-363). Cambridge: Elsevier

GLOW (2008). [Online]. http://www.glowscotland.org.uk/ [Accessed 27 March 2008].

Gorwood, B. (1991). *Primary-secondary transfer after the national curriculum.* London: Croom Helm.

HMSO (1998). *Data Protection Act.* [Online]. http://www.opsi.gov.uk/acts /acts1998/ukpga_19980029_en_1 [Accessed 06 August 2008].

HMSO (2003). *Every Child Matters.* Norwich: TSO.

HMSO (2005). *Statutory Instrument 2005 No. 1437*
The Education (Pupil Information) (England) Regulations 2005. Norwich: TSO

HMSO (2007). *ContactPoint.* [Online]. http://www.everychildmatters.gov. uk/deliveringservices/contactpoint/ [Accessed 04 January 2007].

Implementation Review Unit (IRU) (2003). *tackling Bureaucracy in schools: Interim report.* DfES/0830/2003. Nottinghamshire: DfES Publications.

IRU (2005). The revised edition of the Protocol on Data Sharing and Rationalisation in the Schools Sector. [Online]. www.teachernet.gov.uk/ management/ims/newsinfo/protocol/ [Accessed 20 December 2007].

Keane, T. (2005). CTF Usage in Schools [Online] www.teachers.gov.uk/ _doc/8603/CTF_DCSR_0705.ppt [Accessed 18 December 2007].

Nicholls, G. & Gardner, J. (1999). *Pupils in transition.* London: Routledge.

142 _Alan Strickley and Sue Allen_

OFSTED (1998). *How teachers assess the core subjects at key stage 3.* London: OFSTED.

OFSTED. (2002). *Changing schools: an evaluation of the effectiveness of transfer arrangements at age 11.* London: OFSTED.

OFSTED. (2008). *RaiseONLINE.* [Online]. https://www.raiseonline.org/ [Accessed 23 July 2008].

SIFA UK (2007). *Home page.* [Online]. http://uk.sifinfo.org/ [Accessed 18 December 2007].

Schagen, S. & Kerr, D. (1999). *Bridging the gap? The national curriculum, and progression from primary to secondary school.* Slough: NfER.

Skyrme, D. (2002). Knowledge management: approaches and policies. [Online] http://www.providersedge.com/docs/km_articles/KM_-_Approaches_and_Policies.pdf [Accessed 4 April 2006]

Smith, D & Wild, P. (2001). The future of school information systems. In Visscher, A.J., Wild, P. & Fung, A.C.W. *Information Technology in Educational Management.* (pp. 137-160). Netherlands: Kluwer.

Strickley, A., B. (2004). Factors Affecting the Use of MIS as a Tool for Informing and Evaluating Teaching and Learning in Schools. *Education and Information Technologies* 9 (1): (pp.47-66), March 2004. Boston, Dordrecht, London: Kluwer Academic Publishers.

Strickley, A., B. (2007). *An evaluative case study of the use of management information systems in Birmingham primary schools.* Doctoral thesis. Birmingham: Birmingham City University.

Research Management Systems as an Evolutionary Backwater

A Management System for Australian University Research Quality Framework Data

Arthur Tatnall and Bill Davey

Graduate School of Business, Victoria University, Australia; and School of Business Information Technology, RMIT University, Australia

Abstract: Since 2004 the former Australian Government had been working on developing some means of measuring the quality of research from Australian universities. A recent change of Government has meant that the implementation of a Research Quality Framework (RFQ) in the form proposed by the former government will not now take place. The new Commonwealth Government made an election promise that if elected it would review this controversial plan. It did so and in June 2008 preliminary plans for a new version of the RQF, called Excellence in Research for Australia (ERA) were unveiled. One aspect of the planned RQF that will probably be retained, however, is the creation of digital repositories for storing copies of all research output at the local university level, linked with a central government repository. This paper discusses the RQF with particular reference to the creation of digital repositories and the likely RQF Information Management System.

Keywords: Research Quality Framework (RQF), Excellence in Research for Australia (ERA), information management systems, accountability, journal ranking, quality metrics.

1.   INTRODUCTION

As an example of the application of information systems in university research management, this paper considers a new research quality system that was to be introduced in Australia in 2008. In a study that investigated problems with research management systems in a number of countries, Davey and Tatnall (2007) concluded that: "To properly manage the growth of human capital a knowledge management system must inform the manager of the increase in research output, the emerging new research areas and be able to add research value by using a knowledge management system." The article noted that while the need to provide information to funding bodies cannot be ignored, an added capacity to allow researchers to locate others

Please use the following format when citing this chapter:

Tatnall, A. and Davey, B., 2009, in IFIP International Federation for Information Processing, Volume 292; *Evolution of Information Technology in Educational Management*; Eds. Tatnall, A., Visscher, A., Finegan, A., O'Mahony, C., (Boston: Springer), pp. 143–154.

with similar areas of research interest, both inside and outside their own institution, was often missing. This study showed that many such systems were slanted towards the reporting needs of funding bodies rather than genuinely contributing to the growth and quality of research outputs.

Since 2004 the former Australian Government had been working on developing some means of measuring the quality of research output from Australian universities. The system it came up with was called the Research Quality Framework (RQF) and was to be implemented early in 2008. As future research funding for each university was to be based on its RQF score, this was to be a very significant and controversial development, but a change of government at the Federal election in November 2007 changed all that.

The new government had pledged, as an election promise, to scrap the controversial RQF in its proposed form and develop a new quality measure in consultation with the university sector (Australian Government 2007b). On taking up government this pledge was honoured, and in June 2008 a consultation paper (Australian Government 2008) for the new system: Excellence in Research for Australia (ERA) was released. It is not at all clear, at this stage, exactly what ERA will be like, except that it will probably be based more solidly on some form of quality metric. One aspect of the new system that is unlikely to change from the previously proposed RQF, however, is the need to keep track of research output and manage this in such a way that it can be properly checked, assessed and made generally available. This paper discusses the originally proposed Research Quality Framework and the likely changes in any new system, concentrating on the means that could be used to manage the research output data.

2.   THE ORIGINALLY PROPOSED RQF

In May 2004 the former Prime Minister, John Howard, announced the Federal Government's intention of implementing a new Research Quality Framework for assessing research at Australian universities and other publicly funded research establishments (Howard 2004). After some work, in November 2006 the Minister of Education, Science and Training released an Australian Government document called "The Recommended RQF".

"The Australian Government seeks to ensure that public money is being invested in research of the highest quality that delivers real benefits not only to the higher education and research sectors but also to the wider community. Research conducted in universities by individuals or teams of researchers is supported by the Australian Government through a dual funding system. This system comprises:

- *Direct funding from agencies (including the Australian Research Council and the National Health and Medical Research Council) determined on the basis of competitive peer review; and*

- *University block grants which are performance based and are made up of the Research Training Scheme (RTS), IGS and Research Infrastructure Block Grant Scheme.*

The Research Quality Framework (RQF) provides the Australian Government with the basis for redistributing a significant proportion of the block funding on the basis of ratings for research quality and research impact. Currently, there is no system-wide and expert-based way to measure the quality and impact of research conducted in universities and its benefits to the higher education sector and the wider community.

The existing distribution of university research block funding is based on quantitative measures (i.e. numbers of publications, external research income and Higher Degree by Research (HDR) student load and completions) that have been used as proxies for quality. These particular quantitative measures do not provide sufficient information upon which to identify and reward areas of research excellence or to encourage the wider community to increase its investment in Australian research. Consequently, the Australian Government is committed to the development of a Research Quality Framework (RQF) that will provide a broad assessment mechanism for research quality and impact."

(Australian Government 2006)

The basis of the RQF was to be an expert review process involving the examination of evidence from each university for the **quality** and **impact** of its research output. Researchers were to be grouped into one of the following areas:

1. **Biological Sciences**: Biochemistry and cell biology, Genetics, Microbiology, Botany, Zoology, Physiology, Ecology & evolution, Biotechnology, other biological sciences.
2. **Physical, chemical and earth sciences**: Astronomical sciences, Theoretical & condensed matter physics, Atomic & molecular physics; Nuclear & particle physics; Plasma physics, Optical physics, Classical physics, Other physical sciences, Physical chemistry, Inorganic chemistry, Organic chemistry, Analytical chemistry, Macromolecular chemistry, Theoretical & computational chemistry, Other chemical sciences, Geology, Geophysics, Geochemistry, Oceanography, Hydrology, Atmospheric sciences, other earth sciences.
3. **Engineering and technology**: Aerospace engineering, Manufacturing engineering, Automotive engineering, Mechanical & industrial engineering, Chemical engineering, Resources engineering, Civil engineering, Electrical & electronic engineering, Geomantic engineering, Environmental engineering, Maritime engineering, Metallurgy, Materials engineering, Biomedical engineering, Computer hardware, Communications technologies, Interdisciplinary engineering, other engineering & technology.

4. **Mathematical and information sciences and technology**: Mathematics, Statistics, Other mathematical sciences, Information systems, Artificial intelligence & signal & image processing, Computer software, Computation theory & mathematics, Data format, other information, computing & communication sciences.

5. **Agricultural, veterinary, food and environmental sciences**: Industrial biotechnology & food sciences, Soil & water sciences, Crop & pasture production, Horticulture, Animal production, Veterinary sciences, Forestry sciences, Fisheries sciences, Environmental sciences, Land, parks & agricultural management, other agricultural, veterinary & environmental sciences.

6. **Clinical sciences and clinical physiology**: Medicine – general, Immunology, Medical biochemistry & clinical chemistry, Medical microbiology, Pharmacology & pharmaceutical sciences, Medical physiology, Dentistry, Optometry, Clinical sciences (exc. Psychiatry), mental health.

7. **Public health and health services**: Nursing, Public health & health services (exc. mental health), Complementary/alternative medicine, Human movement & sports science, other medical & health sciences.

8. **Psychology, psychiatry, neurological, behavioural and cognitive sciences**: Neurosciences, Psychology, Psychiatry, Cognitive science, other behavioural & cognitive sciences & Linguistics.

9. **Social sciences and politics**: Political science, Policy & administration, other policy & political science, Sociology, Anthropology, Human geography, Demography.

10. **Economics, Commerce and Management**: Economic theory, Applied economics, Economic history & history of economic thought, Econometrics, Other economics, Accounting, auditing & accountability, Business and management, Banking, finance and investment, Transportation, Tourism, Services, other commerce, management, tourism and services.

11. **Law, Education and Professional Practices**: Education studies, Curriculum studies, Professional development of teachers, Other education, Journalism, communication and media, Librarianship, Curatorial studies, Social work, Other journalism, librarianship & curatorial studies, Law, Professional development of practitioners, Justice & legal studies, Law enforcement, other law, justice, law enforcement.

12. **Humanities**: History & philosophy of science & medicine, Other studies in human society, Art History and appreciation, Language studies, Literature studies, Cultural studies, Other language & culture, Historical studies, Archaeology & prehistory, other history & archaeology, philosophy, Religion & religious traditions, Other philosophy & religion.

13. **Creative arts, design and built environment**: Architecture and urban environment, building, Other architecture, urban environment and building, Performing arts, Visual arts & crafts, Cinema,

electronic arts & multimedia, Design studies, other arts (exc. Art history & appreciation).

(Australian Government 2006)

Each individual researcher would then be allocated by their university to one of these groups, the idea being to find groups of researchers sharing a common focus. Each university Research Group had to have at least five members, and research was then to be assessed for quality and impact.

To provide some means of determining research quality, each of the thirteen research areas was asked to come up with some form of journal ranking. This was done in different ways, but in each case an attempt was made to produce something that would be internationally acceptable.

2.1 Research Quality

For each Research Group, evaluation of research quality was to be based on the four best research outputs for each researcher in the Group, the full list of research outputs for the Group produced in the six-year assessment period and evidence of research quality provided as part of a context statement. Research quality was to be based on the following five-point, criterion referenced scale:

"5 Research that is world leading in its field or makes an equally exceptional contribution in an area of particular significance to Australia.

4 Research that meets world standards of excellence in its field or makes an equally excellent contribution in an area of particular significance to Australia.

3 Research that is recognised internationally as excellent in terms of originality, significance and rigour but which nonetheless falls short of the highest standards of excellence.

2 Research that is recognised as methodologically sound in its field and of high originality, significance and rigour.

1 Research that is deemed to fall below the standard of recognised quality work."

(Australian Government 2006)

2.2 Research Impact

Research impact was defined as "the social, economic, environmental and/or cultural benefit of research to end users in the wider community regionally, nationally, and/or internationally" (Australian Government 2006, 21). The impact assessment for a Research Group would have been based on an impact statement that was evidence-based against generic and panel-specific impact criteria. This would need to have included verifiable indicators to support these claims, up to four case studies that illustrated the Group's claims of impact, and details of end users who could verify the Research Group's claims. It was to be based on this scale:

"A Adoption of the research has produced an outstanding social, economic, environmental and/or cultural benefit for the wider community, regionally within Australia, nationally or internationally.

B Adoption of the research has produced a significant social, economic environmental and/or cultural benefit for the wider community, regionally within Australia, nationally or internationally.

C Research has been adopted to produce new policies, products, attitudes, behaviours and/or outlooks in the end user community.

D Research has engaged with the end user community to address a social, economic, environmental and/or cultural issue regionally within Australia, nationally or internationally.

E Research has had limited or no identifiable social, economic, environmental and/or cultural outcome, regionally within Australia, nationally or internationally."

(Australian Government 2006)

3.   RQF INFORMATION MANAGEMENT SYSTEM

Implementation of the RQF would have required that the research outputs to be assessed be placed in a digital storage system or repository (wherever this was possible). A funding program for the Australian Scheme for Higher Education Repositories (ASHER) was designed to assist individual universities in establishing such digital repositories.

The idea was to allow institutions to put their research outputs, including journal articles and other less tangible outputs, in an accessible digital store for RQF assessment. The funding program was to provide assistance to universities to establish and support the installation or upgrading and population of digital repositories for use in the RQF, as well as technical and administrative support for digital repositories (Australian Government 2007a).

Over the longer term another intended aspect was that these repositories would make information about research more widely accessible to business, the community and the government. A Research Accessibility Framework was to be developed by the Australian Government "to ensure that information about research and how to access it is available to researchers and the wider community" (Australian Government 2006). The RQF Information Management System was to allow for this and be based on the following principles:

*   It should involve research repositories and the standardisation of data acquisition, given that research repositories and reporting systems are still evolving.
*   It should be designed to enable the contents of evidence portfolios and the results of the RQF assessment process to be made generally available at the completion of the process, subject to resolution of issues around intellectual property, privacy and ethics.
*   It should include provision for submission of evidence of non-traditional research outputs such as software development, creative works and designs.

- Universities should be given sufficient advance notice of RQF Information Management System data specifications and submission requirements for the necessary preparation of the evidence portfolios for each of the nominated Research Groups.
- The specifications for RQF data collection, submission, access and retention should recognise the need for cost effectiveness.

(Australian Government 2007c)

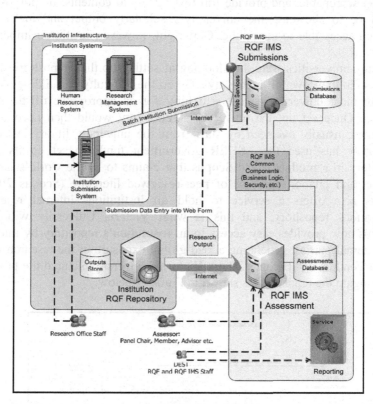

Figure 1: RQF IMS overview

The RQF data submission process was planned to transfer data on the best four outputs for each researcher in each Research Groups from the University's own repository to the RQF Information Management System (IMS), so it was necessary that each university first have its own repository before the system could operate. For the purposes of the RQF the repository would have to be available only to RQF assessors and could remain closed to the general public. Even prior to the announcement of the RQF many Australian universities already had set up some sort of digital repository for their research publications. At Victoria University this was located at: http://eprints.vu.edu.au/. The idea was that the RQF IMS would collect institution-level data and evidence portfolios, using either online or batch interfaces, as part of the university's submission.

What this meant was that the central RQF repository would need secure access and be limited to RQF assessors and authorised university personnel only. Its purpose would be limited to storage of RQF documents, preferably as published PDF versions of journal articles, or at least pre-publication versions from the authors. Copyright agreements needed to be negotiated for RQF purposes, and this has already been achieved for a number of major publishers. An individual university's research repository, on the other hand, would ideally be open access, with no passwords required. It would be Internet searchable, and provide full text access to contents. Its purpose of would be to showcase the university's scholarly output and make this research accessible to the public. Copyright, however, is still an important issue.

Many universities were thus looking at setting up their repositories, but doing so in their own different ways. Given the difficulty of building such a system, most universities went searching for an appropriate off-the-shelf product. Once set up, the university's repository would then need to be populated, usually overseen by staff from the university library. Victoria University has used the ASHER government funds to set up its own repository in a product called Scopus that claims to be the world's largest abstract and citation database of peer-reviewed literature (Scopus 2007). Scopus also offers a service to hold an institutions internal research publications repository, and this is what Victoria University will use. "Scopus now provides easy access to an institution's repository by internal and external parties, generating added global exposure of the research their staff is conducting" (Scopus 2006). Victoria University pictured the process of setting up the repository as shown in Figure 2 below.

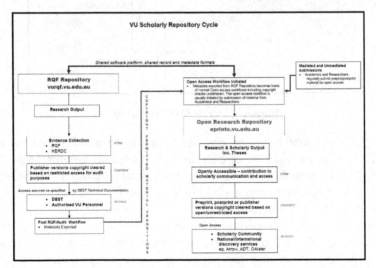

Figure 2: Victoria University's Scholarly Repository Cycle

4. EXCELLENCE IN RESEARCH FOR AUSTRALIA (ERA) – THE REPLACEMENT FOR THE RQF

In June 2008 the new government produced a consultation paper which notes that: "ERA reflects the Government's commitment to a transparent, streamlined approach for evaluation of the excellence of research undertaken in Australia's universities, using readily available information where practical." (Australian Government 2008). The paper states that the new research framework will aim to:

- Identify excellence across the full spectrum of research activity
- Compare Australia's university research effort against international benchmarks
- Create incentives to improve the quality of research
- Identify emerging research areas and opportunities for further development

The consultation paper noted that the first stage of evaluations was planned to access research excellence using a combination of indicators and expert review by committees comprising experienced, internationally-recognised experts (Australian Government 2008). These evaluations will be based on 3 broad categories:

- Measures of research activity and intensity
- Indicators of research quality
- Indicators of excellent applied research and translation of research outcomes

Evaluation of the research is planned to take place in the following discipline clusters:

- Physical, Chemical and Earth Sciences (PCE)
- Humanities and Creative Arts (HCA)
- Engineering and Environmental Sciences (EE)
- Social, Behavioural and Economic Sciences (SBE)
- Mathematical, Information and Communication Sciences (MIC)
- Biological Sciences and Biotechnology (BSB)
- Biomedical and Clinical Research (BCR)
- Public and Allied Health and Health Services (PAHHS)

It is interesting to see what is contained with the cluster for **Social, Behavioural and Economic Sciences** (SBE) as this also covers business, sociology and education: Accounting, Auditing and Accountability; Banking, Finance and Investment; Business Management; Marketing; Services; Tourism; Transport and Freight Services; Other Commerce, Management, Tourism and Services; Economic Theory; Applied Economics; Econometrics; Other Economics; Sociology; Social Work; Anthropology; Human Geography; Demography; Political Science; Policy and Administration; Criminology; Psychology; Cognitive Science; Other Psychology and Cognitive

Sciences; Education Systems; Curriculum and Pedagogy; Specialist Studies in Education; Other Education.

ERA plane to consider all publications within a publication reference period of each the following publication types:

- Book
- Book chapter
- Journal article
- Refereed conference publication

The consultation paper indicates that interdisciplinary research should not be disadvantaged in ERA and will be permitted in more than one cluster where relevant. It goes on to say that it is also important that ERA encourages collaboration across institutions.

5.   RESEARCH QUALITY METRICS

Not everyone, however, agrees that using research quality metrics is a useful path to follow. Alexander et al. (2007) found that systems of quality and impact measurement that were built around journal rankings were not globally consistent. They found that the differences between systems adopted by different countries could be explained by cultural embeddedness, and concluded that "Administrators of business schools that benchmark their faculty's intellectual contributions should identify how a particular journal ranking system reflects the mission, culture, and resources of their own business schools, rather than blindly selecting one journal ranking system over another."

Chen and Hoshower (2006) conducted a survey of 320 faculty members at 10 business schools which showed that faculty members who assign higher importance ratings to both the extrinsic and the intrinsic rewards of research exhibit higher research productivity. Joan Rogers et al. (2006) have created an alternative method for ranking research output that shows different results than some previous methods. Similarly Priscilla Rogers (2007) has found that the discipline area of the research has as much influence on journal rankings as any other measure of research quality. The ability of research output rankings to be manipulated by method demonstrates that research management built around convenience numbers is flawed.

6.   CONCLUSION

In common with many other information management systems in education, information systems designed for handling research are often designed primarily to serve the needs of the funding agencies' demands for accountability (Sessions and Collins 1988; Spurgeon 1994; Tatnall 1995). In this regard, the information system proposed for the Australian Research Quality Framework is no different, except that the funds provided to each university to set up their own repositories do offer other possibilities.

Senator Kim Carr, the new Minister for Innovation, Industry, Science and Research said that the previous government's proposed RQF was "... poorly designed, administratively expensive and relies on an 'impact' measure that is unverifiable and ill-defined" (Australian Government 2007b). He indicated that he wanted "... to implement a less cumbersome and less costly process that still provides the Australian Government and taxpayers with an efficient and transparent process. A process that ensures valuable research dollars are allocated to the university sector using internationally verifiable measures" (Australian Government 2007b).

Like many other information management systems in education, those systems intended for handling research data are often designed primarily to serve the needs of the funding agencies' demands for accountability. We have previously suggested (Davey and Tatnall 2007) that as well as being designed to handle accountability and funding requirements, features to facilitate putting researchers in touch with others working on topics that are possibly related to their own would be useful. It is, however, still too soon to see how ERA will develop, and whether its IMS will be similar to that intended for RQF. Hopefully the new system, whenever it comes into operation, will address this need. At the very least, individual university digital repositories should assist in this.

7. REFERENCES

Alexander, J. K., Scherer, R. F. and Lecoutre, M. (2007). "A global comparison of business journal ranking systems." *Journal of Education for Business* **82**(6): 321 -327.

Australian Government (2006). Research Quality Framework: Assessing the Quality and Impact of Research in Australia - the Recommended RQF. Department of Education; Science and Training, Australian Government.

Australian Government (2007a). Australian Scheme for Higher Education Repositories (ASHER) Fact Sheet. Department of Education; Science and Training, Australian Government.

Australian Government (2007b). Cancellation of Research Quality Framework Implementation. Innovation; Industry; Science and Research, Australian Government.

Australian Government (2007c). Research Quality Framework: Assessing the Quality and Impact of Research in Australia - RQF Technical Specifications. Department of Education; Science and Training, Australian Government.

Australian Government (2008). Excellence in Research for Australia (ERA) Initiative - Consultation Paper. Australian Research Council, Australian Government.

Chen, Y., Gupta, A. and Hoshower, L. (2006). "Factors that motivate business faculty to conduct research: an expectancy theory analysis." *Journal of Education for Business* **81**(4): 179-190.

Davey, B. and Tatnall, A. (2007). Research Knowledge Management can be Murder: University Research Management Systems. *Knowledge Management for Educational Innovation.* Tatnall, A., Okamoto, T. and Visscher, A. J. New York, Springer: 19-25.

Howard, J. (2004). "Backing Australia's Ability - Building Our Future through Science and Innovation." Retrieved January 2008, from http://backingaus.innovation.gov.au/pm_message.htm.

Rodgers, J. R. and Valadkhani, A. (2006). "A multidimensional ranking of Australian economics departments." *Economic Record* **82**(254): 30-44.

Rogers, P. S., Campbell, N., Louhiala-Salminen, L., Rentz, K. and Suchan, J. (2007). "The impact of perceptions of journal quality on business and management communication academics." *The Journal of Business Communication* **44**(4): 403-424.

Scopus. (2006). "Scopus Announces first-of-its-kind Customized Institutional Resources and Digital Archive Searches ", from http://info.scopus.com/news/press/pr_060821.asp.

Scopus. (2007). "Refine your Research - Scopus." from http://info.scopus.com/news/press/pr_060821.asp.

Sessions, R. and Collins, T. (1988). "More Accountability in Federally Funded Academic research: a Costly "Bill of Goods"." *Journal of the Society of Research Administrators* **20**(1): 195.

Spurgeon, D. (1994). "University Censured over Research Accounting." *Nature* **370**(6488): 132.

Tatnall, A. (1995). Information Technology and the Management of Victorian Schools - Providing Flexibility or Enabling Better Central Control? *Information Technology in Educational Management.* Barta, B. Z., Telem, M. and Gev, Y. London, Chapman & Hall: 99-108.

Evolving Forms of Visualisation for Presenting and Viewing Data

Don Passey

Department of Educational Research, Lancaster University, UK

Abstract: Teachers have been 'visualising' ideas or information that emerge from data for a long time. Mark books have provided teachers with 'visual', albeit normally numerical, records of pupil attainment and achievement, which they have used to generate views about progress, trends, or the identification of appropriate learning support, for example. The advent of information and communication technologies (ICT) has brought potential to provide perspectives from data in more visual forms; these visual forms would previously have taken a long time to generate, and would have been unlikely to have been dynamic (that is, updated with regularly changing background data, to offer up-to-date pictures). What differences have been made as a result of this potential? Has it meant that 'visualisation' of forms of presentation have changed, that forms of analyses have been introduced, that reliability and robustness have been more focused on, or that different types of needs have arisen? This paper will explore evolving visualisations of curriculum data, and will conclude that different forms of visualisation are being introduced, but do not necessarily make it easier for the teacher to identify necessary or precise detail (or to consider fundamental statistical questions or specific professional needs).

Keywords: Visualisation of data; data management and visual forms; school management systems and presentation of data; viewing data

1. BACKGROUND

Visualisation of data is clearly an important aspect for those presented with the need to understand and use data (and this includes teachers). It is also clear that the transfer of presented data to information is likely to be supported through forms of visualisation. Indeed, Tufte (1990) in his classic book entitled 'Envisioning information' explores the many ways in which visualisation can support access to and enhance the meaning of data. Teachers are being encouraged to use visualisation of data, both for subject teaching, and for curriculum management purposes. From a research perspective, the literature concerned with visualising data to support subject

Please use the following format when citing this chapter:

Passey, D., 2009, in IFIP International Federation for Information Processing, Volume 292; *Evolution of Information Technology in Educational Management*; Eds. Tatnall, A., Visscher, A., Finegan, A., O'Mahony, C., (Boston: Springer), pp. 155–167.

teaching is more developed than is the literature concerned with visualising data for curriculum management purposes. The Smart Centre in Durham University (2007) is, for example, focusing on projects for "envisioning data and reasoning from evidence"; these to date have focused on subject teaching. The Australian Bureau of Statistics (2007) offers a useful review of the literature concerned with data visualisation to support management practices. However, teacher uses for curriculum and classroom management purposes are not a focus of this review. This paper offers an introductory foray into the field, by exploring forms of visualisation for management purposes that have been, and are becoming, available to teachers.

2.   INTRODUCTION

For the classroom teacher, data are used fundamentally to consider pupil progress and identification of learning support or teaching approach needs. Although teachers have used mark books to record numerical features for a long time, often to give them ideas of how to judge or assess pupil progress and performance, it does not necessarily follow that numerical forms of data about other aspects of curriculum need (such as the estimation of likely future outcomes, or the assessment of appropriate targets and challenge) are as easy for teachers to view or that they are used in particularly useful or analytical ways. As the government department in England said in a document offering advice about data management to secondary schools in 2002:

> *"... teachers can often be daunted when presented with vast spreadsheets containing columns of data. A data-rich school only becomes information-rich when that data is systematically collected and passed to staff in easily digestible forms. A school that manages data well has systems that allow key aspects of student performance to be easily identified - and staff with the training and time to draw appropriate conclusions from the data available to them. Prior attainment data and effective monitoring are used to identify strengths and weaknesses, and set challenging, but attainable, targets." (DfES, 2002, p.3)*

This document suggested that presentation is important, in that information arising from data needs to be easily identifiable, so that strengths and weaknesses, challenges and targets, can be considered and set. It is clear that teachers, when using mark books, have often been able to identify trends with regard to performance and attainment. However, data relating to estimated likely outcomes (future possible attainments) based on prior attainment, or data relating to added value (gains arising from educational experiences and calculated over particular periods of time) have not been accessible to teachers for the same long periods of time. The identification of trends or even the identification of comparative evidence from these forms of data has not been established in long-term practice.

Indeed, there is little evidence to indicate that teachers currently being qualified are being given deep or insightful experiences in using data for predictive or indicative purposes, to support or inform their trial or future practice. Teachers do not necessarily have training experiences that offer them attributes to easily 'visualise' key features of data. Indeed, some teachers admit that they do not understand the basis on which data is often presented. In the Kirkup, Sizmar, Sturman and Lewis (2005) report on uses of data in schools, they concluded that:

> *"The main challenges to the effective use of data for primary schools were reported to be: lack of time, particularly time to update and analyse the data; difficulties in applying data to classroom situations; limitations of data, i.e. that the data collected/recorded was too narrow/academic or did not accommodate individual needs; ICT-related issues, e.g. insufficient resources or restricted access. Challenges to the effective use of data for secondary schools were similar to those experienced by primary schools. However, having sufficient trust in the data was also of concern to secondary schools (some respondents believed either that it was unreliable or arrived too late to be of use). Special schools reported two key challenges to the effective use of data: data systems that do not accommodate the complex needs of individual pupils; insufficient comparable data (year-on-year or with similar schools)." (Kirkup et al., 2005, p.4-5)*

This report did not highlight issues of 'visualisation' or the potential of forms of visualisation in addressing some of the issues raised within the study (as had the study for the DfES by Passey, 2002), but it did raise issues concerned with knowing about underlying fundamental statistical practices and processes: reliability; validity; robustness; and sampling dynamics. When concerns about visualisation by teachers are considered, there has been a distinct lack of studies into this aspect of the field. Neither the importance of visualisation, nor the potential of visualisation have been studied in any great depth (although it is true to say that the importance of background statistical processing has been considered and has been reported much more widely). At the same time, however, it is clear that ICT-based school management information systems (MISs) have increasingly been adopted and used by schools, and that a part of that adoption has been the increasing power brought to users by ranges of forms of visualisation.

Visscher (2002), in discussing a framework for studying school performance feedback systems, stated that there were likely to be differences in features across different school performance feedback systems. The features that he identified that could be different in different cases were concerned with extents of: information validity; information reliability; how up-to-date the information is; data relevance; indicators of relative and absolute school performance; trends, relationships and differences over time; standard and tailored information; presentation in accessible and appealing forms; support in using data correctly; time and effort requirements; complexity and clarity; and user support in solving problems. It is clear that these features relate not only to the concerns raised within the DfES report

(2002) and issues raised in the Kirkup et al. report (2005), but that they also refer to aspects concerned with visualisation and the implications of making data accessible through visual formats. The features identified by Visscher (2002) will be used as a categorisation for discussion of the development of forms of visualisation within school MISs in England.

3.   AN EVOLUTIONARY OVERVIEW

As the Visscher list of features indicate, there is a need to consider both the importance of visualisation in terms of presentational ease and access, and the importance of being able to 'see' that validity, reliability, and relevance are accounted for and considered. However, ease of presentation might mean that some important points remain hidden and are lost to view. It is clear that ease of presentation in itself is not a simple substitute for knowing about the validity of analytical technique when it comes to the need to identify key points for potential action. As Gray (2002) says:

"Judging schools' performance in 'raw' terms may be seen as inappropriate by researchers. Nonetheless, few schools which find themselves in the top half of any resulting 'league tables' will feel threatened by their use, even whilst acknowledging that they do not in reality give an accurate picture of their performance. They may well have learnt to interpret the evidence to their advantage, whatever the actual position. A well-conducted value-added analysis will challenge at least some of these schools, offering little or no comfort." (Gray, 2002, p.149)

This view indicates some concerns about the different ways of indicating and reporting school performance. However, it is just as clear that important points concerned at the pupil level, with pupil performance and challenge, can be also be missed if presentational features are viewed without sufficient consideration being given to analytical background. As Fitz-Gibbon (2002) says:

"Indicator systems may be used in very damaging fashions. By publishing a small number of indicators, attention is focused just on those indicators, and efforts are often directed not at real change but at getting the indicator in the right direction. Thus, the malign effect of the indicator used in England which schools' examination performances were reported in terms of the percentage of pupils achieving Grade C and above. This led to widespread concentration on students likely get a D to push them over the borderline." (Fitz-Gibbon, 2002, p.36)

Visualisation of numerical data can clearly lead to interpretation at a superficial (or selective) level. As Kirkup et al. (2005) suggested, limitations arise not only at the level of ease of presentation, but also at the level of implementation. If visualisation is leading to superficial or selective analysis, and subsequently superficial implementation, then data are clearly not being supportive at an informative level. In the same report, the authors indicate a real potential tension with developments of systems that offer increasing detail, but where the level of reliability, validity and relevance at an individual, group, class, or school level is not made clear to them by the system and visualisation itself:

> *"Some of the needs of special schools are identical to those of mainstream schools; they need systems that are simple to use and allow the easy input and interpretation of data. However, above all they need systems that allow a much finer level of detailed information to be added and that allow progress to be measured in extremely small steps and that accept and recognise that such progress may not be smooth nor linear." (Kirkup et al, 2005, p.81)*

Studies to date, therefore, suggest that there are fundamental questions to ask from a visualisation viewpoint (following the features offered by Visscher). Does visualisation indicate anything about information validity or reliability? Does visualisation indicate anything about how up-to-date the information is? Is anything shown regarding data relevance? Are there indicators of relative and absolute school performance? Does visualisation show trends, relationships and differences over time? Does it present standard and tailored information? Is presentation offered in accessible and appealing forms? Is support offered in using data correctly? Are time and effort requirements considered? How are issues of complexity and clarity addressed? How is user support in solving problems addressed?

4. CONSIDERING SOME INDICATORS OF EVOLUTION OF DATA VISUALISATION

Different visual forms were used in the DfES report (2002), which offered advice to schools on uses of curriculum data. In Table 1 the visual items used have been grouped according to form and type (as shown in the second column).

Table 1: Visual forms contained in an advisory document on data management (DfES, 2002)

Purpose of visual items	Graphical or tabular form of visual item	Page reference in document
Pupil estimated likely outcomes based on end of Key Stage prior attainment shown as a calculated value added line	Graphical form, showing a single line	14
Pupil estimated likely outcomes based on end of Key Stage prior attainment shown as a calculated value added line, with an additional challenge line to consider target setting	Graphical form, showing an estimation line and an additional challenge line in another colour	14
Comparison of school and national baseline data by attainment level for English and mathematics	Graphical form, showing colour and height comparisons	9

Comparison of school and national baseline data by year for English	Graphical form, showing colour and height comparisons	9
Comparison of school with local authority and national residuals by gender	Graphical form, with columns for girls and boys shown in different colours	24
Comparison of national probability of pupils attaining particular average scores at the end of a Key Stage, being able to attain at the end of the next Key Stage, with actual school results in mathematics	Graphical form, with columns for school actuals and national probabilities being in different colours	22
Comparison of national probability of pupils attaining different particular average scores at the end of a Key Stage, being able to attain at the end of the next Key Stage, with actual school results in mathematics	Graphical form, with columns for school actuals and national probabilities being in different colours	23
Comparison of achievement results by levels and grouped by ethnicity	Graphical form, with columns shown in a colour	29
National probability of pupils attaining particular average scores at the end of a Key Stage, being able to attain at the end of the next Key Stage	Graphical form, with columns shown in colour	22
Comparison of school with local authority and national residuals	Graphical form, with columns shown in colour	24
Comparison of pupil added value (prior and current plots) with national median and quartile lines	Graphical form, with median and quartile lines in different colours	20
Comparison of pupil added value (prior and current plots) with national median and quartile lines	Graphical form, with median and quartile lines in different colours, and pupils with different extents of added value highlighted in different colours	21
Comparison of pupil added value (prior and current plots) by gender with national median and quartile lines	Graphical form, with median and quartile lines in different colours	21
Plotting teacher predictions based on prior attainment against a previous year trend line	Graphical form, with pupils with low estimated added value being highlighted in a different colour	27
Transition matrix to indicate the expected percentages of pupils attaining levels at the end of one Key Stage compared to the previous Key Stage	Tabular form, highlighted to show typical expected positive progress	18
Table showing percentages of pupils needing to attain levels of examination results to meet inspection standards, according to school grouping and levels of free school meals	Tabular form, with a column highlighted in another colour	16
Comparison of predicted outcomes against prior results, with actual outcomes against prior results	Tabular form, with actual and predicted numbers shown in different colours	25
Pupil performance recorded by registration group, gender, ethnicity, end of Key Stage 2 results in science, and end of year results in science, and calculated added value	Tabular form, with colour highlighting showing below and above expected achievement, and below and above added value measures	11
Pupil performance recorded by registration group, date of birth, gender, ethnicity, teacher assessments in geography, CAT	Tabular form, with colour highlighting showing below and above expected achievement	11

results, and reading ages		
Numbers of pupils estimated to attain at each level in English based on comparisons of results of the CATs verbal and non-verbal reasoning tests	Tabular form, with colour highlighting showing numbers estimated to attain by only one rather than both test results	12
Comparison of schools' results by achievement levels by gender	Tabular form, with extremes highlighted in another colour	27
Table of subject residuals comparing school with local authority and national figures	Tabular form, with one subject residual highlighted in another colour	23
Differences between levels of attainment given as probabilities, based on prior results, on school grouping, and compared to actual results	Tabular form, with significant differences from expectations highlighted	36
Pupil performance recorded by registration group, gender, ethnicity, end of Key Stage 2 and 3 results, reading ages, and standardised yearly tests	Tabular form, without highlighting	10
Estimated probabilities of pupils attaining levels of examination outcomes based on prior accrued results	Tabular form, without highlighting	16
Spreadsheet to calculate numbers of pupils in a school estimated to attain levels of examination outcomes based on prior accrued results	Tabular form, without highlighting	16
Table of point scores to indicate how 'solid' a level a pupil has attained	Tabular form, without highlighting	18
Table to allow schools to plot their pupil results to compare with a national transition matrix to indicate the expected percentages of pupils attaining levels at the end of one Key Stage compared to the previous Key Stage	Tabular form, without highlighting	18
Table showing measures of typical yearly progress for different groups of pupils	Tabular form, without highlighting	19
Plotting pupils estimated to achieve subject results at the end of a Key Stage by class group	Tabular form, without highlighting	26
Comparison of national achievement levels by gender	Tabular form, without highlighting	27
Comparison of school results by achievement levels by term of birth	Tabular form, without highlighting	28
Estimates of attainment given as probabilities, based on prior results, and on school grouping	Tabular form, without highlighting	35

It is clear from this list that different forms and types of visualisation were used (line graphs, column graphs, and tables). Different features were applied to these different forms of visualisation. The range of different features are identified, grouped and shown in Table 2.

Table 2: Visual forms and highlighting techniques shown within an advisory
document (DfES, 2002)

Graphical or tabular form of visual item	Frequency
Line graphs	
Graphical form, showing a single line	1
Graphical form, showing a single line with pupils with low estimated added value being highlighted in a different colour	1
Graphical form, showing lines in different colours	3
Graphical form, with median and quartile lines in different colours, and pupils with different extents of added value highlighted in different colours	1
Column graphs	
Graphical form, with columns shown in a colour	3
Graphical form, showing colour and column height comparisons	5
Tables	
Tabular form, without highlighting	10
Tabular form, with some figures, cells or columns highlighted	8
Tabular form, with significant differences from expectations highlighted	1

Within the entire document, there were 33 items that were shown in visual form. Of these, 6 were in line graph form, 8 in column graph form, and 19 were in tabular form. Of the 7 line graphs, 6 used forms of colour highlighting to indicate particular features. Of the 8 column graphs, all used colour to highlight columns and, where appropriate, comparisons between columns. Of the 19 tables, 9 used some forms of highlighting (usually colouring of numbers or different forms of background colouring). However, only one of these items (from a research charity source) used colour to indicate statistically significant differences.

Some indication of the shift over time, in terms of visual forms used, can be gained by looking at the types of visual presentations highlighted by a school MIS provider, when showing features of its curriculum facilities to a teacher group. The visual forms shown in the presentation (Sherwood, 2008) are grouped using the same categories as those in Table 2 above, and the results are shown in Table 3.

Table 3: Visual forms and highlighting techniques shown within a
presentation of a school MIS (Sherwood, 2008)

Graphical or tabular form of visual item	Frequency
Line graphs	
Graphical form, showing a single line	0
Graphical form, showing a single line with pupils with low estimated added value being highlighted in a different colour	0
Graphical form, showing lines in different colours	1
Graphical form, with median and quartile lines in different colours, and pupils with different extents of added value highlighted in different colours	0
Graphical form, with median and quartile lines in different colours, and densities of pupils with different extents of added value highlighted by size	5
Graphical form, in star form showing a coloured line	1
Column graphs	
Graphical form, with columns shown in a colour	2
Graphical form, showing colour and column height comparisons	4
Tables	
Tabular form, without highlighting	15
Tabular form, with some figures, cells or columns highlighted	6
Tabular form, with significant differences from expectations highlighted	0

Within the entire presentation, there were 34 items that were shown in visual form (about the same number as those within the advisory document). Of these, 7 were in line graph form, 6 in column graph form, and 21 were in tabular form (again, roughly the same balance within the advisory document). Of the 7 line graphs, all used forms of colour highlighting to indicate particular features. However, 6 of these line graphs used new forms of presentation (one was in the form of a star graph, and five were in the form of trend graphs that showed densities of pupil responses by the differential size of coloured dots). Of the 6 column graphs, all used colour to highlight columns and comparisons between columns. Of the 21 tables, 6 used some forms of highlighting, but none of these items used colour to indicate statistically significant differences (although it is true to say that the MIS did provide access to tools that offered these forms of visualisation). The visual forms in this presentation indicated that colour highlighting was used prominently in line and column graph forms, that new forms of line graphs had been deployed, but that statistically significant differences were not shown within these presentations.

Other sources (such as the Data Enabler Toolkit from the Specialist Schools and Academies Trust, 2008) also provide access to new forms of presentation. In this resource, Venn diagrams are now used to show numbers of pupils attaining numbers of pass grades in Key Stage 4 tests (GCSE grade levels A* to C), and elements of the diagram give an overview of numbers of students gaining one, two, three or more, four or more, or five or more passes. The Venn diagram enables teachers to easily see not only the numbers from across an entire year group who are attaining certain grades, but those subjects limiting the overall number of five or more passes, as well as a facility to show the name of each student when the cursor is placed over an individual 'dot'. Considerations of statistical validity and relevance are also included within resources in the Data Enabler Toolkit: value added measures are shown in terms of current attainment levels compared to previous school attainment levels (allowing comparisons across schools to be identified); and different forms of estimated likely outcomes allow a triangulation of comparison to be made.

Using evidence about visual forms from across these sources, what can be concluded about the development of features of visual forms? A review, focused through questions raised by Visscher features, is shown in Table 4.

Table 4: The status of visual forms with regard to Visscher features

Feature concerned with visualisation	Comments about features observed in sources
Does visualisation indicate anything about information validity or reliability?	Resources do tend to use a range of different techniques, and many resources do indicate ways that different techniques might be used to display data for specific purposes (such as comparisons with previous pupil performance, or performance of other schools). However, aspects concerned with validity and reliability relating to individual visual forms tend not to be completely obvious. It is not always clear when it is appropriate and not appropriate to use a particular form, and indeed evidence suggests that some schools select visual forms that represent positive pictures rather than pictures to determine action. The validity of using visualisations to compare school data with national data, for example, is not generally discussed or considered on the visualisation itself. However, there is a greater tendency now to group schools so that comparing like-for-like (contextual value added, for example) becomes more possible. Reliability is also being considered to greater extents through the use of different forms of contextual value added measures, and the use of comparisons across different statistical techniques. For example, the Specialist Schools and Academies Trust (SSAT, 2008) now provide the comparison of estimated likely outcomes using three different statistical techniques. Reliability is also considered more inherently in those visualisations where probabilities are indicated (in Fischer Family Trust visualisations, exemplified within the DfES report, 2002, for example), or where quartile lines are shown as well as median lines.
Does visualisation indicate anything about how up-to-date the information is?	Generally, the ability to access visual forms that are up-to-date is becoming easier. It is possible through the school MIS that has been reviewed, for example, to link to different data sources (Sherwood, 2008), and to have access to visual presentations on up-to-date data (as MISs often update on at least a daily basis). Visual forms are usually date stamped, and this shows clearly the day that the data were presented.
Is anything shown regarding data relevance?	Relevance is an aspect that tends to be determined to an extent by government department requirements. Although schools do have some scope for selecting forms of presentation, there are some forms that are regularly used by the government department and school inspectorate. The clear labelling of visual forms does tend to show how presentational forms relate to particular curriculum needs (for example, an estimated likely outcome, or a potential future target).
Are there indicators of relative and absolute school performance?	These indicators have been built into a range of systems since at least 2002. It has been possible for schools to compare their performances relative to national attainment and to their previous attainment. More recently, the Fischer Family Trust (Treadaway, 2008) has made available the facility for schools to work in groups or federations, to compare their data and performance, to share their strengths and support their weaknesses.
Does visualisation show trends, relationships and differences over time?	These aspects have been accessible since at least 2002. Trends at pupil, class, subject, school, local authority and national level have been made available. Relationships and differences over time have also been shown through a range of visual forms (see Table 1 above).
Does it present standard and tailored information?	Increasingly, school MISs allow tailored information to be presented as well as standard information (Sherwood, 2008). The SIMS MIS now allows schools to link to other sources of data

	(such as that from the government department, the Fischer Family Trust, and research test sources), and allows schools to enter their own data in fields that can then be analysed through a wide range of selected techniques.
Is presentation offered in accessible and appealing forms?	Increasingly, visual forms are using features to highlight exceptions or differences, and are using techniques that indicate features such as density, strengths and weaknesses. Teachers are voicing fewer concerns about accessibility and appeal of visual presentations, and are now voicing more concerns about aspects such as relevance and validity.
Is support offered in using data correctly?	Data support is available to schools. Local authorities continue to support through courses and help desks, as do national support agencies such as SSAT (2008). There is now a desire to engage with researchers more on aspects of data use. For example, this year a research practitioner course on data handling has been run for the first time (SSAT, 2008), although this course has not focused specifically on visual forms of presentation.
Are time and effort requirements considered?	Schools generally provide access to development time for staff, and some schools are now focusing much more on support for teachers in data handling. Visual forms of presentation have not been a specific focus, but some schools recognise that online forms of visual presentation of data are positively affecting effort and time.
How are issues of complexity and clarity addressed?	Clarity is being addressed increasingly through the auspicious use of visual forms of presentation. Increased clarity is also allowing levels of complexity to be addressed to increasing extents. For example, in trend graphs, densities of pupil performance are now being shown by sizes of dots (Sherwood, 2008), allowing a different level of complexity to be highlighted in a recognisable form.
How is user support in solving problems addressed?	User support is being enhanced increasingly over time with regard to data handling. Increasing numbers of practitioners with wider understanding and knowledge are being trained, and are supporting others. However, with regard to support at the point of use of visual forms, this is not necessarily built into data handling systems, although systems allow visual forms to be regenerated or saved easily, so that users feel more able to engage with others about any issues they identify.

5. DIRECTIONS AND POLICIES

It is clear from the responses in Table 4 that some features of visual forms of data presentation have been addressed to greater extents than have others in terms of an evolution over time. The features that have been addressed more successfully at this point in time are:

- Visualisation often indicates how up-to-date the information is.
- Relevance is often indicated on the labels on presentations of data presented visually.
- Indicators of relative and absolute school performance are accessible and different forms of comparison are widening.

- Visualisation is used to show trends, relationships and differences in a range of ways.
- Standard and tailored information is increasingly accessible.
- Presentation is increasingly offered in accessible and appealing forms.
- Issues of complexity and clarity are being increasingly addressed.

There are features that have not been addressed so successfully, and that should clearly be a focus for future direction and policies (especially for those concerned with the increasing development and uses of visual forms). The features that are worthy of more focus at this time are:

- Visualisation needs to indicate much more information about specific validity and reliability.
- Support needs should focus more on how to use data 'correctly'.
- Time and effort requirements need to be considered when visualisation forms are developed.
- Offering user support in solving problems through appropriate visual forms needs more focus.

The need to focus on these features is becoming increasingly recognised. For example, Treadaway (2008), in a presentation to a conference focusing on school achievement, indicated that more attention should be given to discussion of findings from data (such as the selection of pupil targets from background and estimated future attainment) with pupils, rather than using data to merely take actions. He was pointing to the need for visualisations to be 'smarter', and to indicate points of concern and need, as well as to offer raw data views. Data (particularly statistical data) have perhaps (too) frequently been offered in forms that have assumed that the reader or user is a 'smart' interpreter. Evidence suggests that this can happen, but that it may not happen. Sutherland (1992) pointed out the many ways that data can be used irrationally, or how its uses can lead to irrational views or actions. Can it be assumed that educational users are any different from other users in this respect? The evidence suggests not. However, indicators suggest that the recognition by teachers and managers in schools of the need to be 'smarter' with regard to data handling is in itself a useful and positive trend. There is a clearly a great deal of potential application for a range of focused research in this field.

6.   REFERENCES

Australian Bureau of Statistics (2007). *1211.0.55.001 - Research Paper: Data Visualisation*. Retrieved August 15, 2008, from http://www. abs.gov.au/AUSSTATS/abs@.nsf/Latestproducts/1211.0.55.001Main%2 0Features1Jul%202007?opendocument&tabname=Summary&prodno= 1211.0.55.001&issue=Jul%202007&num=&view=
Department for Education and Skills. (2002) *Releasing Potential, Raising Attainment: Managing Data in Secondary Schools*. DfES: London

Fischer Family Trust. (n.d.). *Data Analysis Project.* Retrieved July 13, 2007, from http://www.fischertrust.org/

Fitz-Gibbon, C.T. (2002). A Typology of Indicators. In A.J. Visscher and R. Coe (Eds.) *School improvement through performance feedback.* Routledge: Oxford and New York.

Gray, J. (2002). Jolts and Reactions: Two Decades of Feeding Back Information on Schools' Performance. In A.J. Visscher and R. Coe (Eds.) *School improvement through performance feedback.* Routledge: Oxford and New York.

Kirkup, C., Sizmur, J., Sturman, L. and Lewis, K. (2005) *Research Report No 671: Schools' Use of Data in Teaching and Learning.* Department for Education and Skills: Nottingham

Passey, D. (2002). *Schools in Exceptionally Challenging Circumstances: ICT Audit.* Lancaster University: Lancaster

Sherwood, C. (2008). *Assessment Manager 7, Performance Analysis 7.* Presentation given at the Second Conference of the Research Practitioner Course in Data Management, Aston University Business School, 30 April 2008

Specialist Schools and Academies Trust. (2007). *Toolkits.* Retrieved July 13, 2007, from https://secure.ssatrust.org.uk/eshop/default.aspx?mcid=22&scid=34&productid=627

Smart Centre (2007). *Smart Centre Durham University.* Retrieved August 15, 2008, from http://www.dur.ac.uk/smart.centre/

Specialist Schools and Academies Trust. (2008). *Data Enabler.* Retrieved July 12, 2008, from www.ssatrust.org.uk/dataenabler

Sutherland, S. (1992). *Irrationality: The Enemy Within.* Constable: London.

Treadaway, M. (2008). *Data visualisation.* Presentation given at the Specialist Schools and Academies Trust Achievement Show, Emirates Stadium London, 17 June 2008

Tufte, E.R. (1990). *Envisioning information.* Graphics Press: Cheshire, CT.

Visscher, A.J. (2002). A Framework for Studying School Performance Feedback Systems. In A.J. Visscher and R. Coe (Eds.) *School improvement through performance feedback.* Routledge: Oxford and New York.

Industry-Based Learning

Kathy Henschke and Patrick Poppins
School of Business Information Technology, RMIT University, Australia

Abstract: Research from the fields of adult learning, workplace education, professional development, organisational learning and co-operative education are drawn on to identify elements that should be considered in the design, implementation, management and sustained improvement of co-op programs. Each work placement is unique meld of stakeholders, the job and the organisational context. Key factors that promote learning in the workplace include the engagement of the work place supervisor in the student's professional development; the learning environment within the organisation; and the student's own motivation, abilities and learning orientation: It is proposed that information systems delivering co-op programs need to manage: (a) the development and performance of industry partnerships, (b) the relationships between key stakeholders; and (c) the professional skills development and learning.

Keywords: Information management systems, Co-operative education, ICT professionals, employability skills, workplace learning, professional development

1. INTRODUCTION

Businesses and governments look to educational institutions to prepare individuals that are job-ready and have the ability to grow in the constantly changing workplace. Co-operative education programs (co-op) or sandwich years within higher education institutions, place students in long term paid or unpaid employment in a relevant job for up to 12 months. These placements aim to provide students with context-based, experiential learning opportunities.

There are a number of stakeholders involved in co-operative education programs: the employers who recruit and employ the student for the period of the co-op placement; the students who take on the job; the co-op personnel who develop and maintain the relationships between the employers, the students and the university; the work-based supervisors and/or mentors who guide the students during the placement; the academics

Please use the following format when citing this chapter:

Henschke, K. and Poppins, P., 2009, in IFIP International Federation for Information Processing, Volume 292; *Evolution of Information Technology in Educational Management*; Eds. Tatnall, A., Visscher, A., Finegan, A., O'Mahony, C., (Boston: Springer), pp. 169–180.

who teach the students before and after the co-op year; the university management that resource the programs; and the professional bodies who accredit the degree programs.

A literature review uncovered differences of opinion on the value of co-op programs. In general, most students gained confidence and self-concept; developed social skills; increased their practical knowledge and skills – all of which enhanced their employment opportunities (Waryszak 2000). However some, students returned to study disillusioned by their work experience. Many employers felt academic programs were not preparing the students adequately with essential skills to be competent in the work placement (Howard 2005; Multimedia Victoria 2005). While many in the academic community viewed co-op practice as limited to vocational development (Cates and Jones 1999, Howard 2005) and a drain on resources (Jancaukas et al. 1999). Academic staff involved in co-op programs reported feeling their work was undervalued and not recognised or rewarded through university promotions. In these cases, the commitment by academics to co-op was sometimes found to take a relatively low priority in their curriculum and work planning (Weisz 1995) and the student learning in co-op often left to chance (Reeders et al. 1999).

The diversity of stakeholder views highlights the inherent difficulties of managing co-op programs. Coll and Eames (2004) observed that co-op programs designed with objectives that are relevant and appropriate to all parties involved, are far more likely to be successful and sustainable. With the growing area of interest (and concern) to governments, industry and universities of the importance of generic employability skills in graduates, it is proposed that co-op programs be designed, delivered and managed around the shared purpose of developing employability skills of the students.

This paper presents the findings of an extensive literature review that investigates the contribution of co-op work placements to the development of employability skills. Key processes needed to manage co-op programs, focussed on developing these skills, are identified. These processes are used in investigating a co-op program found within an existing undergraduate program at an Australian university, to determine its efficacy in developing employability skills.

In the next section the nature of employability skills and how they are developed are explored.

2.   THE NATURE OF EMPLOYABILITY SKILLS

The past 20 years has seen Australian universities making significant efforts to enhance the graduate outcomes of their students by providing them with opportunities to develop generic employability skills within curricula. The Department of Education, Employment and Workplace Relations (DEST) published a report in 2002 in which it identified generic employability skills as: *personal attributes* of loyalty, commitment, honesty and integrity, enthusiasm, reliability, personal presentation, commonsense, positive self-esteem, sense of humour, balanced attitude to work and home life, ability to deal with pressure, motivation and adaptability; and eight key *generic skills*: communication; team work; problem-solving; initiative/ enterprise; planning and organisation; self-management; learning; and technology (DEST 2002).

An earlier report funded by the Department of Employment, Training and Youth Affairs (DETYA) titled Employer Satisfaction with Graduate Skills (DETYA 2000) noted that "... a large proportion of applicants for positions are considered unsuitable" (p.vii) identifying key skill deficiencies of graduates in the areas of oral business communication; creativity and flair; problem solving; independent and critical thinking; and understanding of business practice.

These deficiencies are attributed to a lack of understanding of the nature of generic skills and how they are acquired. Beckett and Hager (2002) propose generic skills be examined within a context-specific, relational perspective. The relational view sees generic skills linking the abilities of individuals (knowledge, skills, dispositions, values) to the demands, tasks and activities that individuals undertake (Gonczi 2004). How a task is completed is influenced by the context it is found in. The interplay of cultural, political, social and economic factors makes the situation each task is found in, unique. The ways generic skills cluster are strongly shaped by particular features of the context in which the work is carried out Hager (1997) cited in Beckett and Hager (2002).

From this perspective, generic skills are acquired through completing a variety of tasks in a range of work contexts. Classroom contexts are limited as are the scope of tasks for execution. There is an assumption that learning the theory of teamwork and then working on a team assignment within a university setting provides students with some teamwork skills that transfer into the workplace setting. However, research evidence suggests knowledge gained in the classroom does not become usable at work without further learning in the workplace (Eraut 2002). Eraut adds that acquired knowledge only has meaning once used; and its meaning is strongly influenced by previous contexts of use. The contextual nature of employability skills (particularly within practical judgement) moves focus from skills acquisition to professional development. From this standpoint, the development of professionals is seen as a life-long endeavour where educational and workplace settings contribute various formal and informal admixtures to shaping the individual. Professional education shifts thinking from training the individual mind to the social setting in which the individual is situated (Gonczi 2004)

As co-op programs are located in the workplace, they provide rich environments for learning and developing generic employability skills. However, many co-op programs struggle for educational recognition and overall viability. Also, there is little written on the learning value of co-op programs. Much of the research literature on co-op tends to reflect the practitioners' orientation that is largely focused on the effects of co-op programs on the personal growth and career development aspects of students. As a result the nature of learning in co-op education is not well understood (Ricks et al. 1993).

Each co-op work placement sits within an organisation where the opportunities for learning are influenced by personal, interpersonal, institutional, social and historical factors (Foley 2004). The nature of learning in workplaces has implications for designing a co-op management system to support the co-op learning experience.

3.   IMPLICATIONS FOR DESIGN

Research literature in the fields of adult learning, organisational learning and workplace learning expose ambiguities, diversities and complexities associated with learning in the workplace. How adults learn can be seen to be influenced by a highly complex set of variables. These variables may be loosely grouped across three overlapping dimensions: the contextual dimension, the social dimension and the learning dimension. A number of variables specific to our discussion on professional development and learning are identified.

1. The **contextual dimension** includes the micro contexts of the organisation. External political, economical and technological forces drive an organisation's strategies. These strategies in turn drive its internal policy, culture, structure, processes and learning orientation. This learning orientation promotes or discourages a learning culture within the company and influences how managers, supervisors and employees share knowledge. Also the type of industry the organisation is involved in, influences the nature of the learning required and how learning is perceived (Smith and Sadler-Smith 2006).

     It cannot be assumed that all organisations have a learning environment with resources and personnel in place to support the co-op student. Nor can it be supposed that the student will learn just by being in the workplace. Through discussions between the organisation offering the work placement and the university, each co-op placement can be tailored to not only accommodate the needs of the workplace but the learning needs of the student.

2. The **social dimension** includes internal and external stakeholders, their interactions and relationships. The assumptions, expectations and concerns held by the stakeholders towards learning, impact the design and implementation of learning programs. Good relationships between all parties depends on clear agreements, two-way, open communications; learning and mentoring support for students; advisory support for workplace supervisors; and a recognition of the value of an ongoing relationship between all parties (Lyons 2007, Gamble et al. 2007, Howe and Patrick 2007).

3. The **learning dimension** brings together the factors regarding the learners and their contexts within the learning program. Learning can be formal, non-formal, informal and incidental (Foley 2004). However, most workplace learning occurs informally, but consciously through experience, or incidentally and unconsciously (Eraut et al. 1998). This means that measurement of learning and capturing individual learner progress is fraught with complexity. The Dreyfus Model of Skill Acquisition charts the incremental changes of a professional over five levels of proficiency: novice, advanced beginner, competent, proficient and expert (Benner 1982). Benner and Smith and Sadler-Smith (2006) found that the learning needs of professionals varies according to their stage of professional development. Novices and advanced beginners require more learning support and scaffolding which decreases as they became more expert.

Most students in a co-op placement are at the novice stage of professional development and require guided instructions, "hand-holding", recognition and affirmation from supervisors and colleagues. Also students should be encouraged to be proactive and take responsibility for their own learning and professional development. Reflective practices can be encouraged through planned curricula (integrated with the university program), individual work and learning plans; and regular performance reviews and feedback.

This brief discussion touches on some of the complexities of workplace-related learning. The co-op placement offers a unique learning opportunity for students. However, a successful learning program in the co-op workplace is the shared responsibility of the student, the employer and the university and is most successful with the active involvement of all parties. Martin in Howe and Patrick (2007) observes the best co-op placements are those where industry and universities are seen as equal partners involved in the planning of the overall experience and student's professional development

Information systems designed to manage the contextual, social and learning dimensions of co-op placements do not currently exist in normal university settings. The requirements to develop partnerships and manage relationships would imply facilities such as those found in customer relationship management systems. The system would also require the ability to capture and organise data arising outside the university in varied industry settings. Learning also needs to be monitored in a situation where formal assessment is not appropriate.

4. TOWARDS A SYSTEM MODEL

It is proposed that a co-op management system designed to promote the learning and development of employability skills, should support the following processes: building and cultivating partnerships between industry and the university; monitoring relationships between students and their workplace supervisors; facilitating learning and development of employability skills; and managing a cycle of continuous quality improvement.

In the next section, the extent to which these processes feature in an existing co-op program is investigated.

5.   IMPLICATIONS FOR PRACTICE

The Bachelor of Business in Business Information Systems (BBBIS) at RMIT University is a 4 year degree that includes a mandatory 12-month industry placement in the third year. The co-op program has been running for over 19 years and has gone through a number of iterations. Experiential learning has always been considered an important aspect of the co-op year. However there has been a general assumption that students learn by "osmosis" with little contact required from the University during the student's placement. The past few years has seen a shift in thinking by the School (and the University) on the unique learning opportunities offered by a workplace setting. The co-op program is now seen as an integral part of the whole BBBIS program curriculum with a number of academics and administrative personnel now involved in its management and delivery. There are roughly 90 students in co-op placements at any one time.

Currently a number of manual and automated systems are employed to manage and deliver the Co-op program. These systems are investigated against the processes proposed in our systems model for the purpose of identifying design, development and implementation issues that require consideration when developing information systems for managing co-op programs.

5.1   Building and cultivating partnerships between industry and university

Jobs are sourced from new and existing employers (usually through email and phone calls from/to the Co-op Manager); or through students own job search efforts. Prospective employers are oriented to the Co-op program and the expectations of their participation outlined. Co-op jobs coming into the School are vetted for their suitability. At a minimum each job needs to be a full-time position; be engaged with information technology skills development; and be allocated a workplace supervisor.

Across the University, there are also a number of separate databases holding industry contact data about alumni, research partnerships and co-op employers that have the potential for developing further job opportunities. However, individuals, programs and schools are reluctant to share contact details with other parts of the University for fear of jeopardising their current relationships. Investigations are underway to identify ways the various databases can be linked without effecting individual relationships.

5.2 Monitoring relationships between students and their workplace supervisors

Each student is allocated an academic supervisor (or "relationship manager") who visits the student at the start, middle and end of the placement. The co-op site visits are an opportunity for all the stakeholders to discuss expectations, review progress, give feedback and identify any issues or concerns.

Co-op site visits are scheduled through emails, phone calls, electronic calendars and spreadsheets. Three data capture forms are sent to the workplace supervisor prior to each site visit - the *Memorandum of Understanding* (refer to Appendix A), the *Mid-Term Co-op Student Workplace Performance Appraisal*, and the *Final Co-op Student Workplace Performance Appraisal*. These forms are designed to promote awareness of the workplace supervisor's involvement in the development of the student's employability skills during the placement period; to promote feedback to the student on their performance; and to discuss career directions. Co-op Site Visit forms are completed and emailed after each visit. Any concerns or issues are flagged for action by the Co-op Office.

The School maintains its own MS Access database and stores data on employers, students, student job applications, and employment details, as well as recording all interactions between the various stakeholders. The current system does not allow students, workplace supervisors or university staff (the data sources) to input co-op data from off-campus locations.

5.3 Facilitating the learning and development of employability skills

During the co-op preparation classes, students are made aware of the DEST set of employability skills as part of their resume writing exercises. Once they start co-op, students are placed in teams with other co-op students. Co-op student mentors (volunteers sourced from final year students or alumni) are allocated to each team to encourage students to share stories, concerns and achievements. Students meet on a monthly basis to participate in facilitated professional development discussions and activities.

Student performance appraisals are carried out at during and at the end of the placement in order to chart employability skills development (refer Appendix B). Workplace supervisors provide input into the student's final assessment grade.

The course website is designed around academic and student requirements. It supports student reflection (e-journals blogs); team discussions; open forums; learning resources; and assessment information. It does not however allow for ready access by non-RMIT participants such as workplace supervisors, alumni and other industry-based individuals.

5.4   Managing a cycle of continuous quality improvement

Feedback is sought from all stakeholders in three key areas: the delivery of the co-op experience; the administration and management of the co-op program; and the relevance of BBBIS program curriculum to the co-op year. The feedback is collected through paper-based forms (refer Appendix C); emails; student journals and reflection papers; and face-to-face meetings. There is no electronic repository for capturing feedback data for analysis and just-time reporting. Improvements are implemented on an ad-hoc basis.

There are a number of separate, disparate systems involved in the management of the current BBBIS Co-op program. The above discussion raises a number of issues and concerns and highlights the need for a more collaborative, holistic approach to the design, development and management of co-op management systems that cross program, School and University boundaries. Information systems supporting and managing co-op partnerships should:

- Allow for and support, two way communication and discussion between all stakeholders (within and outside the university);
- Provide on-line learning resources for all stakeholders;
- Permit data to be captured directly from data sources, located at on and off-campus locations, in a format that allows analysis and reflection by key stakeholders;
- Support local and remote, multi-user access to relevant databases;
- Allow just-in-time reporting; and
- Be responsive to changes and improvements.

6.   CONCLUSIONS

Co-op programs have been around for over 100 years yet have struggled for recognition in university curricula. Research studies purport knowledge and skills gained in the classroom do not become usable without further learning in the workplace. It is argued, that generic employability skills, in particular, are developed through completing tasks in a variety of situations. Co-op programs are located in workplaces and offer a rich source of learning contexts. A curriculum integrating workplace and classroom learning suggests a good foundation for on-going professional development.

The most successful co-op placements are those where industry and universities are seen as equal partners involved in the planning of the overall experience and in monitoring and guiding day to day development. Information systems supporting and managing these partnerships need to allow for and support open, two-way communications and discussions between all stakeholders; contain relationship management systems; track student placements and monitor progress of employability skills development; provide on-line learning resources and mentoring support; permit data to be captured directly from data sources, located at on and off-campus locations, in a format that allows analysis and reflection by key stakeholders;

support multi-user, remote access to relevant databases; allow just-in-time reporting; and be responsive to changes and improvements. New industry partnerships can be cultivated at a number of levels, within and outside the university. Systems that track previous industry engagements in research, co-op and projects endeavours have the potential to promote stronger links with industry.

Co-op programs provide a bridge between universities and industry and are in a unique position for building sustainable programs, developing existing industry relationships and promoting new partnership opportunities. The design, development and management of co-op systems should be considered beyond program, School and University boundaries.

7. REFERENCES

BECKETT, D. & HAGER, P. (2002). *Life, Work and Learning: Practice in post modernity.* London & New York, Routledge.

BENNER, P. (1982). From Novice to Expert. *The American Journal of Nursing,* 82, 402-407.

CATES, C. & JONES, P. (1999). *Learning outcomes: The educational value of cooperative education,* Colombia, MD, Cooperative Education Association.

COLL, R. & EAMES, C. (2004). Current Issues in Cooperative Education. IN EAMES, R. K. C. A. C. (Ed.) *International Handbook for Cooperative Education.* Boston, USA. World Association for Cooperative Education, Inc.

DEST (2002). Employability Skills for the Future. Commonwealth of Australia.

DETYA (2000). Employer Satisfaction with Graduate Skills: Research Report 99(7), Feb 2000 Evaluations and Investigations Program. Higher Education Division (Ed.). Canberra.

DRESSLER, S. & KEELING, A. E. (2004). Student Benefits of Cooperative Education. IN EAMES, R. K. C. A. C. (Ed.) *International Handbook for Co-operative Education.* Boston, USA, World Association for Co-operative Education, Inc.

ERAUT, M. (2002). The interaction between qualifications and work-based learning. IN K. EVANS, P. H., L. UNWIN (Ed.) *Work to Learn.* London, Kogan Page.

ERAUT, M. E., ALDERTON, J., COLE, G. & SENKER, P. (1998). Development of Knowledge and Skills in Employment. East Sussex, UK, University of Sussex.

FOLEY, G. (2004). Introduction: The state of adult education and learning. IN FOLEY, G. (Ed.) *Dimensions of Adult Learning: Adult education and training in a global era.* Crows Nest, NSW, Allen & Unwin.

GAMBLE, N., THOMPSON, K. & ZDENKOWSKI, S. (2007). Sustainable Partnerships and Meeting Expectations: What Keeps Industry Coming Back for More? *Proceeding for the Asia-Pacific Conference on Cooperative Education.* Singapore, WACE.

GONCZI, A. (2004). The new professional and vocational education. IN FOLEY, G. (Ed.) *Dimensions of Adult Learning: Adult education and training in a global era.* Crows Nest, NSW, Allen & Unwin.

HOWARD, A. (2005). Cooperative Education and Internships at the Threshold of the Twenty-First Century. IN LINN, P. L., HOWARD, A. & MILLER, E. (Eds.) *Handbook for Research in Cooperative Education and Internships.* Mahwah, NJ, Lawrence Erlbaum Associates.

HOWE, C. & PATRICK, C. (2007). The importance of the customer relationship to Industry in Work-integrated-learning programs. *Proceeding for the Asia-Pacific Conference on Cooperative Education.* Singapore, WACE.

JANCAUKAS, E., ATCHISON, M., MURPHY, G. & ROSE, P. (1999). *Unleashing the potential of work-integrated learning through professional trained academic and industry supervisors.* World Association of Cooperative Education.

LYONS, F. (2007). Developing Sustainable Education Partnerships with Industry. *Proceeding for the Asia-Pacific Conference on Cooperative Education.* Singapore, WACE.

MULTIMEDIAVICTORIA (2005). ICT Skills Snapshot: The State of ICT Skills in Victoria. Melbourne, Department of Infrastructure.

REEDERS, E., ATCHISON, M., POLLOCK, S. & RIZZETTI, J. (1999). Structured work experience: Habit, cargo cult or Cinderella? *Practicum Colloquium.* Flinders University, SA.

RICKS, F., CUTT, J., BRANTON, G., LOKEN, M. & VAN GYN, G. (1993). Reflections on the cooperative education literature. *Journal of Cooperative Education,* 29, 6-23.

SMITH, P. J. & SADLER-SMITH, E. (2006). *Learning in Organizations: Complexities and diversities,* London and New York, Routledge.

WARYSZAK, R. Z. (2000). Before, during and after: International perspective of students' perceptions of their cooperative education placements in the tourism industry. *Journal of Cooperative Education,* 35.

WEISZ, M. (1995). How to motivate and train academic supervisors: Find the missing link to the partnership in co-operative education. *9th World Conference on Co-operative Education.* Jamaica.

Appendix A – Memorandum of Understanding

Agreement regarding the Co-operative Employment / Internship Program

1. *The employment period for a student needs to be a minimum of 40 weeks full time.*
2. *During the industry placement, students are employees of the organisation and are required to observe the same standards and conditions of work within the company as would any other regular employees, or face disciplinary action as would any other employee within the organisation (warnings, directives and dismissal). The student also risks failing their Co-operative Employment Year.*
3. *If there are any problems that are inhibiting the student from reaching their expected potential, RMIT should be contacted and after consultation, undertake appropriate action.*
4. *The employer should arrange for the payment of tax & superannuation, and provide Workcover, professional indemnity insurance and ensure all standard Australian/Victorian employment conditions apply.*
5. *The employer agrees that the student is working in areas that are predominantly (~90%) in software, and that students have an IT qualified or experienced supervisor to lead them throughout the placement.*
6. *Students must complete assignments throughout the year. These are expected to be completed outside business hours.*
7. *Students are requested to attend monthly forums (outside normal working hours) at RMIT University during the year as a class group (not applicable to interns outside Melbourne).*
8. *An RMIT representative agrees to attend the workplace at a minimum, three times during placement to appraise and discuss progress of the internship. RMIT will speak openly to employers, supervisors and students regarding questions, problems or issues concerning the internship.*

I have read and accept the Agreement regarding the Co-operative Employment / Internship Program

Employer Representative		Supervisor
Name		Name
Position		Signature
Signature		Date
Date		
Student		**RMIT Representative**
Name		Name
Signature		Signature
Date		Date

Appendix B – Student Performance Review Forms

Personal & Professional Skills (Excerpt from Student Performance Forms)

	Below Average	Average	Above Average	Outstanding
Interest in work	☐ Interest spasmodic, occasionally enthusiastic	☐ Satisfactory amount of interest	☐ More than average amount of interest and enthusiasm	☐ High interest, very enthusiastic. Takes pride in doing work well
Problem solving skills	☐ Exhibits marginal problem solving ability	☐ Satisfactory problem solving ability	☐ Adept at solving problems	☐ Highly adept and innovative
Interpersonal skills	☐ Sometimes antagonises others, tends to be uncommunicative	☐ Relations with others are harmonious at most times	☐ Works well with associates	☐ Always works in harmony with others, an excellent team worker.
Creativity	☐ Rarely offers new ideas	☐ Has average imagination	☐ Frequently offers new ideas, imaginative	☐ Continually offers new ideas, extremely imaginative
Desire to learn	☐ Requires more than average instruction	☐ Grasps instruction with average ability	☐ Usually quick to understand and learn	☐ Exceptionally keen and alert
Work Quality, Attention to detail	☐ Make many errors	☐ Usually accurate	☐ Is almost always accurate	☐ Work is always accurate
Work Quantity	☐ Does just enough to get by	☐ Volume of work is satisfactory	☐ Produced a good volume of work	☐ Very industrious, does more than required
Dependability	☐ Sometimes needs prompting	☐ Usually takes care of tasks and completes them fairly promptly	☐ Requires little supervision and completes tasks promptly	☐ Requires absolute minimum supervision
Work knowledge	☐ Lacks knowledge of some phases of work	☐ Moderately informed	☐ Understood most work challenges presented	☐ Understands all phases of work
Communication Oral	☐ Sometimes encounters difficulty in speaking clearly and concisely	☐ Satisfactory verbal skills	☐ Clear well organised and clearly understood	☐ Exceptional verbal expression.
Communication Written	☐ Sometimes encounters difficulty in writing clearly and concisely	☐ Satisfactory written skills	☐ Clear well organised and clearly understood	☐ Exceptional written expression.

Appendix C – Workplace Supervisor & Student Feedback

(Excerpt from Student Performance Forms)

Overall Level of Satisfaction

☐.Outstanding	Major strengths are:
☐.Very good	1.
☐.Satisfactory	2.
☐.Unsatisfactory	Areas for improvement:
	1.
	2.

If employment was available would you support the placement of this student in a permanent position within your company?   ☐.   Yes.   ☐. No

Other Supervisor Comments

I have discussed this evaluation with the student. . ☐. Yes. .☐. No

Supervisor's signature: Date:

Student Comments

Were your personal expectations for growth and development during this work experience:
☐.Accomplished. . . . . ☐.Somewhat accomplished. . . . . ☐.Not Accomplished

Other Student Comments

Student's signature: Date:

Feedback to BBBIS Program Team

Did you find the student's knowledge or skills lacking in any particular area?. ☐.Yes .☐.No
If so in what areas.

Feedback to Co-op Education Team

Could the student have being prepared for the work placement in some way? .☐.Yes .☐.No
If so, please specify
Is there a possibility of a further Co-operative Education Placement next semester/year? ☐.Yes .☐.No
Contact Name:
Contact Details:

RMIT, School of Business Information Technology

The Future of School Performance Feedback Systems

Conference Discussion Group Paper

Don Passey, Andreas Breiter and Adrie Visscher
Lancaster University, UK; University of Bremen, Germany; and University of Twente, The Netherlands

Abstract: This paper introduces a simple categorisation of school performance feedback systems. It explores how a cross-national review of systems in each category, using a number of selected criteria, can identify features that warrant development, if user accessibility is to be enhanced in the future. The paper indicates potential value to be gained from both a deeper and a wider cross-national study.

Keywords: School performance feedback systems; school performance; pupil performance and monitoring; future developments

1. INTRODUCTION

The discussion group explored issues that face researchers wanting to undertake future studies on school performance feedback systems (SPFSs). Coe and Visscher (2002) define SPFSs as: "information systems external to schools that provide them with confidential information on their performance and functioning as a basis for school self-evaluation". The uses of SPFSs are clearly related to a range of features that are constructed by developers, as well as those features and uses that are promoted or supported by advisers and trainers. Having said that, it is certainly possible within this overall definition of SPFSs to distinguish two different types of systems, dependent upon the focus for the self-evaluation within a school: the first focus is concerned with pupil performance and attainment at individual, class, year group and school levels, while the second focus is concerned with other aspects of school performance (including school leadership, school climate and the characteristics of classroom processes).

In terms of looking at the uses and outcomes of SPFSs, the discussion group felt that there are a number of key questions that are of fundamental importance to future research in this area, irrespective of whether a system is

Please use the following format when citing this chapter:

Passey, D., Breiter, A. and Visscher, A., 2009, in IFIP International Federation for Information Processing, Volume 292; *Evolution of Information Technology in Educational Management*; Eds. Tatnall, A., Visscher, A., Finegan, A., O'Mahony, C., (Boston: Springer), pp. 181–187.

focused on pupil attainment or on school performance in a wider sense. The key questions identified by the discussion group were:

- What are the main features of current SPFSs?
- What are the future needs for SPFSs, to improve utilisation and impact?

It was felt that the sharing of details about different national SPFSs, in conferences such as ITEM, indicated that certain forms of more intensive study (cross-national comparative studies) would be likely to aid researchers in the short-term as well as to potentially support those concerned with policy and practice in the longer-term. From details emerging during the ITEM 2008 conference, it was clear that there were differences and similarities in terms of features and approaches across systems used in different countries, and that some issues faced by some countries had been addressed in particular ways in other countries. The discussion group felt that a useful approach would be to undertake an initial small-scale review of systems in three countries to illustrate these forms of principle, and to begin to identify some indicators that might address the three key questions that the group identified. The approach reported here is to select three national SPFSs in each of the two categories (pupil attainment, and school performance in a wider sense), one from each of the countries represented by members of the discussion group (Germany, The Netherlands, and England). The remainder of this paper will briefly describe the SPFSs selected, identify criteria selected to draw comparisons across the systems, provide a table of comparisons using these criteria, and indicate conclusions drawn and recommendations made on the basis of the results shown.

2.   BRIEF DESCRIPTION OF SYSTEMS

The SPFSs selected that focus on pupil attainment or monitoring are:

- In The Netherlands – The CITO Leerlingvolgsysteem (CITO Pupil monitoring system) (Vlug, 1997).
- In Germany – Vergleichsarbeiten (VERA) (Schrader et al., 2008; Hosenfeld et al., 2008).
- In England – Reporting and Analysis for Improvement through School Self-Evaluation (RAISEonline) (some features are reviewed in the paper by Passey, in this book).

The SPFSs selected that focus (also) on other aspects of school performance are:

- In The Netherlands – Zelfevaluatie in het basisonderwijs (ZEBO) (Hendriks et al., 2002).
- In Germany – Selbstevaluation in Schulen (SEIS) (Stern et al., 2008).
- In England – Self-Evaluation Framework (SEF) (DfES and Ofsted, 2004).

3. CRITERIA FOR COMPARISONS

The discussion group selected fifteen criteria to describe these six SPFSs. They were:

1. The source provider (for example, a government, university or commercial group)
2. The purpose (for example, for school improvement, accountability, certification, or inspection of policy implementation)
3. Extent of use (for example, nationwide, statewide, regional or local)
4. Number of data sets used or involved
5. Interoperability with other systems (for example, school management information systems)
6. Indicators (the elements of focus that the data relate to)
7. Forms of presentation offered (for example, tabular, graphical or pictorial)
8. Whether comparisons, trends or benchmarking are offered
9. Whether psychometric analysis provides indicators of reliability or confidence levels
10. Flexibility for users, in terms of data analysis
11. Targeted users, including collaborative use
12. User friendliness for (non-) occasional users, concerned with data entry, analysis, retrieval and interpretation
13. Ownership issues with regard to the data (for example, privacy and security)
14. The time lag between data collection and data access by users of the system
15. Instruction, guidance and support (technical and non-technical) as well as training for use

4. TABLE OF COMPARISONS

Table 1 shows a comparison of the six SPFSs, using criteria listed above.

Table 1: Comparison of six SPFSs using selected criteria

Criteria	School performance			Pupil attainment and monitoring		
	ZEBO	SEIS	SEF	CITO pupil monitoring system	VERA	RAISEonline
The source provider	Developed by the University of Twente, now sold by a commercial company	The Bertelsmann Foundation	The schools' inspectorate	CITO	University of Koblenz-Landau	The government department
The purpose	Provides information on school process variables and on classroom variables for school self-evaluation	Instrument for self evaluation in schools, provides questionnaires (online/paper-based) to gather data about school quality (teachers, students, senior staff, parents)	Provides a framework to allow schools to gather the range of evidence to allow self-review as well as independent inspectorate review	A pupil monitoring system for 4 to 12 year olds and for schools (with benchmarking against similar pupils and schools)	Feedback of results from standardised tests at the end of the third grade (in mathematics and German)	Provides online analysis and reporting of pupil attainment, comparison to other similar schools nationally, as well as target

						setting and monitoring facilities
Extent of use	About 150 primary schools	Optional for schools, but recommended by some States	All schools in England must complete this form regularly	70 to 80% of Dutch primary schools (about 5,000 schools)	Accessible for all primary schools in participating States (16)	All schools in England have access to this facility
Number of data sets used or involved	One data set is used	One data set, involving in the region of between 30 and 80 questions for each stakeholder	A data set gathered about the school is supplemented with national test results, pupil and parent comments	One data set is used	One data set gives results of tests and comparison data between grades, schools with the same socio-economic status, and other States	One data set gives pupil attainment data from national tests, at a question level as well as a complete mark level
Interoperability with other systems	None	Data can be imported to and exported from MS Excel	The format allows the document to be copied and pasted	Data on pupils can be imported from and exported to other CITO tests and school administration systems	None	Data can be imported into or out of the system
Indicators	Indicators cover: consultation on school functioning; educational leadership; professional development; achievement orientation; team cohesion; pupil care; didactic methods; pupil achievement evaluation; and adaptive education	6 dimensions of school quality: results, teaching and learning, school culture, leadership and management, teacher's professionalism, goals and strategy. Each dimension has a set of indicators	Levels of pupil attainment, including those for specific groups, progress over time, personal development and well-being, assessments of teaching, the curriculum, care and guidance, leadership and management, school objectives, and links with other groups	Pupils' progress in the core subjects is shown at an individual, lesson group and whole school level	Ability tests, norm-reference models (the Rasch scale) in two subjects, plus socio-economic status (with a separate questionnaire)	Pupil attainment, in each subject area, by gender, ethnic group, gifted and talented, special educational needs, and those in care
Forms of presentation offered	Box and whisker plots	Raw data, tables with comments, bar graphs	Textual and tabular only generally	Graphical forms, and in numbers and percentages	Aggregated data (Rasch scales), tables, graphs	Graphical and tabular
Whether comparisons, trends or benchmarking are offered	Benchmarking is made with a reference group (an average Dutch primary school)	Between participating schools, and between different stakeholders, annually	None are offered within the online framework, but schools are given benchmarks	Yes, there are comparisons with pupils' previous scores, with other pupils and with other schools	Comparisons within school, and between schools with the same socio-economic status, and benchmarks	Comparisons with other school groups with similar socio-economic status or previous results can be made
Whether psychometric analysis provides indicators of reliability or	Yes	No	The data are from the one school alone, so this form of analysis does not	Yes	Yes	Indicators of reliability and confidence levels are shown in some reports

confidence levels				apply		
Flexibility, in terms of data analysis	Standard reporting only	Schools can add additional questions, but there is no additional data visualization	Schools can review the data in their own ways, but there are no online facilities to do so	Part of the system is computer-supported and part is not. There is limited flexibility in terms of analysis	There is a fixed set of data and its representations	There are a set number of reports and analyses that can be used
Targeted users, including collaborative use	Teachers and school teams	School management, parents, teachers, local community	School managers and governors	Teachers and school managers in primary schools	Teachers and school managers	Teachers and school managers
User friendliness for (non-) occasional users	Few complaints have been raised about user-friendliness	Said to be well designed, easily accessible, but the output is not very flexible	Users would almost certainly be regular school manager users	Parts of the system are accessible to occasional users	The first version had many reported problems, a revised version was much better, but a high level of knowledge (both computer use and psychometrics) is expected	Reports suggest that occasional users find the facilities quite difficult to use
Ownership of the data	The school that uses the system	Schools	The data must be shared with the inspectorate	Schools can use the data to improve the quality of instruction, but Inspectorate can use the information for judging the schools' performance level	University and schools	Schools have access to their own specific data alone, but comparisons with grouped data are possible
Time lag between data collection and data access by users	Access is possible as soon as data has been entered	Immediate response after data collection and entry	Access is possible as soon as data has been entered	Access is possible as soon as data has been entered	Three to six months	There has been a delay of several months between tests being taken and results being accessible through this system
Instruction, guidance, support (technical and non-technical) and training	The company offers some support and will offer a training course to promote system use	Website support, manuals, and in some States there are regional co-ordinators	Online help and support, documentary support and guidance, and training through local authority groups are all accessible	There is a training course providing information on the more basic level of use	Website support, hotline, and in some States there is individual discussion with schools	Online help and support, documentary support and guidance, and training through local authority groups are all accessible

5.   CONCLUSIONS AND RECOMMENDATIONS

In terms of main features of current SPFSs, if the systems selected are representative of the provision within each of the three countries, then it is clear that systems to support both school performance and pupil attainment monitoring processes are available in each of the three countries. Government and government agencies provide systems in England, but the provision in Germany and The Netherlands is through university and commercial companies. In most cases, use of the systems by schools and teachers is optional and dependent upon school involvement. Data sets from schools are commonly used, but in some systems national data sets are used for comparative purposes. Comparisons or benchmarking are used commonly within systems in all three countries, while indicators of reliability and confidence appear to be shown where these apply to data collected in relevant forms. Schools generally own their data, but sharing with other groups is sometimes necessary (with inspectorates) or possible (with other schools). Training and support are generally offered across all three countries, but the focus of that support varies from basic user training to the specific analysis of data reports.

In terms of the future needs for SPFSs, to improve utilisation and impact, the review suggests that future focus would be worthy in certain areas. Across all three countries, interoperability with other systems is generally at a low level, while user-friendliness appears to vary, and would be worthy of further exploration also. Flexibility of systems is currently low (it is not easy for teachers or managers to ask questions outside a range accommodated by providers). Time delays reported in England and Germany to data about pupil attainment suggest that the use of these systems by teachers may well be increased consequently if this aspect was addressed. A cross-country analysis could be mutually supportive in a number of additional areas: indicators that are used within the data are generally comparable across all three countries, but some systems focus more on indicators allowing specific groups of pupils to be selected and their attainments viewed for comparative purposes; forms of presentation of data reports vary, but some basic (and some more precise) visual forms are used in some systems; systems focus on school managers and teachers as users, while parents and governors can access the school self-evaluation systems in Germany and England, and the outcomes of these different forms of access could well be of wider interest.

A cross-country study looking at certain aspects of systems would be potentially worthy, and consideration and identification of appropriate research methods would be needed for a focus on, in particular, features of interoperability, user-friendliness for occasional as well as regular users, flexibility of systems to support questions outside a specific range, ways to address time delays in accessing data, the review of attainment for selected pupil groups, uses of visual forms of presentation, and outcomes of use of such systems by parents, governors or pupils themselves.

6. REFERENCES

Coe, R. and Visscher, A. (2002). In A.J. Visscher and R. Coe (Eds.). *School improvement through performance feedback*. Routledge: Abingdon

Hendriks, M.A., Doolaard, S. and Bosker, R.J. (2002). In A.J. Visscher and R. Coe (Eds.). *School improvement through performance feedback*. Routledge: Abingdon

Hosenfeld, I., Koch, U., Groß Ophoff, J. and Scherthan, F. (2008). Projekt VERA: Ergebnisorientierte Unterrichtsentwicklung durch internetgestützte externe Evaluation? In A. Breiter, A. Lange and E. Stauke (Eds.). *Schulinformationssysteme und datengestützte Entscheidungsprozesse*. Peter Lang: Berlin

DfES and Ofsted (2004). *A New Relationship with Schools: Improving Performance through School Self Evaluation*. DfES: Nottingham

Passey, D. (2008). First no choice, then some choice, and finally overload: A reasonable data management evolution? In A. Tatnall and Davey, B. (2008). (Eds.). *Evolution of Information Technology in Educational Management*. Springer: New York

Schrader, F.-W., Helmke, A. and Hosenfeld, I. (2008). Stichwort: Kompeten-zentwicklung im Grundschulalter. *Zeitschrift für Erziehungswissenschaft, 11*(1), 7-29

Stern, C., Ebel, C. and Müncher, A. (Eds.). (2008). *Bessere Qualität in allen Schulen. Praxisleitfaden zur Einführung des Selbstevaluationsinstruments SEIS in Schulen, 3. vollständig überarbeitete Auflage*. Bertelsmann Stiftung: Gütersloh

Vlug, K.F.M. (1997). Because every pupil counts: the success of the pupil monitoring system in the Netherlands. *Education and Information Technologies, 2*(4), 287-306

ITEM Evolution

Conference Discussion Group Paper

Greg Baker, Christopher D. O'Mahony, Ian D. Selwood and Alan Strickley
Scotch College, Australia; Uppingham School, UK; Birmingham University UK; Birmingham City Council UK

Abstract: This paper presents the output of a discussion group formed at the ITEM 3.7 Working Conference. The main theme of the discussion group was to consider the evolutionary nature of IT in Educational Management.

Keywords: School information systems, Evolution, Stages of Growth, Educational Management, information technology

1.   INTRODUCTION

The 'shape' of our discussion group is longitudinal. Essentially we considered ITEM in terms of "past, present, and future". The paper commences by reviewing core theoretical foundations – stages of growth theories and evolutionary models.

With this as a basis, we then use these models to interpret the recent history of ITEM developments in a number of countries. "Stories" from each case/country can be mapped to different stages of evolutionary sophistication.

Having reviewed the 'past', we then turn our attention to the present. In this section, we highlight the perception that ITEM in schools is on a journey. We certainly haven't arrived, and it's questionable whether one can ever "arrive". We acknowledge that evidence of 'success' is thin, although we cannot now conceive running a school without ICT as a core service. The mixed evidence from School Performance Feedback Systems is indicative of this journey.

The discussion group then turned to consideration of perspectives on future evolutionary paths for ITEM. Areas of discussion included Web 2.0, School/Home partnerships, IT Consumerisation, MLEs, Technology integration and unification, Privacy and Personalisation.

Please use the following format when citing this chapter:

Baker, G., O'Mahony, C.D., Selwood, I.D. and Strickley, A., 2009, in IFIP International Federation for Information Processing, Volume 292; *Evolution of Information Technology in Educational Management*; Eds. Tatnall, A., Visscher, A., Finegan, A., O'Mahony, C., (Boston: Springer), pp. 189–199.

The discussion group concluded by noting that the future of ITEM looks exciting and daunting. The past and present have witnessed amazing developments in IT in Educational Management. These developments do indeed exhibit evolutionary characteristics.

2.   THEORETICAL FOUNDATIONS

When analysing the evolution of ITEM it is perhaps wise to do this within a theoretical framework. The problem here is – "What framework to use?" In two papers in the late 1970s Nolan (1977, 1979) presented a theory concerning the growth stages through which it automates its data processing activities. This theory was transferred to the field of office automation by Zisman (1978) an area that Visscher (1991) argued has many similarities to the type of application that takes place in schools, when they introduce ITEM. Based on the work of Nolan and Zisman, Visscher (1991, 1995) outlined four stages or levels of what was then called the development Computer Assisted School Administration (CASA). The four levels were defined as 'initiation', 'expansion', 'integration' and 'stabilisation' and have strong similarities with Fullan's (1991) "Simplified Overview of the Change Process" in education.

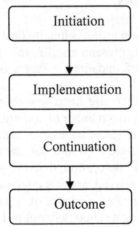

Figure 1: A simplified overview of the change process (Fullan 1991, p 48)

According to Visscher (1991, 1995) the initiation level is characterised by software for CASA being developed by a few amateurs working in isolation. As more schools and educational authorities become aware of the potential benefits of the computer the expansion level commences, the numbers of software packages grow, and commercial software developers start to enter the market. However, at this level integrated school information systems are not available and software consists of independent stand-alone applications. Thus, little or no information can be transferred between applications, data entry may be duplicated, and there is little or no possibility of investigating relationships between various types of data. The goal of automation "in the first two levels is improvement of the efficiency of clerical activities" (Visscher, 1991: p.3) or the improvement of administration.

Whilst it is difficult to disagree with his first two levels of initiation and expansion Visscher claims that: the third level integration can be "characterised by 'integrated modules' and 'the production of management information'"(Visscher, 1995: p.16); and that the fourth level of stabilisation is characterised by computer assistance reaching its full potential with the focus shifting to systems maintenance and refinement. Selwood & Drenoyianni, (1997) argued that these final two levels were somewhat open to debate and that it was possible that systems, even though they may comprise of "integrated modules" may not be flexible enough to provide information for management decisions (Mitchell and Wild, 1993).

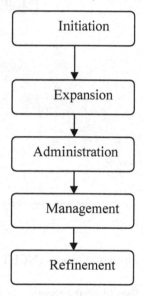

Figure 2: Interim theoretical model for progress in ITEM

With the benefit of hindsight Selwood & Drenoyianni, (1997)I suggested that in England and Wales it would appear that the third level of the evolution of CASA was administration - the use of computers to aid school administration and that the fourth level is management – IT being used to aid decision making. The stabilisation level still remained but moved to become the fifth level. However, whether this level is achievable is debatable, as Visscher (2001) states "it presupposes the accomplishment of the full potential of computer-assisted school administration and management..." and ".......software for the full support of managerial work is still elusive" and new technologies ".....promote new types of support for administrative and managerial school staff" (p.14). Selwood (2004) suggested that, as it would appear unlikely that progress in ITEM would cease, the stabilisation level should be replaced with a "refinement level" where applications and uses are refined. This led to an interim theoretical model.

However Selwood (2004) noted that his interim theoretical framework had strong similarities with that put forward by the MITs 90 Research Group (NCET, 1995) to model the extent of IT integration within business organisations. The MIT model was adapted by the NCET Educational Technology Project (NCET, 1995) into the Tranformative Model (see Figure 3), to provide a model to map the development of IT in schools. The model was primarily used to map the development of IT use in teaching and learning but ITEM was not entirely ignored and the description of some levels include a very brief, and generally not very useful, reference to it.

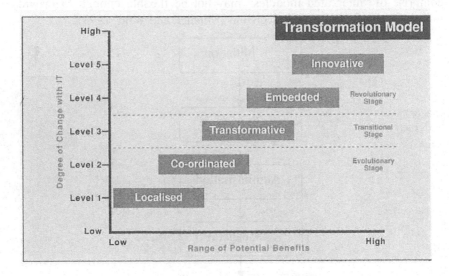

Figure 3: Transformation model (NCET 1995, p8)

- Evolutionary Stage
  - o Initiation and
  - o Expansion;
- Transitional Stage
  - o Administration
- Revolutionary Stage
  - o Management and
  - o Refinement

Figure 4: Theoretical framework for the progress of ITEM

Selwood (2004) compared Figure 3 to his interim theoretical framework and noted that the "Evolutionary Stage" could well cover "Initiation" and "Expansion". The administration level in the interim theoretical framework could definitely be seen as a "Transitional Stage". With the final two levels of the interim framework being regarded as *revolutionary* because they enable significant changes to be made in the processes of education. Therefore a new theoretical framework for the development of ITEM is presented in Figure 4 (above).

However it should be apparent that all education systems will not progress through the stages and levels of the framework at the same rate. Also, different sections of a a school will probably progress through the stages at different rates. For example, the Senior Management Team may well be using ITEM for management purposes whilst teachers in the same school may not even be using ICT for administration.

3.   REVIEW OF PAST EXPERIENCES

There have been a number of significant studies of school Management Information Systems (MISs) internationally over the last 15 years. Amongst them are those focussed on systems in Hong Kong, New Zealand, England and Wales, the Netherlands and Australia covering both primary and secondary school phases and using a variety of research methods.

The School Administration and Management System (SAMS) in Hong Kong has been the subject of 3 studies (Fung et al, 1998; Ip Tsang & Lee, 1997; Fung & Ledesma, 2001a&b) and in the Netherlands Visscher and Bloemen (2001) carried out research using a multiple case study approach to compare patterns in one school against similar and contrasting cases.

In New Zealand research into the Massey University School Administration by Computer (MUSAC) system has included three case studies at a primary, secondary and combined school (Nolan et al. 1996) a further case study of three primary schools (Nolan & Lambert, 2001) and a survey of acquisition and usage patterns (Nolan & Ayres, 1996).

In England the study of the School Information Management System (SIMS) by Wild & Walker (2001) and commentary by Visscher, Wild and Smith (2003) involved a large scale survey of secondary schools whilst Selwood (1995) used a survey based on questionnaires distributed in 1989 and 1991/92. A second study (Selwood, 2004) involved detailed interviews and questionnaire responses from one primary and one secondary school in the spring of 2003 and this was followed by (Selwood, 2005) a study into primary school teachers use of ICT for administration and management. Also in England Strickley (2007) undertook an evaluative case study of primary schools in Birmingham and Hay-Campbell (2006) carried out research with primary teachers.

Finally O'Mahony (1998) referencing research from 1995 (a&b) and 1996 (a&b) describes how schools in New South Wales, Australia, have evolved in their use and perception of MISs.

Although the above cover a variety of different countries and practices general themes emerged from all of them. As O'Mahony (1998) comments, he found similar trends in the Australian studies to those observed by Barta, Telem and Gev (1995) in other countries.

Whilst progress is clearly marked across the last decade and a half some common elements requiring development remain. In particular the following issues were common in the research:

- use of the MIS limited to administrative tasks;
- lack of MIS availability to all teaching staff;
- unsuitable training and support;
- inappropriate software interface;
- usability and functionality limitations;
- inadequate reporting and decision support facilities;
- lack of user-centric implementation;
- minimal interoperability with other systems.

This is reinforced by Strickley (2004) who notes that systems still need accessibility, ownership, training, trust, and usability and Selwood, in 2005, who suggests that a lack of quality training, time and ICT resources are resulting in low levels of teacher usage of ITEM systems.

4.   CURRENT STATE

Anecdotal and research evidence in 2007 and 2008 suggests that the use of an evolutionary framework for understanding ITEM development is useful, but at the same time specific ITEM examples may not clearly 'fit' into pre-defined evolutionary stages. Good 'stages of growth' models should have the following characteristics:

- The model should be descriptive, enabling individual cases to be understood;
- The model should be predictive, enabling future development and growth to be projected;
- The model should be prescriptive, enabling ITEM planners to make recommendations and develop policy and strategy.

Examples drawn from across the world demonstrate mixed progress through arbitrary stages accepted in the literature. In particular, two areas of disconnect were noted by members of the discussion group:

a) Ongoing lack of integration between ITEM solutions
b) The difficulty faced by ITEM systems to keep pace with techno-logical change

4.1   Dis-Integration

ITEM solutions are developed to support a wide range of activities at different phases of education – primary, secondary, further education, higher education and adult learning. The broad spectrum of ITEM needs faced by different education providers presents two main problems. Firstly, there is no single ITEM product that meets the needs of all (and in fact, seeking such a product now appears naïve and unachievable.) Secondly, if it is accepted that multiple products need to be developed to meet multiple needs, there is currently a distinct lack of integration between them. For example, a recent study conducted in the German region of Bremen identified 800 different databases used for supporting educational processes (Breiter, 2008)

4.2   Pace of Change

Historically, the nature of ICT implementations in education is reactive, rather than proactive. That is, the education sector in general is a consumer of ICT innovation, rather than an active developer. As a result, a technological lag exists between ICT innovation and ITEM implementations. One example of this is the emergence of MLEs (Managed Learning Environments), which necessitate dynamic links between VLEs (Virtual Learning Environments) are more traditional ITEM management information systems. Whereas the theoretical benefits of MLEs are clear, the programming and developer effort required from educational decision-makers means that the benefits are still many years from being realised. Other examples of technological change are presented in the following section.

The message from a review of the current state of ITEM suggests that some progress has been made in terms of evolution and sophistication, but at the same time much still needs to be done.

5.   SOME PERSPECTIVES ON THE FUTURE

Many factors continue to impact the use of ITEM – technological, social, statutory, political and financial, among others. The discussion group highlighted some of these perspectives, which are briefly discussed in the following sections:

- **Web 2.0**
  Many schools block sites such as Myspace, Youtube, Bebo and the like, yet outside of the school environment students see these as the usual method of communication. School leaders and IT Managers grapple to find the balance between effective use of these new collaborative tools, and the duty of care required for vulnerable groups.
- **Home/school relationship**
  Home access to the internet is now very high and still growing, but effective leverage of this access by ITEM systems is patchy. Issues exist surrounding equity of access, authentication, privacy, licencing, supervision and control.
- **Consumerisation – private devices on school networks**
  The consumerisation of IT presents new problems to schools and other educational institutions. Students and staff can now purchase a range

of IT enabled devices over the counter in local stores or online. The iPod, iPhone, Smartphone and many other handheld devices are now being brought into schools and there is no way this can be avoided. Issues of security and authentication need to be addressed.

- **Regulatory and reporting issues**
Increasingly there is a greater regulatory and reporting requirement. Schools are being required by governments and authorities to report on a range of aspects of school life. Many ITEM systems include reporting capabilities, but not always as flexible as required.

- **Privacy and personalisation**
Student and parent portals need to be increasingly personalized to allow access to appropriate information. Privacy legislation requires personal information to be stored securely and accessed only by a defined range of people.

- **MLEs**
Managed Learning Environments are evolving from content management systems and learning management systems to become all encompassing. For example, Blackboard has developed from a tertiary directed product into a product for K-12 schools as well and now uses Web 2.0 technologies to develop learning communities. As well as requiring an additional wave of staff professional development, these systems pose system integration issues as referred to below.

- **Systems integration and unification**
With the increased complexity of school life, many different information systems are developed. Over time, those that are useful must be integrated into the main ITEM system to ensure data integrity, interoperability and to enable the development of a complete picture of each student. Unified communications products also provide the potential to better develop immediate communication using: Email, Voicemail, Telephone, Software phones, Instant messaging, On line conferencing from the desktop, Presence, and others. These systems are increasingly integrated into the standard desktop environment.

6.   CONCLUSIONS

ITEM in schools has exhibited evolutionary characteristics. Evidence from case studies around the world demonstrates this. However, the current state of ITEM in schools suggests that we're still on a journey, and it's not clear what the end point will be (if ever there can be an end-point). Certain elements emerging now, and highlighted through this discussion group, will influence future evolution of ITEM. As a consequence, ITEM as an area of research continues to be valid, vibrant and relevant.

7.   REFERENCES

Barta, B. Z., Telem, M., & Gev, Y., (Eds.) (1995). *Information technology in educational management.* London: Chapman & Hall.

Fullan, M. (with Stiegelbauer, S.). (1991). *The New Meaning of Educational Change. 2nd Edition.* Cassell, London

Fung, A.C.W., & Ledesma, J. (2001a) SAMS in Hong Kong: A centrally developed SIS for primary and secondary schools. In Visscher, A.J., Wild, P. & Fung, A.C.W. *Information Technology in Educational Management.* (pp. 39-53). Netherlands: Kluwer.

Fung, A.C.W., & Ledesma, J. (2001b) SAMS in Hong Kong: A user acceptance audit. In Nolan, C. J. P., Fung, A.C.W., & Brown, M.A. (Eds.), *Pathways to Institutional Improvement with Information Technology in Educational Management* (pp. 121-145). Boston, Dordrecht, London: Kluwer Academic Publishers.

Fung, A. C. W., Visscher, A. J., Wild, P., & Selwood, I.,D. (1998) SAMS in Hong Kong school: The first evaluative findings of a large-scale implementation of school management information systems. In Fulmer C., B. Barta, & P. Nolan (Eds.), *The Integration of information for educational management,* Whitefield, ME: Felicity Press, (pp. 19-38).

Hay-Campbell, R. (2006). *Primary teachers' use of and attitudes to management information systems.* MA dissertation. Institute of Education: University of London.

Ip Tsang, B. C. H. & Lee, S.Y.F. (1997) Implementation of the school administration and management system: a Honk Kong experience. In Fung, A.C.W., Visscher, A.J., Barta, B.Z., & Teather, D.C.B. (Eds.) *Information Technology in Educational Management for the Schools of the Future* (pp. 83-89). London: Chapman and Hall.

NCET (1995). *Managing IT – A Planning tool for Senior Managers.* NCET, Coventry

Nolan C.J.P & Ayres D.A (1996) Developing a good information system for schools: the New Zealand experience *International Journal of Educational Research* Volume 25(4) 1996. (pp. 307-321). Milton Keynes: Elsevier.

Nolan C.J.P, Ayres D.A, Dunn S and McKinnon D.H (1996) Implementing computerised school information systems: case studies from New Zealand *International Journal of Educational Research* Volume 25(4) 1996. (pp. 335-350). Milton Keynes: Elsevier.

Nolan C.J.P & Lambert, M. (2001) Information systems for leading and managing schools: Changing the paradigm. In Nolan, C. J. P., Fung, A.C.W., & Brown, M.A. (Eds.), *Pathways to Institutional Improvement with Information Technology in Educational Management* (pp. 72-85). Boston, Dordrecht, London: Kluwer Academic Publishers.

Nolan, R.L. (1977). Restructuring the data processing organisation for data resource management in *Information Processing 77. Proceedings of IFIP Congress 1977.* Edited by Gilcrist, B. North Holland, Amsterdam.

Nolan, R.L. (1979). Managing the crisis in data processing. *Harvard Business Review,* 57(2), p. 115-126.

O'Mahony, C. D., (1995a). *Measuring school information systems management.* Macquarie Computing Report 95-169C. Sydney: Macquaire University: School of MPCE.

O'Mahony, C. D., (1995b). *Improving schools information systems management: The quest for quality.* Sydney: Australian Catholic University.

O'Mahony, C. D., (1996a). IS effectiveness and organisational culture: An underlying model for ITEM evaluation. In Fung, A.C.W., Visscher, A.J., Barta, B.Z., & Teather, D.C.B. (Eds.) *Information Technology in Educational Management for the Schools of the Future* (pp. 122-130) Chapman and Hall, London.

O'Mahony, C. D., (1996b). *Collegial or Adversarial? An investigation of the relationship between organisational culture and information systems management in NSW secondary schools.* Research Report: Department of Computing & Technology: Australian Catholic University.

O'Mahony, C. D., (1998). *Key functions for integrated school IS management.* In C. Fulmer, B. Barta & P. Nolan (Eds.), *The integration of information for educational management.* (pp. 105-117). Maine: Felicity Press.

Selwood, I. D. (1995). The development of ITEM in England and Wales. In Barta, B.Z., Telem, M., & Gev, Y. (Eds.), *Information technology in educational management,* (pp. 85-92) London: Chapman Hall.

Selwood, I.D. (2004). *Information technology in educational management in schools in England and Wales: Scope progress and limits.* Doctoral Thesis, Birmingham: University of Birmingham School of Education.

Selwood, I. D. (2005). Primary school teachers' use of ICT for administration and management. In Tatnall, A., Visscher, A. and Osorio, J. (Eds.), *Information Technology and Educational Management in the Knowledge Society.* (pp.11-22). New York: Springer.

Selwood, I.D. (2004). *Information Technology in Education Administration and Management in Schools in England and Wales: Scope. Progress and Limits.* Unpublished PhD Thesis. University of Birmingham.

Selwood, I.D. & Drenoyianni, H. (1997). Administration, Management and IT in Education. In *Information Technology in Educational Management for the Schools of the Future.* Edited by Fung A, Visscher A, Barta B and Teather D. Chapman & Hall for IFIP. London.

Strickley, A., B. (2004). Factors Affecting the Use of MIS as a Tool for Informing and Evaluating Teaching and Learning in Schools. *Education and Information Technologies* 9 (1): (pp. 47-66), March 2004. Boston, Dordrecht, London: Kluwer Academic Publishers.

Strickley, A., B. (2007) *An evaluative case study of the use of management information systems in Birmingham primary schools.* Doctoral thesis. Birmingham: Birmingham City University.

Visscher, A.J. (1991). School Administrative Computing: A Framework for Analysis. *Journal of Research on Computing in Education.* 24(1) p. 1-19.

Visscher, A.J. (1995). 'Computer assisted school administration and management: where are we and where should we go?' In *Information*

Technology in Educational Management. Edited by Ben Zion Barta, Moshe Telem and Yaffa Gev. Chapman Hall for IFIP, London.

Visscher, A.J. (2001). Computer-assisted school information systems: the concepts, intended benefits, and stages of development in *Information Technology in Educational Management: Synthesis of Experience, Research and Future Perspectives on Computer-Assisted School Information Systems.* Edited by Visscher, A.J., Wild, P. and Fung. A.C.W. Kluwer Academic Publishers, Dordrect, Holland

Visscher, A.J. & Bloemen, P.P.M. (2001) CSIS usage in school management: A comparison of good and bad practice schools. In Nolan, C. J. P., Fung, A.C.W., & Brown, M.A. (Eds.), *Pathways to Institutional Improvement with Information Technology in Educational Management* (pp. 87-97). Boston, Dordrecht, London: Kluwer Academic Publishers.

Visscher, A.J., Wild, P. and Smith, D. (2003). The results of implementing SIMS in English secondary schools. In Selwood, I., D., Fung, A., C. W. & O'Mahony, C., D. (Eds.), *Management of education in the information age: the role of ICT.* (pp. 33-45). Dordrecht: Kluwer Academic Publishers.

Wild, P. & Walker, J. (2001). The commercially developed SIMS from a humble beginning. In Visscher, A.J., Wild, P. & Fung, A.C.W. *Information Technology in Educational Management.* (pp. 19-38). Netherlands: Kluwer.

Zisman, M. (1978). Office automation revolution or evolution? *Sloan Management Review.* 19(3), p. 1-16.

Requirements of University ITEM Systems

Conference Discussion Group Paper

Bill Davey, Tuulikki Paturi, Eduard Kostolansky and Ronald Bisaso
*RMIT University, Australia; HAAGA-HELIA University of Applied Sciences, Finland;
University of St. Cyril and Methodius in Trnava, Slovakia; University of Tempere, Finland*

Abstract: This paper addresses the issue of requirements of University ITEM systems. A
guide to characteristics is presented which is supported by two international
cases.

Keywords: University, Management systems, educational support

1.   BACKGROUND

This paper arises from a desire to look at the specific requirements of
ICT systems that support University education management. This appears to
be a domain in which there are both general needs that apply to all
educational institutions and particular needs for the University sector. This
paper looks first at requirements of systems then compares these requirements
with two major projects in Finland and Slovakia.

2.   THE PANEL

The paper arises from an extensive set of meetings between researchers
and practitioners. Included were; researchers in ITEM Ronald Bisaso and
Bill Davey, and Practitioners Tuulikki Paturi and Eduard Kostolansky
holding senior positions in Tertiary institutions in Finland and Slovakia
respectively. This mix of theoretically oriented and practically oriented
participants led to a lively debate. The conclusions presented here represent
those formed by contrasting the theoretical considerations moderated by
practical experience of implementing University systems. The panel decided
to limit recommendations to two simple questions:

1.   What are the characteristics of a University ITEM system required to
     support the educational effort?

Please use the following format when citing this chapter:

Davey, B., Paturi, T., Kostolansky, E. and Bisaso, R., 2009, in IFIP International Federation for
Information Processing, Volume 292; *Evolution of Information Technology in Educational Management*;
Eds. Tatnall, A., Visscher, A., Finegan, A., O'Mahony, C., (Boston: Springer), pp. 201–205.

2. What are sensible functional areas that such a system should include?

The results of these questions were contrasted with two major projects for implementing systems in University environments.

3.   CHARACTERISTICS OF ITEM SYSTEMS

The panel first decided that a design philosophy needs to be articulated. Experiences around the panel indicated that often an ITEM system is created because it is seen to have some intrinsic value. That is, some Universities seem to have chosen to implement a product or system not out of some educational need, but because it was thought to be a good idea to have a system (Tatnall, A. and Pitman, A. (2002), Davey, B. and Tatnall, A. (2003), Tatnall, A. and Davey, B. (2005), Sandy, G. and Davey, B (2005), Davey, B; Visscher, AJ & Wild, P, (2001), Tatnall, A. and Davey, B. (2001)). From a systems point of view an ITEM system is pointless unless it can both influence the environment and adapt to the environment. This means that a system must both influence the decisions of the educational manager and then be able to incorporate new directions that the manager may have set in train. This can be achieved within the original design or by design based on change and modularity (Tatnall, A and Davey, B, (2001)).

To make this a more concrete discussion the panel identified a minimum set of characteristics.

- **Organisational alignment**: An ITEM system should reflect the structure of University. Experience has shown that systems written for the USA University sector often contain assumptions about the way an organisation is structured that are difficult to accommodate in other systems. This precludes packaged solutions that are difficult to modify. Organisational alignment also implies that the system captures data and delivers information that is relevant to the objectives of the University.
- **Timely response to forces**: The panel believes that globally Universities are becoming more prone to outside forces such as government funding requirements and market forces. This requires systems that can be changed to accommodate partnership requirements in short time-frames.
- **Integration:** The various functional areas need to be able to interconnect so that information can be created using the disparate functional systems. This is often achieved using a data warehouse.
- **Upgrade and update paths built into design**: the panel commented on the rapid generational change inherent in hardware and software. Systems need to be built with an eye to platform and architecture changes.
- **Generation of management consolidation reports**: scorecard or other report types must be included in the design philosophy.

- **Regulating inputs to affect consolidated outcomes**: If ITEM systems are to be useful in management then they need to be able to do more than provide the manager with information. The decisions of the manager should be supported by the system and the manager should be able to trace the effect of decisions on educational outcomes.

- **Built-in roles that allow self-service for all stakeholders**: academics, students and those with a relationship to the system must be supported by the system. This is most clearly achieved by designing the system with built-in roles. These roles can be implemented by views, but must incorporate the common tasks that each stakeholder relies upon if the system is to produce quality data.

- **Systems for teaching, research and administration**: One of the peculiar aspects of Universities is that they have research as a function in addition to other normal educational roles. A University system must recognise this tripartite nature of the organisation.

- **Allow external connections**: Universities are commonly more integrated with the industrial community than other educational institutions. Functions such as Praxis, joint research efforts, industry sponsorships and the alumni function require a system to allow permeability with partners.

- **Inclusion of undergrad, masters, PhD**: Another peculiarity of Universities that should be an underlying design requirement is the very wide range of types of educational program from under-graduate, with a largely formal learning role through to PhD with a mostly research focus. All of these are student roles, but the information requirements and management decisions to be supported for each vary greatly.

4.   FUNCTIONAL AREAS

The panel was presented with the following model of functional areas by Tuulikki Paturi. You will find a detailed explanation of this model in her paper elsewhere in this book. The panel considered this model from the view of inclusiveness of functional areas and sensible division into modular groups. This model was unanimously supported as containing all features that would be required by a system.

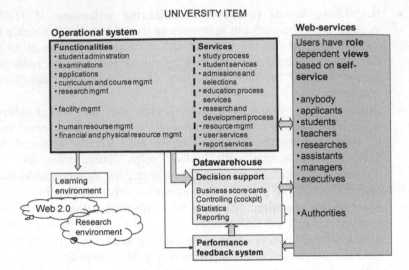

Figure 1: University Information Technology in Educational Management

5.　GETTING THE SYSTEM GOING

The panel reported on a number of cases globally of systems that had great merit but became failed implementations. It was thought that a list of actors that affect the possible success of an ITEM should be compiled. The panel identified at least ten different issues that had caused systems to fail:

- Influence of committees and other groups external to the University
- Data purity
- Multiple data sources and data capture
- Privacy and IP considerations
- Security and testing
- Local needs and conditions
- Special transactions should be contained in loosely coupled modules
- Change management
- Migration path
- Nature and change life cycle.

6.　A SUCCESSFUL IMPLEMENTATION

In contrast to the last point of discussion we were able to identify one system that had been implemented as a National system. In Slovakia the decision was taken to implement a system at the National level with complete ownership of the data at the institution level. This system was implemented as a phased implementation using the SAP (R/3) database as a foundation. The system was commenced with a student records module providing a central database of Slovakian student enrolment. This was seen as adding immediate value as a student could take courses anywhere in Slovakia with minimal problems. The system was then rolled out in stages:

- Personal records
- HR then added for 3 months trial
- Research and other grant related data
- Financial system (linked with government funding system).

7. CONCLUSION

The panel found that the problems inherent in creating a useful university ITEM system are a globally common. The factors identified are more general in nature than are normally considered when creating a set of requirements. The panel feel that taking a wider philosophical view of what an ITEM system is intended to provide will lead to more appropriate system being created.

8. REFERENCES

Davey, B, Visscher, AJ & Wild, P, (2001) `Conclusions, reflections and the road ahead', Information technology in educational management', Visscher, AJ, Wild, P and Fung, ACW (eds.) Kluwer Academic, Dordrecht, Netherlands, 2001, pp. 161-

Davey, B. and Tatnall, A. (2003). Involving the Academic: A Test for Effective University ITEM Systems. Management of Education in the Information Age: The Role of ICT. Selwood, I., Fung, A. C. W. and O'Mahony, C. D. Assinippi Park, Massachusetts, Kluwer Academic Publishers: 83-92.

Sandy, G. and Davey, B (2005) 'Data quality in educational systems for decision makers', in Information Technology and Educational Management in the Knowledge Society, Springer, New York, pp. 111-120

Tatnall, A and Davey, B, (2001) 'Open ITEM Systems are Good ITEM Systems', in Pathways to Institutional Improvement with Information Technology in Educational Management, Kluwer Academic Publishers, Boston, 2001

Tatnall, A. and Davey, B. (2005). Future Directions in ITEM Research. Information Technology and Educational Management in the Knowledge Society. Tatnall, A., Visscher, A. J. and Osorio, J. New York, Springer: 209-217.

Tatnall, A. and Pitman, A. (2002). Issues of Decentralization and Central Control in Educational Management: the Enabling and Shaping Role of Information Technology. TelE-Learning: The Challenge of the Third Millennium. Passey, D. and Kendall, M. Assinippi Park, Ma, Kluwer Academic Publishers: 233-240.